JEWISH RESPONSES TO EARLY CHRISTIANS

HISTORY AND POLEMICS, 30–150 C.E.

CLAUDIA J. SETZER

Fortress Press   **Minneapolis**

JEWISH RESPONSES TO EARLY CHRISTIANS
History and Polemics, 30–150 C.E.

Scripture quotations, unless otherwise noted, are from the New Revised Standard Version of the Bible, copyright © 1989 by the Division of Christian Education of the National Council of the Churches of Christ in the United States of America.

Cover design: Nancy Eato
Interior design: Ann Elliot Artz Hadland

Library of Congress Cataloging-in-Publication Data

Setzer, Claudia.
   Jewish responses to early Christians : history and polemics, 30-150 C.E. / Claudia J. Setzer.
      p. cm.
   Includes bibliographical references and index.
   ISBN 0-8006-2680-X
   1. Bible. N.T.—Criticism, interpretation, etc. 2. Jews in the New Testament. 3. Christianity in rabbinical literature. 4. Judaism—Relations—Christianity. 5. Christianity and other religions—Judaism. 6. Church history—Primitive and early church, ca. 30-600. 7. Judaism—History—Talmudic period, 10-425. I. Title.
   BS2545.J44S47   1994
   296.3'872—dc20   94-564
                                                                  CIP

The paper used in this publication meets the minimum requirements of American National Standard for Information Sciences—Permanence of Paper for Printed Library Materials, ANSI Z329.48-1984.   ∞™

Manufactured in the U.S.A.   AF 1-2680
98   97   96   95   94   1   2   3   4   5   6   7   8   9   10

JEWISH RESPONSES
TO EARLY CHRISTIANS

CONTENTS

Preface

Overworked undergraduate professors should never underestimate their impact on students. This book, I now realize, began in an introductory New Testament course I took at Macalester College in 1973. Calvin Roetzel taught me the tools of critical study, as well as rehabilitated the image of the Pharisees and early Judaism in my eyes. These two interests—New Testament and early Judaism—guided me through graduate school and have dominated my subsequent teaching and scholarship.

When I was experimenting with ideas for a dissertation topic, my adviser Raymond E. Brown suggested I gather all the explicit statements about what Jews and Christians were saying and doing about one another. As my work evolved, it proved unwieldy. Since many others had considered Christian attitudes toward Jews and Judaism, I chose to leave aside that half of the equation. Jewish attitudes toward Christians, however, have not received a systematic treatment. Because of the paucity of early sources directly from Jews and Judaism, few have ventured into this area.

I have joined the few Jewish sources with information of Christian (and occasionally pagan) provenance to identify a spectrum of trends in Jewish attitudes toward early Christians. I do not automatically discount (or accept) Christian testimony of Jewish responses, but consider issues of bias, theological and literary utility, and external corroboration. My hope is to provide a useful sourcebook for the field, as well as to contribute nuance to our understanding of early Jewish-Christian relationships.

Many people contributed directly and indirectly to this work. In particular I would like to thank my advisers, Raymond E. Brown and Robin Scroggs, for their constancy and thoughtful care. J. Louis Martyn, Shaye Cohen, and John Koenig read large portions of the work and helped clarify my thinking. David Weiss Halivni, Richard Kalmin, and David Kraemer kindly helped me with rabbinic literature and Justin. Many of my colleagues at Columbia University and Union Seminary gave freely of their friendship, advice, and encouragement, especially Alexandra Brown, Celia Deutsch, Susanne Lehne, and Michael Winger. My editor, Charles Puskas, has smoothed out many a rough phrase and sharpened my presentation.

My children, Leora and Alexander, have brought continual joy and balance to the process of producing this book, as they do to my whole life. My parents took a lively interest in the project and offered their support. Between the defense of an earlier version of this work as a dissertation and the publication of this book, my beloved father died. I am certain he would have read this book from cover to cover and offered his own enthusiastic and insightful responses. His intellectual vitality and personal largesse are qualities I dearly hope to emulate. I dedicate this book to his memory.

Introduction

This book examines the ways Jews who did not share the belief that Jesus was the long-awaited Messiah of Israel reacted to people who did hold this belief in the first and early second centuries, ca. 30–150. What did they say and do about them? More specifically, when did Jews begin to see other Jews who believed in Jesus as beyond the pale of the people of Israel, no longer eccentric or deviant Jews, but outsiders? When did Christians begin to see themselves as distinct from other Jews?

For convenience, I use the term "Jew" to denote someone who identifies with the people of Israel but does not identify Jesus of Nazareth as the Messiah, God's Son, or a divine being. I use the term "Christian" to mean someone who holds one or more of these beliefs, and who may be Jewish or Gentile in origin. Many people, of course, were both Jews and believers in Jesus; they would readily identify with the term "Jew" and wonder at the term "Christian" altogether. Yet the majority of people who called themselves Jews did not believe in Jesus. Those who did believe in him at some point became "Christians" (Acts 11:26) even if they did not coin the term themselves or use it from the very start.

The issue of how Jews who did not believe in Jesus reacted to their Christian neighbors has frequently been part of the study of early Christian writings, either as an attempt to better understand a particular Christian work[1] or to illuminate a particular issue.[2] Often scholars have been quite sympathetic to Judaism,[3] but their aim has been to understand early Christianity. This is not surprising, since the bulk of available references are from Christian texts. The Blessing against the Heretics (*Birkat ha-Minim*) has loomed large as an issue in the Jewish context of early Christianity, partly because it seems to represent a certain specific measure taken by Jews.[4]

Scholars who consider Jewish reaction to Christians as an aspect of Jewish history generally rely on later texts—third century or beyond. Historians of Judaism have tended to minimize Christianity's impact on Judaism, and treated Christianity as one of many Greco-Roman cults or as an expression of sectarianism.[5] Even in the second century and later, some argue, Judaism affected Christianity far more than the reverse.[6] For scholars of both early Christianity and Judaism, the recent trend has been away from an attempt to pinpoint a time of Christianity's separation from Judaism and to assume a gradual process whereby many kinds of Christians related to and separated from many kinds of Jews. The existence of Jewish Christianity into the fourth century presents an obstacle to the identification of a certain irrevocable religious divorce of all Christians from Judaism.[7]

Simultaneous with these developments, an interest in the ancient origins of modern anti-Semitism has flourished. Scholars consider the enduring effect of New Testament images of Jews and Judaism and debate Christian culpability for modern anti-Semitism.[8] Baldly stated, the issue seems to be whom to blame for ancient anti-Judaism, the pagans[9] or the Christians[10] or both?

The Holocaust is the single most obvious cause for this soul-searching in both popular and scholarly circles. Yet this examination also fits with a current trend that recognizes that history is largely written by the "winners" and projects their understanding of early conflicts. Many scholars now attempt to see "the other side" of social relationships and focus on perspectives that have previously been ignored.[11]

An appreciation for the other's religion in their ancient expressions is clear in the work of recent Jewish and Christian scholars.[12] For the first and early second century, the focus still remains more on the Christian attitude toward Judaism. To my knowledge, no one has systematically gathered and evaluated the material that reports Jewish reaction to Christians.[13] The present study seeks to fill this lacuna.

The vast majority of relevant statements come not from Jewish sources but are filtered through Christian materials. To investigate the question of Jewish responses to Christians, I will: (1) evaluate pre-150 materials that report Jews saying or doing things to or about Christians; (2) look for trends that emerge in these materials; (3) ask which of these references point to Jews viewing Christians as outsiders; and 4) briefly survey later, post-150 materials to see if they support my findings in the earlier works.

The criteria I use to select materials are early dating and specificity of reference. The focus of this study is on materials redacted from about 30–150, or the post-resurrection Christian community up to the earliest apologists. While earlier data is embedded in later texts, there is no foolproof method for identifying it.[14] In chapter 10 we shall look briefly at certain later materials that shed light on this time period.

The passages must also give fairly specific information about Jewish reaction to believers in Jesus. I do not consider, for example, Christian attitudes toward Jews and Judaism, so I exclude general remarks about Judaism that appear, for example, in Hebrews or the *Epistle of Barnabas*. Often such remarks relate to Christian self-identification vis-à-vis biblical Israel, Scripture, or the covenant, and need not signal flesh-and-blood Jews actually doing or saying things to Christians.

Nor do I consider Jewish reactions to Jesus. While there is frequently a relationship between the portrayal of Jewish reaction to Jesus and the portrayal of Jewish reaction to Christians, the two kinds of references are not, on the face of it, identical. The Gospels are not primarily allegories, and Jesus is not always a "stand-in" for early Christians. At junctures where the portrayal of Jesus and the Jews seems especially pertinent I treat it as a related issue.

Once a text has been identified as pre-150 and bearing some specific reference to Jewish reactions to Christians, I evaluate its relative reliability and meaning. In order to determine historicity, I look for four things: corroboration, contradiction, literary convention, and theological tendency.

Of the materials that seem reliable, I must judge on which level of historicity to use them. Even an event or attitude that is inaccurate on the simplest level can be useful to the historian. The *Gospel of Peter*'s depiction of "the Jews" personally executing Jesus and witnessing his resurrection is doubtless unhistorical. Yet the work is useful as an index of popular attitudes and offers a hint of some of the content of Christian-Jewish propaganda and polemics. The nature of my sources presents a problem. With the exception of the historian Josephus (and the nonliterary evidence) all the early (pre-150) extant evidence comes from Christian writers. We only hear directly one side of the encounter. The reactions and attitudes I attempt to track are those of the non-Christian Jews; yet the reports are from the objects of those reactions. I must extrapolate as to what the Jews thought they were doing from what Christians said they were doing.

Having gathered and evaluated the material, I look for trends to emerge. What are the various reactions that Jews had to Christians? Are they all negative or do some positive reactions echo in the texts? Which trends have greater claims to historicity? Do various trends organize themselves geographically or chronologically? Are Jewish reactions primarily to Christian Jews or to Christian Gentiles? Are Jewish reactions to other Jews who profess Jesus generalized by Christian writers to apply to all Christians?

In particular, I consider the question of when Jewish actions or statements imply that Jews considered Christians total outsiders to the Jewish community, no longer authentic Jews or part of the people of Israel. Many other Jews might be outsiders to a particular synagogue, the Jewish community of a certain city, or a certain elite group, but would still be regarded as Jews by their coreligionists. Did Christians develop a sense of themselves as set apart from other Jews, outsiders to the larger Jewish community, at the same time Jews began to see them in this light, or did Christians begin to withdraw earlier? The presence of the Roman government is a constant factor: our actors belonged to two cults within a multiplicity of groups that made up Greco-Roman society.

Last, I consider certain materials from a later period that shed light on our texts. Do later writers confirm and carry out the images gleaned from our material, or have the issues changed? Do they provide perspectives that do not exist in our materials, such as the pagan or rabbinic view?

I have excluded materials that some readers might expect to see discussed here—namely most pagan testimony, a letter from Bar Kochba, works of Christian self-definition, and materials that reflect inner-Christian debates. Although pagans have a great deal to say about Jews[15] and a certain amount to say about Christians,[16] they have almost nothing to say about how Jews and Christians treated one another. I do not think that Suetonius is referring to controversies in the Jewish community over Jesus when he mentions disturbances over "Chrestus" (*Claudius* 25.4),[17] but rather I accept the arguments of D. Slingerland and others.[18]

Similarly, I reject the reference in a fifth-century church writer, Sulpicius Severus, which some people attribute to Tacitus (*Chronica* II, 30.3, 6, 7). Since the attribution is tenuous and its use of Pauline symbolism of Judaism as the root and Christianity as its offspring suggests a Christian origin, clearly nothing can be based on this as a historical description.

Bar Kochba's letter to Yeshua ben Galgula (*DJD* 2.159–61), according to my reconstruction, says "If any one of the Galileans who are with you causes harm, I will put fetters on your feet, as I did to ben Aphlul." In addition to the difficulty of establishing the correct reading, a survey of early literature provides little evidence that "Galileans" was a common early name for Christians.[19]

I have also excluded materials in which Christians try to define themselves relative to biblical Israel or Judaism, but make no clear references to Jewish activities. Many of these works show Christians working out their own theology including their orientation to the symbols of Judaism, Scripture, the Temple, and the commandments, but the works may have nothing to do with Jews reacting to Christians. Many works belong in this category—Paul's letters, Hebrews, *Barn.*, 2 *Clem.* 2.3, *Lives of the Prophets* 2.8–14. Virtually every original Christian thinker had to make some judgment about biblical Israel and its covenant.

Similarly, I have excluded materials about Judaizing—Christians of Gentile origin adopting Judaism or Jewish practices. In this category I include Galatians, the Pastoral letters (1 Tim 1:6; 2 Tim 3:8-13; Titus 1:10, 14), Colossians (2:16-22), Ephesians, Ignatius's letters (*Smyrn.* 5.1; *Magn.* 8.1, 9.1, 10.3; *Phld.* 6.1, 8.2), and *Did.* (8.1-2). These references show Christians attracted by Judaism or some of its rituals. They also show other Christians' disapproval of their fellow Christians' infatuation with Judaism. These quarrels are primarily internal Christian matters; they do not necessarily point to the activities of non-Christian Jews.

Ancient materials that touch upon the topic of this study in a general or indirect way are nearly innumerable. Any reference to Judaism or its symbols in a Christian work might spring from a historical situation. My task, however, is limited to the examination of rather specific responses of early Jews to believers in Jesus. Thus, many passages are not included here because they fail the tests of early dating or specificity or because they belong to one of the four categories of excluded materials mentioned above, pp. 4-5.

PART ONE

Materials That Report Jewish Reactions to Christians

CHAPTER ONE

The Pauline and
Deutero-Pauline Letters

Paul's letters contain relatively few remarks about the treatment of
Christians by Jews who did not share the belief in Jesus. Paul's
main concern with Judaism relates to his self-understanding or to
the winning of Gentile converts. Most of his difficulties with other
Jews are with those Jews who are fellow-Christians.

I have excluded the material in Galatians that relates to Paul's
arguments with Christian Jews over circumcision of gentile converts, since it reflects an inner-Christian dispute. Romans 3–4 and
9–11 represent a Christian Jew's reflection on the ultimate fate
of all Israel, but lend no specific information on what those
Jews thought and did about Christians. Similarly, 1 Cor 9:20–21
is excluded because it is primarily a statement of Paul's self-
understanding. I have also dismissed certain material from a
Deutero-Pauline letter—Col 2:11–23—that merely reflects an attraction to certain Jewish practices such as the observance of food
laws, the Sabbath and special days (as well as philosophy, angel-
worship, visions, asceticism, and a host of religious phenomena).

PAUL AS A FORMER PERSECUTOR OF CHRISTIANS

1 Cor 15:9: For I am the least of the apostles, unfit to be called
an apostle, because I persecuted the church of God.

Phil 3:5–6: . . . as to the law, a Pharisee; as to zeal, a persecutor
of the church; as to righteousness under the law, blameless.

Gal 1:13–14: You have heard, no doubt, of my earlier life in

9

Judaism. I was violently persecuting the church of God and was trying to destroy it. I advanced in Judaism beyond many among my
people of the same age, for I was far more zealous for the traditions
of my ancestors.
    Gal 1:22–23: . . . and I was still unknown by sight to the
churches of Judea that are in Christ; they only heard it said, "The
one who formerly was persecuting us is now proclaiming the faith
he once tried to destroy."

These statements are the only first-person accounts from a (former) non-Christian Jew of measures he took against Jewish Christians. Naturally he views these activities through the filter of his
present life as a believer in Jesus and missionary for the cross of
Christ.
    Whether or not one calls these anti-Christian measures "perse-
cution" or "discipline" depends on whether or not one believes in
Jesus. When Paul relates his former pursuit of Christians in
Galatians, he makes it sound as if his primary aim was to annihilate
the church. This is a retrospective assessment, however. At the
time he might have phrased it as correction of wayward Jews and
promotion of proper adherence to Torah. In Phil 3:6, for example,
Paul couches the reference to his persecution of the church between two statements underlining his fervent observance of the
law: "as to the law, a Pharisee," and "as to righteousness under the
law, blameless." Persecuting the church appears to be one aspect of
Paul's passion for the law. Similarly, in Gal 1:13–14, Paul links
persecuting the church to being a zealot for his ancestral traditions.
The term "zeal" is often linked to the word "law," whether the
Torah (Acts 21:20; Philo, *Spec. Laws* 2.46.253) or the secular laws
(2 Macc 4:2; Josephus, *Ant.* 12.6.2 § 271). Paul's defense of the
law against Christian assaults could have revolved around issues of
observance of particular commandments, as well as the broader
issue of a christological claim that God's Messiah is one whom the
law declares cursed due to his death on a cross. The two possibilities do not exclude one another.
    Paul simply does not say why he persecuted believers in Jesus.
Even the designation of his victims as "the church" is a function of
his vantage point as a Christian. Some of his own subsequent sufferings at the hands of non-Christian Jews seems to be linked to

his preaching to Gentiles, encouraging them to believe in Jesus and join in community with Jewish believers in Jesus without requiring their circumcision (Gal 5:11; 6:12). E. P. Sanders assumes that since circumcision in the mission to the Gentiles is the only issue identified by firsthand evidence, other Pauline references to persecution (including his own pursuit of the church) point to the same problem.[1] But we do not know whether Christians had stopped circumcising their Gentile converts as early as the 30s, when Paul pursued them; Acts does not encourage us to think so (15:1-5; 21:20-25).

Possibly Paul was prosecuting certain members of the church for what he regarded as assaults on Torah-observance, but we lack clear evidence for this early period. Christian Jews clearly disagreed on the relative authority of the Mosaic commandments for gentile converts to Christianity (Galatians; Acts 11:2; 15:5, 13-29; Phil 3:2-3).[2] We do not know how these people felt about their own or other Christian Jews' obligation to observe the commandments.

A. Hultgren argues that it was not failure to circumcise, or laxity in law-observance, but the proclamation of Jesus as Messiah that Paul and other Jews labeled as apostasy and sought to uproot.[3] Hultgren uses the testimony of Acts to support his case (7:5—8:3; 9:1-4; 22:4-7; 26:9-11, 14-15) as well as Paul's own testimony in Gal 1:13, 23. Paul's reference to his attempts to destroy "the church" and "the faith" suggest to Hultgren that it was the active proclamation of Jesus as the Messiah that offended Saul the Pharisee, not infelicities in legal observance. I have already noted the retrospective nature of Paul's testimony. Further, if confession of Jesus' messiahship were the crime that precipitated the wrath of Paul and others, that would not explain why the apostles remained untouched by the persecution that arose after Stephen's death (Acts 8:1). Surely they too proclaimed Jesus' messiahship.

Paul might have persecuted some early Christians for disloyalty to the Jerusalem Temple. Stephen's speech (Acts 7:44-50) and the charges against him (6:13-14) reflect a rejection of the continuing validity of the Temple and its rituals. Stephen and others suffered a selective persecution (Acts 7:54—8:1), while the apostles probably escaped persecution because they remained loyal to the Temple.[4] These many possible objections do not exclude one another.

The practice of circumcision and the rituals of the Temple are, after all, both aspects of Torah-observance. Even the objection to claims of Jesus' messiahship may stem from the pronouncement in Deut 21:23, "for anyone hung on a tree is under God's curse." Acts reports a list of overlapping charges against Christians in the 30s— proclaiming Jesus' resurrection (4:2), teaching in Jesus' name (5:28), blasphemy, speaking against the Temple, speaking against the Law, changing Mosaic customs (6:11–14). Similarly, Paul alludes to both circumcision and "the cross" as problematic issues that engendered persecution (Gal 5:11; 6:12). The proclamation of Jesus' messiahship and death on the cross provided the rationale, in some cases, for a rejection of the obligation to perform parts of the Law.

Nor does Paul say how he persecuted Christians, whether by verbal threats and harassment, flogging, imprisonment, stoning, or some other method. The testimony of Acts suggests Paul imprisoned Christians, consented to Stephen's violent death, threatened and wanted to kill members of the Way, wanted to bring individuals to Jerusalem for trial, and voted for the death penalty against them. Moreover he punished them in synagogues and tried to make them blaspheme. The evidence of Acts, however, has secondary status, since it derives from Luke's image of Paul, not from Paul's own testimony.

Galatians 1:13 and Phil 3:6 link persecution of Christians with Paul's statement of his former zeal for Judaism, as if one is proof of the other. Paul's rhetoric may be at work as he tries to make starker the contrast between his present and former life by exaggerating the severity of his former persecutions. Or he may be experiencing the "cognitive dissonance" that Segal suggests characterizes a convert like Paul. A person reduces the uncertainty and discomfort surrounding a major decision by disparaging the "way not taken."[5] For Paul, the "way not taken" was a continued life of Torah-observance as the means to salvation. Instead he cast his lot with a sect that he formerly considered heretical. Thus the severity of his earlier persecutions serves a function beyond mere reporting of his autobiography. Rather it heightens the wisdom of his present choice by exaggerating the negative aspects of the former one. Nonetheless, the basic tradition of Paul's persecution of some Christians in the 30s is fairly trustworthy. He probably did not invent it since he seems to feel some remorse about the persecution (1 Cor 15:9). Furthermore, Luke has a tradition of Paul as a reformed persecutor of Christians that seems independent of Paul's letters.

Coupled with the testimony of his own suffering for failure to demand circumcision of Gentile converts (Gal 5:11; 6:12), his fear of the "unbelievers" in Judea (Rom 15:31), and to a lesser extent, the evidence of Acts, Paul's references to his former life serve as witness to pressures exerted on some early Christian communities by other Jews. The material in 1 Thess 2:14-16, if reliable, suggests that Paul was not the only Jew to do so. However, the evaluation of this pressure as "persecution" comes entirely from Paul's post-conversion perspective. He hints that before his call, he considered these same activities part of his zeal for Torah-observance.

PERSECUTION BY THE JEWS

2 Cor 11:24–26: Five times I have received from the Jews the forty lashes minus one . . . on frequent journeys, in danger from rivers, danger from bandits, danger from my own people, danger from Gentiles, danger in the city, danger in the wilderness, danger at sea, danger from false brothers. . . .

Gal 5:11: But my friends, why am I still being persecuted if I am still preaching circumcision? In that case the offense of the cross has been removed.

Gal 6:12: It is those who want to make a good showing in the flesh that try to compel you to be circumcised—only that they may not be persecuted for the cross of Christ.

Rom 15:30–31 . . . join me in earnest prayer to God on my behalf, that I may be rescued from the unbelievers in Judea, and that my ministry to Jerusalem may be acceptable to the saints.

In these letters, probably written from Ephesus in the early 50s (Galatians and 2 Corinthians) and Corinth in the mid-50s (Romans), Paul reports being persecuted by his own people. The dispute in Galatia is primarily an inner Christian one between Paul and the "teachers," Christian Jews who advocate circumcision for their gentile converts and therefore is outside the scope of this study. Two references are intriguing, however. Galatians 5:11 implies that Paul's failure to preach circumcision to Gentiles resulted in his persecution. Who persecuted him? If he means the teachers themselves, then this verse refers only to an inner Christian dispute. But v. 11 may signal two groups. Some teachers are claiming that Paul really does preach circumcision for Gentiles, but he replies that his persecution by non-Christian Jews proves he does not. Paul complains that those who persecute him would remove the scandal of the cross by pressing circumcision, and it is the Jews who find the cross a scandal (1 Cor 1:23). Galatians 6:12 does not mention Jews outright, but Paul implies that Christian Jewish teachers were persecuted if they failed to circumcise their gentile converts. Non-Christian Jews would probably not care about the status of gentile Christians per se, but rather about the Christian Jews joining fellowship with Gentiles and all that fellowship implies—eating together, praying together, and intermarrying.[6] Paul does not reveal the identity of these people. Romans 15:31 is not specific and only tells us that Paul fears trouble from "the unbelievers in Judea."

2 Corinthians 11:24 is the only text where Paul ever specifies the nature of the punishment he endured or meted out. The thirty-nine lashes refers to the standard discipline delineated in Deut 25:2-3, that, by the tannaitic period, applied to the violation of a variety of prohibitions.[7] Paul's receiving this punishment implies his continued inclusion in a Jewish community.[8] There would be no reason or possibility to discipline an apostate or outsider with this particular punishment. From the Jewish point of view, then, the punishment was a gesture toward a fellow Jew that implied an expectation (or hope) for his reform and continued participation in the community. Paul does not say whether this punishment of thirty-nine stripes was for his failure to circumcise gentile converts or some other transgression. Nor does he indicate whether the "danger from his own people" was limited to synagogue floggings or included other forms of pressure. The umbrella term, "persecution," might mask a whole spectrum of activities, from inner-synagogue discipline to mob violence. Possibly Paul submitted to synagogue punishment at one stage, but later feeling against him took a turn for the worse when he remained intransigent and a "lynch mob" mentality took over. He would describe all these actions with the same words, particularly since he seems to have a penchant for seeing himself and other Christians as victims of persecution (1 Cor 4:12; 2 Cor 4:9; 8:2).[9]

Paul's testimony of his own suffering at the hands of some Jews does not contradict evidence from elsewhere. Acts gives a much more detailed picture of the pressures against him, though it never shows him as subject to orderly synagogue discipline. The likelihood that Paul and other early Jews who believed in Jesus sometimes came under the punishment of flogging is supported by Acts 5:40, where the Sanhedrin beats Peter and the other apostles before sending them away and by the prediction in Mark 13:9 (Matt 10:17) that "you will be beaten in synagogues." Although the mention of the Jewish punishment in 2 Cor 11:24 appears as part of a "catalog of circumstances" or "tribulation list"—a literary form probably used by Paul's opponents to promote themselves—the detail of flogging is not demanded by the form and need not be discounted because it is part of a literary convention.[10]

In the Pauline letters, most references to Jewish ill-treatment of believers are nebulous about the treatment and the transgressions of the believers. The only specific transgression mentioned is the failure to require circumcision of gentile converts (Gal 5:11; 6:12). The only punishment specified is the mention of flogging (2 Cor 11:24).[11] No single reference provides all the pieces of the puzzle—why Christians were punished (for laxity in law observance or failure to circumcise their gentile converts, an anti-Temple stance, or proclamation of a crucified criminal as the messiah); who punished them (the Sanhedrin, a Jewish court, the local Jewish populace, a radical fringe group); or how they were punished (flogging, harrying, social ostracism). We should be wary of generalizations from the few scraps of information Paul gives us and not assume that circumcision was the only issue, flogging the only response, nor the Jews always the persecutors. The Romans, for example, might punish a gentile Christian who underwent circumcision and tried to claim the shelter of Judaism.[12]

We can only speculate as to Paul's own view of his connection to the people of Israel as he experienced their discipline. Did he "submit" to synagogue discipline because he still saw himself as part of the community, as Sanders suggests? Or did it serve a practical purpose as part of his program to "become a Jew to the Jews" in order to win them, while becoming law-free to those who were law-free? He may have continued to see himself as an insider within the Jewish community, perhaps as a reformer. But he interprets all Jewish pressure against Christians, including his own pre-conversion actions as "persecution." This interpretation, quite understandable in itself, implies a consciousness of himself and other Christians as a separate, misunderstood minority. Such a consciousness is a stepping stone to the later development of Christians' self-identity as distinct from the Jews and Judaism around them, expressed by terms like a "third race" or the "true Israel."

1 THESSALONIANS 2:13–16

13 We also constantly give thanks to God for this, that when you received the word of God that you heard from us, you accepted it not as a human word but as what it really is, God's word, which is also at work in you believers.

14 For you, brothers and sisters, became imitators of the churches of God in Christ Jesus that are in Judea, for you suffered the same things from your own compatriots as they did from the Jews,

15 who killed both the Lord Jesus and the prophets, and drove us out; they displease God and oppose everyone

16 by hindering us from speaking to the Gentiles so that they may be saved. Thus they have constantly been filling up the measure of their sins; but God's wrath has overtaken them at last.

Authenticity

Embedded in a pastoral letter of thanksgiving, comfort, and exhortation,[13] these severe remarks about Jewish treatment of Christians relay three pieces of information; the churches in Judea suffered something from the Jews, the Jews drove those represented by "us" out of somewhere, and the Jews in some way obstructed Christian preaching to Gentiles. The earliest of Paul's letters, 1 Thessalonians was probably composed around 50 C.E.[14] and dispatched from Corinth. Thus vv. 14–15 would be the earliest recorded statements about how Jews reacted to other Jews who believed in Jesus (Paul's reminiscences about his life as a Pharisee give earlier chronological material, but are recorded later).

Due to characteristics of content and structure, some scholars have questioned whether 1 Thess 2:14–16 is authentically Pauline. B. Pearson has made the most comprehensive and persuasive case for interpolation, arguing eight points.[15]

1. Verse 16c refers to an event, now past, that is final and cataclysmic. The destruction of Jerusalem in 70 C.E. is the only real candidate.

2. The notion that the Jews killed Jesus sounds like other post-70 Christian ideas that interpret the destruction of Jerusalem as God's punishment inflicted on the Jews for killing the Christ.

3. Paul nowhere else attributes the death of Jesus to the Jews.

4. The ad hominem attack on the Jews in v. 15 smacks of Gentile anti-Judaism. It is difficult to ascribe to Paul, who is proud of his accomplishments in Judaism.

5. Paul does not think God has abandoned the Jews forever (Rom 9:1; 11:26).

6. No other evidence indicates that the churches in Judea suffered at the hands of the Jews between 44 and 70 C.E.

7. The mimesis terminology in v. 14 does not correspond to the way Paul uses it elsewhere. Normally he adjures his hearers to imitate him and the Lord (1 Cor 4:16; 11:1; Phil 3:17; 1 Thess 1:6), not other churches.

8. If vv. 13–16 are authentic, then there are two "thanksgiving" sections in 1 Thess. No other Pauline letter shows a doubling of this form.

In response to Pearson, several scholars have defended the Pauline authorship of 1 Thess 2:13–16. Pearson, they argue, imposes a false consistency on Paul's thought and use of epistolary form. On the form-critical problem of the double thanksgiving, K. Donfried, J. Orchard, and R. Schippers maintain that the anomalous patterns in this passage are the result of Paul's use of pre-synoptic traditions and formulae.[16] Others solve the problem of an apparent double thanksgiving by pronouncing it a "repetition" or "double climax,"[17] part of a "double triptych,"[18] part of a rhetorical pattern,[19] or further proof that a pure epistolary form did not exist.[20]

The questions of Paul's apparent anti-Judaism and his contrasting views of Israel's fate are thornier. The utterly negative portrayal of the Jews and sense of estrangement in this passage contradict the discussion in Romans 9–11, where there is hope of Israel's ultimate salvation and an appreciation of its role in God's plan. Witness also the contrast between the anguish Paul asserts over Israel's "hardening" in Rom 9:2–3 and the apparent satisfaction at the downfall of the Jews evident in 1 Thess 2:16c.

My position is close to that of Pearson, but with certain modifications. First, I would minimize the importance of his first point, that *hē orgē* must refer to the destruction of Jerusalem.[21] Although in retrospect, the destruction of 70 seems the most obvious candidate, "the wrath," could mean almost anything—a limited persecution of a local Jewish community, a reversal of economic conditions, a bad harvest, a plague of disease. From our retrospective vantage point, the destruction of 70 C.E. eclipses earlier disasters.[22]

Pearson's third point is, in my judgment, particularly weighty. The statement that the Jews killed Jesus is, to say the least, unusual for Paul. Although the crucified Christ is of paramount importance to Paul, nowhere does he rehearse the historical details surrounding Jesus' death. Either he did not know all the particulars, did not care, or assumed everyone already knew them. In 1 Cor 2:6–8 he assigns responsibility for Jesus' death to "the rulers of this age," a term that may stand for (a) the Romans,[23] (b) demonic powers, or (c) a combination of the religious and political establishment acting as agents of demonic powers.[24] As Paul uses it, the term is determinedly general and includes some human powers, but does not single out the Jews.

The strongest point against Pauline authorship of this passage is, in my judgment, the presence of a standard gentile anti-Jewish stereotype, namely that the Jews "set themselves against all men" (Pearson's point 4 see above, p. 17).

A classic pagan accusation against the Jews was that of misanthropy, "odium generis humani" or "misoxenia." Adherence to food laws in particular was often interpreted as antisocial behavior. For example, Diodorus Siculus, writing in the half-century before the common era, commends the actions of Antiochus IV Epiphanes against the Jews: "Antiochus himself detested this universal misanthropy and made it a point of honor to abolish their usages. He therefore sacrificed a large sow before the statue of the founder (Moses) and the outdoor altar and poured the blood over them. . . . He also forced the high priest and the other Jews to partake of the meat" (*World History* 34.1). Tacitus also connects Jewish customs with misanthropy: "Among themselves there is unswerving loyalty, ready compassion, but hostilty and hatred toward all others. Eating apart, sleeping separately, though a people most prone to lechery, they abstain from sexual relations with women of another race."[25]

It seems highly unlikely that Paul, a Jew who mentions himself as still part of the Jewish people and shows some pride in his pedigree (Phil 3:4–6; Gal 1:14; Rom 11:1), would indulge in such an anti-Jewish stereotype. Nowhere else in his letters does he echo pagan anti-Jewish charges.

On the whole, vv. 13–16 give the impression that "the Jews" are a group to which the author does not belong, and to which he feels no kinship. Paul, on the other hand, never denies his Jewish origins, even when lamenting Israel's mistakes (Phil 3:4–6; Gal 1:13–14; Rom 9:3; 11:1). Coupled with anomalies of form and structure, the incongruities of thought between 1 Thess 2:13–16 and the rest of Paul's letters lead me to suspect it is a post-Pauline interpolation.[26]

If 1 Thess 2:14–16 did not originate with Paul, when did the interpolation arise? It occurs in the earliest manuscript (P46, Chester Beatty papyri) around 200 C.E., which provides a definite terminus ante quem. Marcion, writing around 140, has at least part of v. 15, which he alters to "who killed the Lord Jesus and *their own* prophets,"[27] providing a probable terminus of 140. Obviously an interpolation is harder to fix in time and place, yet these verses deserve consideration as information about Jewish reactions to Christians, penned by an early Christian before 150 C.E.

Evidence for Jewish Pressure on Jewish Christians in 1 Thess 2:13–16

> For you, brothers and sisters, became imitators of the churches of God in Christ Jesus that are in Judea, for you suffered the same things from your own compatriots as they did from the Jews. . . . (v. 14)

Jewish Christian churches in Judea, the author says, were suffering from their Jewish neighbors. The passage does not specify which churches were involved, what kind of suffering they endured, when it occurred, how long it lasted, and how it was organized.

Few sources tell us anything about how Jewish Christian

churches in Judea got along with their neighbors. Certain individual cases of toleration surface, such as the "law-observers" seeking redress for James's death (*Ant.* 20.9.1 § 200) or Gamaliel's defense of the Christians (Acts 5:34–39). As we noted in our evaluation of Pearson, the notion that some Christians in Judea were harassed by some Jews coincides with information from a few other sources (Gal 1:22–23; Rom 15:31; Acts 8:1).

We know little of the nature of the trouble in Judea, whether it was verbal harassment, legal pressure, violent attacks, or simple banditry. With the exception of Saul the Pharisee we also do not know the identity of the Jews who opposed the Christians. If the 1 Thessalonians reference is pre-70, "the Jews" could stand for organized legal opposition by the high priests or Sanhedrin, as envisioned in Acts 4. Alternatively they could represent the brigands who terrorized the countryside in the anarchy of the late 40s until the war broke out in 66. Josephus reports a number of incidents of political terrorism (*Ant.* 20.5.4 § 113; *J. W.* 2.13.3 §§ 254–57, §§ 264–65; 4.5.4 §§ 335–44). Only a fine line seems to have separated acts of sedition from outright banditry.[28] The distinction was probably lost on the victims. Josephus states that the Roman procurator Gessius Florus gave them a free hand as long as he received a share of the booty. Their power was so great that leaving the country became the only remedy for some (*Ant.* 20.11.1 §§ 255–56; *J. W.* 2.14.2 §§ 278–79). The Pharisees are a real possibility before 70 C.E., judging from Paul's own testimony of his pursuit of the church, but after 70 they would not exert much power in Judea. Justin accuses Bar Kochba of persecuting Christians during the revolt of 132–35. Possibly Jews of no particular label were responsible.

The mention of the suffering of the churches in Judea does not fulfill any literary convention, formula, or sterotype except to provide a model for mimesis. But the mention of the Jews or Judea is not necessitated by the form or content of the surrounding material. Any suffering church would suffice for comparison. Indeed it would be more characteristically Pauline to compare the sufferers to Paul himself. We do not, therefore, suspect our passage is invented for literary reasons. Thus the tradition that Christian churches in Judea encountered some trouble from Jews seems relatively reliable, although the specifics elude us.

What about the second tradition—that Jews drove out Christian missionaries?

> [The Jews] who killed both the Lord Jesus and the prophets, and drove us out; they displease God and oppose everyone by hindering us from speaking to the Gentiles so that they may be saved. (1 Thess 2:15–16)

In this text, "the Jews" who are the objects in the first part of the sentence, now become the subjects. The locale need no longer be Judea.

I have already discussed the charge that the Jews killed Jesus. Though unusual for Paul, it is an implicit theme in the Gospels and explicit in Acts 3:12–15 and the Johannine Gospel. The charge shows up later with some frequency, often linking Israel's "no" to Jesus to the destruction of Jerusalem.[29]

The killing of the prophets—a standard motif in early Jewish literature—is here adapted to a Christian context. O. Steck traces the Deuteronomic tradition of the violent fate of the prophets (Neh 9:26; Ezra 9:11) and follows it through late biblical books, Apocrypha and Pseudepigrapha, Josephus and New Testament (Matt 5:12; 23:29–31, 35, 37; Luke 6:22–23; 11:47, 50–51; 13:34; Rom 11:3; Acts 7:52; Heb 11:32–37). Mark 12:1–12 may represent a parallel to this verse, since one plausible motive for the killing of the son is to hinder the gentile mission.[30] H.-J. Schoeps shows the motif of the murder of the prophets to be a traditional one in Jewish circles that surfaces in apocryphal literature.[31] Steck's work, however, refutes Schoeps's contention that the motif is unknown in the canonical Hebrew Bible. Originally, of course, the theme was an in-house critique.

The idea of Christian missionaries being driven out of a particular place meshes with Paul's testimony about himself (1 Cor 15:9; 2 Cor 11:26; Gal 1:13; 5:11; 6:12; Rom 15:31) as well as with the image of him in Acts as a perpetrator and victim of mob actions (8:1–3; 11:19; 13:45, 50; 14:2–5, 19; 17:5–9). It also harmonizes with Josephus' report of revolutionaries making life unbearable for more moderate members of the community in Judea in the midst of general anarchy and intolerance.

Possibly some kind of official expulsion from the Jewish community lies behind the charge of harrying. At Qumran, exclusion is the most frequently mentioned punishment (1QS 6.24—7.25), ranging from temporary exclusion from table fellowship to permanent excommunication from the community. Temporary punishments ranged from ten days to two years, so clearly the return of the recalcitrant member was expected. Later tannaitic materials show various levels of expulsions, some permanent, some temporary (m.Mid. 2.2; m.Mo'ed Qat. 3.1-2). Interestingly enough, the bans of niddui and ḥerem stipulate that the one under the ban observe the laws of mourning, not washing, cutting hair, or wearing shoes, as well as entering the Temple from the left side. So the person under a ban had to cooperate in the process.

As in the example of the suffering of the Judean churches, however, the identity of the Jews and the nature of their activity are unclear and could be anywhere on the spectrum from organized, legal action by community leaders to spontaneous violence from individual troublemakers. Equally possible is the chance that the "driving out" refers to social ostracism.

The charges of persecution, impiety, and misanthropy culminate in the final charge that the Jews were trying to prevent Christian missionaries from preaching to the Gentiles. Why might Jews concern themselves with Christian activity among Gentiles? What is at issue here may be any of the possibilities we have raised for the other Pauline materials—the failure of some preachers to demand circumcision of their gentile converts to Christianity, laxity in Torah-observance, proclamation of a crucified criminal as the Messiah, or preaching against the Jerusalem Temple. At least three of these issues caused problems among Christian Jews themselves. Would not non-Christian Jews have had even less reason to be sympathetic?

Fear of Roman reaction is another possible motive for Jewish resentment of Christian preaching. Events in the diaspora took place within the triangle formed by the Jews, the local gentile populace, and the Roman government. The Jewish community relied on Rome to continue to proffer certain privileges and to protect them from the intolerance of their gentile neighbors. Possibly Christian Jewish missionaries were stirring up the Gentiles and threatening the hard-won, delicate stability of the Jewish community. Local Jews were therefore anxious to eject them to remove a threat to their stable position and to openly dissociate themselves from the troublemakers.

Since the 1 Thessalonians 2 passage lacks detail and admits of so many interpretations, it is difficult to answer the broader question of how these Jews who did not believe in Jesus viewed the Christian preachers. The evidence is especially unyielding in the case of the first charge—that Jews in Judea somehow persecuted Christian Jews. Paul says he persecuted the church, but not why or how (cf. Stephen in Acts). It is nearly impossible to know if from the point of view of the Jews the anti-Christian action was meant as punishment of unruly insiders—implying their continued inclusion—or is meant to widen the distance between the community and people it views as outsiders, but may not be considered so by Rome. If the verses in 1 Thessalonians refer to the simple brigands Josephus writes about, surely the issue of insider-outsider does not even apply. Robbers do not spend much time considering their relative solidarity with their victims. Furthermore, extremist political elements like the Zealots surely considered nearly everyone else an outsider.

The second example of harrying could be directed at outsiders or insiders, depending on the motives. If the Jews were motivated by fear of Roman reaction, that would mean there was enough contact between the Christians and other Jews that the Romans were capable of seeing them as still part of the same community. One could say the same about the specific issue of speaking to the Gentiles. The Jews may have worried that they would be guilty by association with Jewish Christian missionaries and incur Roman displeasure. Or the Jews may have had their own theological investment in discouraging preaching to Gentiles; they might not have appreciated gentile converts to Christianity calling themselves "the true Israel" or the "chosen people" (1 Pet 1:2). Either case almost demands that the other Jews saw Christians as still "their own." If the Christians were total outsiders, why would other Jews have prevented them from preaching to Gentiles? Moreover, how could they prevent them?

In contrast, the Christian author of 1 Thess 2:14–16 shows no evidence of maintaining connection to the Jewish community. At least one pagan anti-Jewish stereotype appears. The passage is heavily couched in terms like "them" and "us," with the Jews playing the role of persecutors. Nor is the author particularly concerned with Israel's ultimate fate.

We have uncovered a certain disparity in 1 Thess 2:14–16 between how Jews seemed to evaluate other Jews who believed in Jesus and their place in the community, and how Jewish Christians evaluated themselves. From the Jewish point of view, two possibilities arise: either Jews who believed in Jesus were still within the broader Jewish community and subject to its discipline, or these believers were on their way to becoming outsiders, but not yet to the extent that the Romans would distinguish them from other Jews. From the point of view of the author of the interpolation, however, Christians were utterly distinct from the Jews.

Observations

The evidence from Paul's letters yields several pieces of information:

1. Paul the Pharisee persecuted the church in the 30s, before his conversion. He does not say why or how. At least some of this activity took place in Judea (Gal 1:22–23). His actions were compatible with his zeal for the Law and his ancestral traditions.

2. Paul the believer suffered a number of things including the Jewish punishment of thirty-nine stripes. The failure of Paul (and others) to preach circumcision brought on some form of persecution (Gal 5:11; 6:12). Some non-Christians in Judea posed a threat to Paul, and the teachers in Galatia tried to avoid persecution, but otherwise Paul does not specify the locale of persecution. Whether we can coordinate these bits of information into a coherent picture is debatable. Paul may have been flogged for some offense other than failure to preach circumcision for Gentiles, for example. The persecution to which he alludes in Gal 5:11 and 6:12 may be something other than synagogue discipline.

3. If 1 Thess 2:13–16 is authentically Pauline (not likely in my judgment), then it supports the picture already evident in other Pauline materials of some Jews making life difficult for their Christian Jewish neighbors in Judea. Christian missionaries were particularly targeted for going to the Gentiles either because they failed to circumcise these Gentiles, yet lived in community with them, or because some part of their message was unacceptable. Perhaps they did circumcise their gentile converts but taught them to

forgo other observances, proclaimed a crucified criminal as messiah, or denigrated the Jerusalem Temple.

If this passage in 1 Thessalonians is, as I suspect, a later interpolation, it might still support any of the Pauline material mentioned above, because it represents a memory of the same events to which Paul refers. It may, however, refer to later difficulties between Jews and Christians in Judea or the diaspora up to the year 200. Since the nature, motive, and scope of the anti-Christian activities are so vaguely stated in 1 Thess 2:13–16, other sources must supply the particulars of these activities.

CHAPTER TWO

The Synoptic Gospels

Between the testimony of Paul in the 50s and the testimony of Josephus in the 90s stands the evidence of Jewish reactions to Jesus' followers reported in the Synoptic Gospels. The priority of Mark and the Two-Source hypothesis are assumptions in this section.[1]

Mark, the earliest Gospel and source for Matthew and Luke, was probably written near 70.[2] Many scholars propose Syria as a likely candidate for the Gospel's provenance.[3] Rome and Galilee[4] are also possibilities.

Most scholars date the Gospel of Matthew around 80–90 because it relies on Mark and alludes to the destruction of the Temple (22:7), but it lacks Mark's hope for imminent deliverance. It was probably written in Antioch.[5]

I shall discuss the issues of origin and date of Luke-Acts in the section of this study devoted to Acts. I place Luke's Gospel in the 80s, but do not identify provenance, except to exclude Palestine.

Nowhere are the problems of historicity more acute than in the study of the Gospels. Because they narrate the story of Jesus' life, ministry, and death, the reliability of their accounts has naturally been an issue since the dawn of New Testament critical scholarship. Which stratum do the evangelists most faithfully record, the time of Jesus' ministry in the 30s, the period of the early church before the final composition of the Gospels—ca. 30–70—or the time of the Gospels' final composition—about 70–90?

R. Bultmann's influence has shifted attention to the second stratum, for he concludes that the Gospels spring from the kerygma of the early church, not from the life of Jesus.[6] Two more recent works take opposite views. C. Blomberg, summarizing the work of the Gospels Research Project, concludes that the Gospels are relatively trustworthy in their information about Jesus' life and ministry.[7] Conversely, B. Mack argues that the layers of the Gospels' formation and composition are the *only* available levels for study.[8] He wonders if the earliest "Jesus people" were not simply Jewish reformers with memories of Jesus' sayings and miracles. The more dramatic elements in the Jesus story were supplied by the imagination of the early Christians, who read back into Jesus' life the drama of Jesus' death and resurrection, the existence of the disciples, disputes with the Pharisees, Jesus as God and Savior. Mack asks what social and historical circumstances transformed these "Jesus people" into a "Christ cult." Most scholars take a position somewhere between these two scholars.

How then, do we evaluate the stories of Jesus' disputes with the Pharisees in the Synoptics? To take Blomberg's view, they reflect traditions that go back to Jesus' ministry and therefore do not relate to our topic, which only considers reactions to Christians after Jesus' death. To take Mack's view, conflicts between Jesus and the Pharisees *only* reflect the later Christian retrospective imagination of these conflicts and their ideal resolution.[9] Jesus is a mythic figure. While we might discover something of the Christian response to certain social factors using Mack's method, we glean little specific information about Jewish views of Christians. To take Bultmann's approach, nearly every conflict story would be crucial for our discussion, because it really tells us about pre-70 conflicts between Jews and Christians in the period before the Gospels' composition.

My position combines elements of all three views. The Gospel materials must be shaped in part by the experiences of Christians in the early church and in the communities of the Gospel authors. Yet to assign every bit of material to the compositional level seems overly skeptical about the process of transmission.[10] Surely the evangelists sometimes passed on traditions about Jesus because they thought they had happened, and not necessarily because they cloaked conflicts in the early church (at the pre-compositional stage) or in the time of the evangelists. Jesus must sometimes play the part of himself; he is not always a stand-in for later Christians.

I have chosen to exclude the many "pronouncement stories" where Jesus is in conflict with Pharisees or scribes or Jewish leaders, because I assume the Gospel author is frequently telling a story that he thinks took place in Jesus' lifetime and not necessarily reflecting a contemporary dispute between Jews and later Christians. Some pronouncement stories about Jesus are communicated because of their implications for later believers and some are not, but there is no sure methodological way to separate them.

I do, however, treat materials in the Gospels that show Jesus' disciples and followers in contact with other Jews. Bultmann is right, I think, that when the disciples are attacked and Jesus defends them, "it is the Church which defends itself by appealing to its Master."[11] Followers of Jesus in the Gospels are better candidates to represent later Christians and their relationship to other Jews a more likely cipher for conflicts of the later church. By appealing to the authority of the founder, these accounts justify then-current Christian practice.

By and large in the Gospels, other Jews react to Jesus and not to his followers. This is not surprising, since the aim of the Gospel genre is to narrate the story of Jesus. The followers appear in a vague way in the presence of the crowds, but the crowd normally plays no visible role or speaks any words (except Matt 27:25, where they represent opposition). The crowd forms a backdrop to more focused disputes. Let us examine the few relevant cases.

QUESTIONING THE DISCIPLES' OBSERVANCE OF LEGAL TRADITIONS

I have alluded to at least three layers of material in the Gospels—the level of the historical Jesus, the level of oral traditions circulating in the primitive church (pre-compositional), and the redactors' use and shaping of early oral and written materials in composing the Gospels (compositional). I will attempt to stratify our materials to aid in dating them, but with no access to Mark's sources, my conclusions will be tentative. Further, my interest is not the composition of the Gospel per se, but rather Jewish reactions to Christians. If, for example, material at the compositional level does not inform our topic, but material at the pre-compositional level does, then I will focus on the latter.

In the first set of references (Mark 2:18; 2:23–24; 7:1–5; and their parallels; see chart 1) Pharisees, scribes, John's disciples, or unspecified Jews query Jesus about his disciples' legal observance. None of the actions attributed to the disciples are specific transgressions of the Mosaic Law, but must reflect laws or customs that arose alongside or subsequent to the written Torah. Jesus' successful rebuttal of these halakic objections justifies the practice of the disciples (and later Christians) with the assertion of Jesus' greater authority.

The basic issues in the conflict stories probably belong to the pre-compositional stage. Features of Mark's Gospel suggest that his community was largely made up of gentile Christians.[12] Pharisees or other Jews would not criticize gentile Christians for breaches of Jewish legal traditions—fasting, Sabbath law, or ritual purity; these laws do not apply to Gentiles. Possibly the issues changed by the time of the Gospel's final composition, yet a certain animosity toward Jews remained alive in the Markan community.

The first example is Mark 2:18 and parallels:

> Now John's disciples and the Pharisees were fasting; and people came and said to him, "Why do John's disciples and the disciples of the Pharisees fast, but your disciples do not fast?"

At the earliest stratum, this was probably a pre-Markan memory of some discrepancy between fasting practices of John's people and Jesus' people, but it may yield information at the compositional level as well.

This tradition is fairly trustworthy at the pre-compositional level. Mark would have no reason to invent a story that underlines a conflict between the authority of Jesus and the authority of John, where John's people are more punctilious.[13] The mention of the Pharisees was probably added at the redactional level to help the story conform to Mark's other Galilean controversy stories or to reflect fasting as a controversial issue in Mark's own church. The phrase "disciples of the Pharisees" is otherwise unknown. Nor are the Pharisees ever categorized elsewhere with the disciples of John, but quite the opposite (Matt 3:7–10; Luke 7:29–30).

The author underlines discrepancies between the fasting practices of John's disciples (alluded to in Matt 11:18) and those of

Chart 1—Group A: Questioning Disciples' Observance of Legal Traditions

Context	Place	Jewish Participants	Activity of Jews
Mark 2:18 Jesus' teaching and healing	Galilee	"people"	ask why disciples do not fast
Matt 9:14 "	"	John's disciples	"
Luke 5:33 "	"	"they"	"
Mark 2:23–24 disciples pluck grain on Sabbath	Galilee	Pharisees (addressing Jesus)	ask why they are doing what is forbidden
Matt 12:1–2 disciples pluck grain on Sabbath and eat	"	"	"
Luke 6:1–5 disciples pluck grain on Sabbath and rub between hands	"	"	"
Mark 7:1–5 Jesus' teaching and healing	Galilee	Pharisees & scribes from Jerusalem	ask why disciples are eating with hands defiled and not observing the tradition of the elders
Matt 15:1–9	"	"	"

Jesus' disciples, as well as discrepancies between practices of the Pharisees and Jesus' disciples with consequent criticism from those quarters. We do not know if the practices of John's disciples and those of the Pharisees were identical, although the Synoptics seem to equate them.[14] Matthew and Luke report traditions that both Jesus and his disciples did fast (Matt 4:2; 6:16–18; Luke 4:2), but they are absent from Mark.

At the pre-compositional level then—ca. 30–70—we have evidence that Christians were criticized for not fasting as John's people did. The question to Jesus implies that the Jews expected some level of observance of extra-scriptural traditions from the disciples, and that they would have some practices in common with other Jews.

At the stage of Markan composition—around 70—things are not so simple. Mark, as we have said, may well have introduced the mention of the Pharisees to bring it in line with the other pronouncement stories that feature the Pharisees.

Yet this may also point to friction in Mark's community. Some of his people may have been criticized by Pharisees or other Jews, for whom "Pharisees" is a code word, for failure to fast, fasting on different days, or fasting in a different manner. We have three early references that suggest the Pharisees fasted (*Did.* 8.1; Luke 18:12; Matt 6:16). They or other Jews may have criticized Christians for their fasting practices. Possibly Mark's people did fast and he attempts to reconcile later church customs (*Did.* 8.1) with a known saying of a founder who (according to Mark) did not fast. Pharisees or other Jews may have criticized some Markan Christians for other reasons. Lastly, the hostility of the Jews may be a motif inherited from earlier, pre-70 churches but maintained in Mark's community regardless of whether or not any Jews were still in proximity. A combination of two or more of these factors is also possible.

By the time of Matthew and Luke, fasting among Christians certainly took place (Matt 6:16–18; *Did.* 8.1), so those Gospels are less hesitant to show Jesus or the disciples fasting. The Markan tradition is less readily applicable to those communities and its presence may show a simple desire to transmit Markan material. Neither Gospel alters the basic contours of the story, although Matthew changes the anomalous "disciples of the Pharisees" to "Pharisees."

The second example in this group is Mark 2:23-24 and parallels:

> One sabbath he was going through the grainfields; and as they made their way his disciples began to pluck heads of grain. The Pharisees said to him, "Look, why are they doing what is not lawful on the sabbath?"

In Luke's version (6:1-5) they are also rubbing the grain in their hands, or threshing. Harvesting grain and threshing are two of the thirty-nine labors forbidden on the Sabbath according to the Mishnah (m. Šabb. 7.2), and our passage suggests that they were already forbidden by some Jews as early as the New Testament period.[15] As in the first example, the charge against the disciples springs from a discrepancy between the way particular Jews observe the oral law and the way the disciples observe it. The objection of the Pharisees here assumes the disciples are, or should be, in some way bound by the law. The answer that Jesus gives—"the Son of Man is even Lord of the Sabbath"—may be authentic. Mark invokes it here to justify actions of the disciples that contravene some Jewish Sabbath laws. Redaction and tradition are especially difficult to separate here. The early Palestinian church likely encountered criticism from Jews for their distinct form of Sabbath observance. Yet similar scenes over Sabbath observance may have been played out again in Mark's time. Mark's church relied on the authority of the founder to counter objections to their form of law-observance or lack of law-observance.

The third example appears only in Mark (7:1-8) and Matthew (15:1-9).[16] Some Pharisees and scribes from Jerusalem challenge the disciples' failure to wash their hands before eating and accuse them of transgressing the tradition of the elders.[17]

> Why do your disciples not live according to the tradition of the elders, but eat with defiled hands?

The charge here is a matter of ritual purity, since it uses the word koinos.

J. Booth perceives a disjuncture between the two parts of the question in v. 5.[18] The second part of the question which asks specifically about ritual purity is probably pre-Markan and earlier than the more general question about the tradition of the elders.

Some scholars have questioned the reliability of this tradition, presuming that only the priests in the Temple were required to eat consecrated food in a state of ritual purity.[19] However, the custom of eating ordinary food in a state of ritual purity arose among the *haverim,* societies in some way related to the Pharisees.[20] The sources show the *perushim* (Pharisees) were distinguished from other Jews in part because of their scrupulousness about ritual purity.[21] Mark mistakenly says these strictures applied to all the Jews (7:3). He does not relate a current conflict. Either he was ignorant that ritual hand washing applied only to the *haverim* or he chose to expand and generalize the hand washing debate into an issue that is more basic and substantive for the pre-Markan church or his own community, namely the authority of the "tradition of the elders."

The Pharisaic criticism of Jesus' followers that they failed to observe cultic purity derives from the pre-compositional stage. Were it a live issue for Mark's audience, they would not have required his explanation of the custom. Some Jews apparently expected followers of Jesus to observe customs similar to the *haverim.* The second criticism—that Christians ignore the "tradition of the elders"—may derive from the pre-Markan or Markan strata. Our preceding two examples in this section showed that the authority of oral legal traditions was a source of dispute in the primitive church. The issue did not necessarily disappear. Some of Mark's people could be censured by Jews over law-observance, the Jews citing extra-scriptural traditions that the Christians did not accept, and the Christians citing the authority of Jesus.

Matthew's version of this pericope takes it out of the realm of cultic purity. The disciples did not eat with "impure" hands, but "unwashed" hands. Matthew moves the logion of Jesus in Mark 7:19-20 elsewhere (15:17–18). He removes "thus he declared all foods clean," and "what comes from outside does not defile a man." As Booth suggests, Matthew may have been trying to forestall an interpretation of Jesus' saying that would deny the validity of the laws of *kashrut.*[22] Matthew, who is writing out of a Jewish-Christian milieu, couches the story only in terms of a dispute over the validity of oral traditions. His community, too, may be an object of criticism for failing to accept these traditions as binding.

Thus we see several levels—the pre-Markan level that recalls disputes in the early church over the relative authority of oral traditions, the Markan compositional level that combines memories of those disputes with Mark's interpretation of them and their meaning for his community, and the Matthean level, where disputes over the oral law again come to the fore. In Matthew's Jewish-Christian diaspora church, the same drama that took place in the primitive Palestinian church is replayed. The details of the issues may not be identical, but the question of the validity of the "tradition of the elders" remains the same.

The three sets of references in this section attest to traditions—from the time before Mark's composition around 70 through the Matthean church of the 90s—that some Jews criticized Christians for their failure to observe certain laws that these Jews considered binding, though they were not part of the written Torah. Jesus' messiahship is not expressed outright in these disputes, but may be implicit in the Christian response to these objections that claims the authority of Jesus.

External evidence supports this notion of halakic disputes between Jews and Christians at or near 70. The oral law was not fixed until the codification of the Mishnah around 200 C.E. The tannaitic corpus records a myriad of conflicting interpretations even at the time of its fixing. Surely not all the laws and customs that arose to complement the written Torah appeared just before 200, but have roots in an earlier period.

Sectarianism was a reality in the period just before 70. According to Josephus, the Pharisees and Sadducees differed in part over the status of oral traditions. The Essenes criticized the "seekers after smooth things" (probably Pharisees) and their interpretations of Scripture. Given the fact that these three groups of sectarians seem to have partly defined themselves on the basis of how they interpreted Scripture, it would be very surprising if disputes did not arise over which oral traditions faithfully interpreted the written Torah. So the notion of Pharisees disagreeing with Christians over which extra-scriptural laws are binding is entirely plausible.

These three stories follow the "pronouncement story" form, similar to the Cynic *chreia*, where the master responds to an event, a situation, or an opponent's query with a memorable, unconventional saying.[23] More specifically, they follow the same form as Mark's other controversy stories in this section.[24] This form practically demands a challenge from an adversary, which could mean the Pharisees and their questions are mere types and extracting historicity is hopeless. In my judgment, however, the disciples and not Jesus bear the brunt of the the Pharisees' objections precisely because Mark is reflecting the time of the early church (and possibly his own time period) when Christians are under scrutiny from other Jews for their practices that contravene the extra-scriptural "tradition of the elders." Jesus' authority is invoked by Christians in their own defense. Pharisees apparently felt that the early Christians ought to be bound by their same traditions and show some surprise when they act otherwise. Surely these Jews saw Christians as part of Israel, subject to her strictures.

Criticism of the disciples is either implied or explicit in these several examples and limited to verbal queries. Similarly, the examples in the next group allude to simple lack of acceptance of Christian missionaries among Jews.

NONACCEPTANCE OF THE TWELVE AND THEIR TEACHING

Another kind of reaction appears in Matt 10:14: "If anyone will not welcome you or listen to your words, shake off the dust from your feet as you leave that house or town." Although this is a Markan saying linked to the commissioning of the Twelve, also transmitted by Luke, only the Matthean context specifies the mission is to "the lost sheep of the house of Israel," and therefore I treat only the Matthean reference. The verse clearly means that some of the house of Israel will not welcome the disciples or listen to their message. This nonacceptance of the messengers and the message is echoed in Acts, along with the prescribed shaking off the dust from the disciples' feet (13:51; 18:6), although there the reaction includes persecution. Jesus' prediction in the Synoptics neither gives a hint of any further reaction to the disciples, nor suggests that they are driven out.

Another prediction of nonacceptance appears in Matt 10:25b: "If they have called the master of the house Beelzebul, how much more will they malign those of his household!" Luke transmits the

Chart 2—Group B: Nonacceptance of the Twelve and Their Teaching

Context	Place	Jewish Participants	Activity of Jews (Predicted)
Matt 10:14 comissioning of the 12	Galilee	anyone of "the lost sheep of the house of Israel"	do not receive the 12
Matt 10:25b ″	″	"they"	will call those of Jesus' house "Beelzebul"

earlier saying, "A disciple is not above the teacher" (Matt 10:24; Luke 6:40), but is missing the Beelzebul saying. In Matthew's area, one of the weapons of Jewish-Christian polemic apparently is to link one's opponents with the devil. Association of Jesus with the devil or a demon (Mark 3:22; Matt 9:34; 12:24; John 8:48, 52) is probably related to charges of witchcraft and magic. Here the charge is extended to include his followers, the "partisans of Beelzebul." Christians employed the same barb against Jewish opponents (Matt 23:15; John 8:44). The New Testament has several accusations and counter-accusations of demon possession or association with the devil.[25] Likewise some at Qumran called their enemies "sons of Belial." It seems an obvious charge to bring against one's religious adversaries and was a frequent weapon in disputes between Christians and Jews. Neither of these examples suggests anything beyond verbal polemic. We will now turn to examples where Jews are said to have moved beyond debate to physical actions against Jesus' followers.

PHYSICAL ACTION AGAINST CHRISTIANS

Two sets of references point to explicit acts against Christians by Jews (chart 3). As with the previous group of examples, they are predictions for the future placed in Jesus' mouth, pointing to the time of the editing of the Gospels.[26] The first example occurs in Mark as part of the apocalyptic discourse of chap. 13 (v. 9) and is

Chart 3—Group C: Physical Actions against Christians

Context	Place	Jewish Participants	Activity of Jews (Predicted)
Mark 13:9 private meeting with Jesus	Jerusalem (Mt. of Olives)	they (in synagogues)	will beat you
Matt 10:17-18	———	men	will deliver you up to councils and flog you in synagogues
Luke 21:12	Jerusalem	they	(will lay hands on you and persecute you), delivering you up to synagogues (and prisons)
Luke 12:11	a village	they	will bring you before synagogues (rulers and authorities)
Matt 23:34 woe against Pharisees	Jerusalem	you (scribes and Pharisees)	will scourge and persecute prophets, wise men, and scribes)

paralleled in Matt 10:17 and Luke 21:12: "As for yourselves, beware; for they will hand you over to councils [*synedria*]; and you will be beaten in synagogues; and you will stand before governors and kings because of me, as a testimony to them." Luke 12:11 transmits a Q saying and alters it to include synagogues: "When they bring you before the synagogues, the rulers, and the authorities, do not worry about how you are to defend yourselves or what you are to say."[27]

Two elements that clearly refer to Jews include "they will hand you over to councils" and "you will be beaten in synagogues."

Paradidomai (hand over) is the same term used for Jesus and John the Baptist (Mark 1:14; 9:31; 10:33) and this is likely a conscious attempt to draw parallels between the sufferings of Jesus and John and those of a later generation of Christians. "Sanhedrins" probably refer to *gerousiai*—local councils with some authority to govern the Jewish communities in the diaspora. The Gospel author probably means *gerousiai*, but uses the slightly less appropriate *synedria* to draw a conscious parallel between later Christians, tried by local *synedria* and Jesus, who was condemned by the Sanhedrin at Jerusalem.[28]

The second element refers to some form of beating in synagogues. Matthew transmits the Markan saying, but changes the colloquial *daresō* (to skin) to the more technical *mastigoō*. The latter term translates the Roman punishment *verberatio* and here, the synagogue punishment of thirty-nine stripes, thus implying a judicial context. This, and the reference to another judicial body, the *synedria,* suggests that these are floggings imposed by a court, not spontaneous actions. These are likely the same kind of judicial floggings that Paul received (2 Cor 11:23–24).[29] Matthew also adds *auton* to synagogues, rendering it "their synagogues," a designation that many commentators say signals a distance between Matthew's church and the Jewish community.[30]

Matthew's hearers would not be subject to judicial flogging by Jewish councils, nor likely to submit to it, were they not still seen by the authorities as members of the Jewish community. As I argued in dealing with the Pauline material, there would be little reason or opportunity to discipline people who declared themselves outsiders. Whether Matthean Christians stayed in the community after this discipline, we do not know. Paul remained long enough to undergo the punishment five times. "Their synagogues" in Matt 10:17 may simply be opposed to "our synagogues" and refer to particular Jewish groups Matthew considers antagonistic to Christians, rather than to all Jewry.

In the context of one of the woes against the scribes and Pharisees, Matt 23:34 refers to the scourging of the prophets, wise men, and scribes. Luke's version, which does not mention flogging (11:49) is probably closer to the original Q saying, since it is more likely that a redactor would take an anonymous Wisdom saying and attribute it to Jesus (so Matthew), than that a redactor would take a saying of Jesus and attribute it to anonymous Wisdom.[31] Matthew is clearly using the tradition of the persecution and martyrdom of the prophets—a standard Jewish motif in both canonical and apocryphal sources.[32]

"Crucifying" in Matthew is a reference to Roman methods and may reflect again the motif of opposition from both Jews and Gentiles, as in the previous example. "Scourge in your synagogues" is an outright reference to judicial flogging, and also uses *mastigoō*. "Harrying from town to town" may or may not refer to Jewish persecution. B. Garland argues that the disciples are aligned with the prophets in Matthew's Gospel (5:11–12; 10:6–8).[33] The present participle form of *ekchynō* in v. 35 implies the blood is still being shed. This, combined with Jesus' direct predictions to the disciples, implies that some Christians underwent flogging and possibly death in Matthew's place and time.

Interestingly, the notion of Israel's collective guilt and subsequent suffering is echoed in 1 Thess 2:14–16, which contains the same themes as Matt 23—Israel's persecution of the righteous and prophets, filling up the measure of Israel's sins and Israel's present affliction as punishment for her guilt. "His blood be on us and on our children" (27:25) further underlines Israel's culpability and conscious acceptance of guilt for Jesus' death.[34] Possibly the themes of persecution of Christians and Israel's present suffering as punishment are also implied in Israel's cry.

Matthew does not merely transmit the Markan pericope but makes it more immediate to his setting. Writing twenty years after Mark, he uses the more technical term for flogging and locates the punishment in *their* synagogues. Quite possibly he is reflecting Christian confrontations with other Jews in his own community in Antioch. Luke, on the other hand, adapts the Markan tradition in a much more detached and general way. He eliminates the reference to flogging and adds the mention of prisons, which meshes with descriptions of Paul's and others' actions in Acts (4:3; 5:18; 8:3; 9:2; 12:4; 22:4; 24:27; 26:10).[35]

In light of Pauline corroboration, especially 2 Cor 11:23–24, I find little reason to doubt the Markan and Matthean traditions that Christians in certain places were subject to synagogue discipline, particularly in pluralistic places like Antioch. Major cities contained a number of house churches whose individual traditions must have varied. Perhaps some were entirely Jewish-Christian and saw themselves as part of the larger, local Jewish community. Some Christians were apparently considered part of the Jewish community by Jews (and perhaps also by Romans) and were seen as insiders in some way.

CIRCULATION OF A RUMOR THAT JESUS' BODY WAS STOLEN

Only the Gospel of Matthew contains the intriguing evidence of a Jewish rumor that Jesus' body was actually stolen by the disciples, who then proclaimed his resurrection (27:62–65; 28:11–15). The details of both references are historically problematic,[36] but the charge that the resurrection was a fraud would not have been a surprising one from nonbelievers. Verse 15b makes clear that this was a live rumor in Matthew's time. Such an accusation would obviously deny Jesus' resurrection and strike at the root of Christian belief.

We have no examples from early Jewish sources of this particular anti-Christian rumor. The medieval *Toledoth Yeshu* transmits a tradition that the gardener Judah (Judas) took the body.[37] In Christian sources, Tertullian alludes to two Jewish claims—that the disciples stole Jesus' body in order to claim his resurrection and that a gardener removed Jesus' body so crowds of visitors would not trample his lettuces (*De spectaculis* 30.6). H. von Campenhausen argues that the latter claim underlies John 20:15 where Mary Magdelene at first mistakes Jesus for the gardener.[38] Justin refers to a Jewish claim that the disciples stole the body (*Dial. Try.* 108), but he may be dependent on the Matthean verses.[39]

The unhistorical elements and Matthew's own mention of his contemporary situation point away from this being a genuine recollection of Jesus' death. Nor is there any congruence with the other Gospels. The *Gospel of Peter* contains an even more developed tradition of the chief priests and Pharisees asking for a guard for the tomb to prevent theft of Jesus' body.[40]

These traditions have more historical utility as hints of what Jews and Christians may have been saying about one another in Matthew's community and elsewhere. Matthew may have had

Chart 4—Group D: Circulation of a Rumor that Jesus' Body Was Stolen

Context	Place	Jewish Participants	Activity of Jews
Matt 27:62–65 before Pilate (Sabbath)	Jerusalem	chief priests and Pharisees	persuade Pilate to make sepulchre secure, lest disciples steal Jesus' body and claim his resurrection
Matt 28:11–15 meeting after guard's report of Jesus' resurrection	"	chief priests and elders	take counsel, bribe soldiers to tell people disciples stole Jesus' body while they slept
Matt 28:11–15		the Jews	this story has been spread among the Jews to this day

access to popular polemical and apologetic traditions that would have been more extreme and clumsier than literary ones. The resurrection would be an obvious point of attack for Jews who did not believe in Jesus. It is a main tenet of Christian belief and clearly difficult for nonbelievers to accept. A "naturalistic" explanation for the empty tomb had to be found. The idea that someone stole the body is an obvious solution. That the disciples took the body and forged the resurrection fits in with charges that Jesus and his followers were deceivers (*planoi*).[41]

How does this passage fit in with the broader question of whether non-Christian Jews saw Christian Jews as part of their community? Other Jews objected to the claim of Jesus' resurrection. They saw Christian Jews as wrongheaded, misguided. But whether they saw them as outside Israel, or Jewry as a whole, because of their unusual belief, we cannot know. Matthew's anomalous (for him) use of the term "the Jews" in this story suggests Christian Jews like him felt themselves alienated from Jewry because of their belief.

Observations

The charts above illustrate the four categories of reaction to followers of Jesus. The first may be characterized as halakic objections
to practices of the disciples. Group B deals with verbal jibes and
nonacceptance of the disciples and their preaching. The examples
in group C predict Jewish discipline or persecution of Christians.
The final category is a story from Matthew that identifies certain
Jews as the source of a rumor that the disciples stole Jesus' body
from the sepulchre while claiming his resurrection. All the examples, except those in group A, consciously point to a period after
Jesus' death; they are phrased as predictions or are said to continue
"to this day."

I observe the following points:

1. The earliest traditions, pre-Markan, or say, pre-70 to 70, are
disputes between Christians and other Jews specifically linked to
the observance of *halakah,* or legal practice. Other issues might
have been present, but are not expressed in disputes between Jesus
and the Pharisees over the disciples' behavior.

2. By the time of Matthew, in the 90s, Jews objected to claims
about Jesus, specifically, that he rose from the dead. This probably
relates to the claim of his messiahship. Matthew's many fulfillment
citations attempt to prove claims about Jesus from Scripture. While
these are partially for the sake of the Christian community itself,
they also suggest polemics with Jews who did not accept Jesus.
Claims about Jesus were doubtless points of contention from the
earliest days.[42]

3. The references to floggings and *synedria* suggest that some
Jews translated their disagreements with Christians into action.
This was happening in Mark's time, but was heightened in
Matthew's era. We do not know whether these punishments were
for offenses against practice or making claims about Jesus.

4. References in the Synoptics to Jewish reaction of any kind to
Jesus' followers are relatively scarce. The Gospels primarily tell the
story of Jesus' life. I have uncovered only seven cases (fifteen if
each Gospel account is counted separately). The great majority of
Jewish reactions are to Jesus himself. Because of the inability to
separate incidents that are recorded because they represent genuine
recollections of Jesus from those that are largely emblematic for

later followers, I have excluded disputes between Jesus and the Jewish authorities.[43]

5. All the above references depict a negative reaction to Jesus' followers, although the reactions range from mere nonacceptance to floggings. The gamut of reactions from sympathetic to negative (observable in Acts) is absent here. Yet no action by a Jew toward a follower of Jesus in the Synoptics indicates the follower was an outsider to Israel, although particular communities or synagogues might not have welcomed Christians.

CHAPTER THREE

The Book of Acts

Majority opinion places the composition of Acts in the 80s or 90s,[1] though a tremendous range of variation in the dating of Acts persists.[2]

The provenance of Acts is, as Fitzmyer remarks, "anyone's guess."[3] At best, we can say Acts was probably composed in a locale where the Pauline and Petrine traditions were strong—Antioch, Ephesus, or Rome.

I assume Luke relied on a variety of written and oral sources in composing his work because he includes material that he could not have known firsthand, or material that does not coincide with his broader themes.[4] These sources must remain hypothetical, since no parallel material exists for Acts as it does for the Gospels. Isolation of sources is not crucial for our question in any case, since certain kinds of relations between Jews and Christians often span more than one hypothetical source. We cannot dismiss any portrayal by assigning it to a source.

I am chiefly interested in questions of the historical reliability of Acts, an issue often wrongly linked to the issue of the identity of the author. If the traditional ascription to Luke the physician and/or companion of Paul is correct, that does not guarantee his accuracy or that of his traditions.[5] If the author is anonymous, he could still report reliably.[6]

For the purposes of this study, questions of who wrote Acts or where it was written are less crucial than the question of how reliable are the traditions it presents. In current scholarship, Luke the historian has taken a backseat to Luke the theologian and Luke the creative author.[7] Luke's literary and theological aims occupy the main focus of attention today. Yet the debate over the historicity of Acts has been a long one. British scholarship has been relatively positive about Acts' historicity, from Lightfoot and Ramsay to W. L. Knox and Bruce. German scholarship has, for the most part, evaluated negatively the historical worth of Acts, from Baur and his school to Dibelius, Conzelmann, and Haenchen.[8] North American scholars show a range of opinion. Mattill and Gasque align with the British approach to Acts. Cadbury and Lake take a moderate line and to some degree sidestep the question of accurate historicity. Cadbury notes the basic fitness of the narrative to its time, but recognizes "fatal discrepancies" in Acts.[9]

The confusion over the historical reliability of Acts is in large measure a confusion over genre. Genre is a clue to intent. If Luke is writing history we would expect a certain scrupulousness in reporting that we would not demand if he were writing a popular historical novel. Luke says in his prologue that he is trying to report what is true (Luke 1:3) but in what way is it true and at what level?[10]

Ramsay considers Luke a great historian largely because many of the details of the setting of Acts are borne out by Ramsay's archaeological work. Yet Luke may have achieved verisimilitude in the setting of Acts without necessarily intending to report actual events. Hengel classifies Acts as a "historical monograph," as accurate as the work of any other ancient historian.[11] Cadbury thinks Luke is closest to being a historian, but writes on a popular level.[12] Others compare Luke to the ancient historian Thucydides, particularly in the matter of composed speeches that strive for verisimilitude.[13] L. Donelson characterizes Luke as a cult historian who travels from place to place gathering traditions, setting down the origin of the sect.[14] Pervo observes that even scholars such as Haenchen who rate Luke as highly unreliable nevertheless classify him as a historian.[15]

C. Talbert argues that Luke-Acts follows the form of the ancient biography, which narrates the lives of eminent founders of philosophical schools and their successors.[16] Pervo's recent work theorizes that Luke's closest model is the popular historical novel, meant to instruct and entertain. It did not narrate events as an eyewitness, but wove together typical events to achieve verisimilitude. Lastly, Fitzmyer notes Luke's use of biblical models like genealogies or chronicles of Israel's history.[17] My judgment is that the attempt to isolate one and only one genre for Acts will fail. Acts fits no model perfectly. Luke probably did not choose one model to imitate, but as an educated person, used many of the conventions of his time. He drew from Hellenistic forms as well as biblical ones. He transmitted popular traditions. Some of his scenes are probably not historically accurate but typical of historical situations.

Acts contains some mistakes and discrepancies, but we should not exaggerate their significance. Even if the author was not Paul's companion, he possessed certain traditions about him. These traditions, written and oral, no doubt varied in historical value. The author himself may have also confused certain details. We can neither accept nor reject all the material of Acts *en masse,* but must evaluate individual elements.

My method in this study is to look for external corroboration or contradiction, literary convention, and theological tendency. Acts is a particularly difficult text to evaluate for historicity on the question of Jewish reactions to Christians. Little external evidence exists either to corroborate or contradict the material of Acts. Luke appears to use a number of literary conventions. As for the theological tendency of Acts, scholars seem to be at an impasse on the question of Luke's view of Jews and Judaism, particularly on the question of a continued mission to Jews.[18]

In considering Jewish reactions to Christians in Acts, attention has often focused on negative aspects of the depiction of Jews who do not accept Jesus. The material is variegated, however, as the charts below indicate. I detect at least five different portrayals of the Jews and their reactions to Christians. In addition to stratification of the material by type of reaction, I will note distinctions of time and place within those groupings that may point to development of relations.

NEUTRAL CURIOSITY

One category of reactions by Jews who do not believe in Jesus to Christians shows these Jews as mainly curious about Christians.

The examples that show these traits of neutral curiosity are set out on chart 1. Within this category are two kinds of references. In a handful of references in chaps. 2–5, Jews react to words or deeds of Christian preachers with wonder and amazement, similar to the ways in which they reacted to words and deeds of Jesus in the Gospel of Luke (2:47–48; 4:22, 32, 36; 5:9, 26; 8:25, 56; 9:43; 11:14; 20:26). The same words are often used, forms of *existēmi* or *thaymazō*. The setting in Jerusalem (save 9:21–22) and the identification of characters as rulers, elders, scribes, high priests, and captain of the Temple also parallel events in the life of Jesus as set out in Luke's Gospel.

Also within this group, I have included references to thousands of Jews in Jerusalem who believed in Jesus in the early days (2:41, 47; 4:4; 5:14; 8:5). Technically, these reports of conversions are outside the scope of this study (hence they appear in parentheses on the chart), because I consider reactions of Jews who did *not* believe in Jesus, but it would present a misleading picture of Jewish reaction in Acts to ignore the statements that Christian preachers met with a warm reception and considerable success in the early days in Jerusalem.

How reliable are these references that show Jews astonished and amazed at miraculous happenings associated with Christians? Luke's portrayals of Jewish reaction to Christian preachers in Acts may simply be imitating reactions to Jesus in the Gospels. Miracles often serve an aretological function in ancient novels, justifying the heroes and pointing to the god who is the source of their triumph.[19] In Acts, too, miracles vindicate Peter and Paul and link them to their master. Thus Luke could have included these incidents to serve both literary and theological aims.

Yet I do not dismiss a possible chronological factor. For the most part Luke places these incidents in the early days in Jerusalem. If Jews were astonished by Jesus' words and deeds in his lifetime, it is plausible that those who preached his message in the years just after his lifetime in Judea would also provoke astonishment and curiosity. In the thirties in Judea, Jewish believers in Jesus would still have been within the Jewish community and reaction to them would be an internal matter. Nor would it be surprising, in this period of sectarianism, if some groups such as the

Chart 1—Group A: Neutral Curiosity

	Activity of Christian Preachers	Place	Jewish Participants	Reaction of Jews	Further Reaction
2:5–13	speaking in other tongues	Jerusalem	devout men, multitude	bewildered, amazed, wondered, (others) mocking	
2:14–37	Peter's address	"	men of Israel, Judea all who dwell in Jerusalem	cut to the heart	received his word, were baptized
(2:41)	"	"		3,000 baptized	
(2:47)	community of believers	"		added daily to their number	
3:9–10	Peter heals man lame from birth	"	all the people	wonder and amazement	
(4:4)	Peter and John preach	"	the people	5,000 believed	
4:13–15	Peter, filled with Holy Spirit, speaking	"	rulers, elders, scribes, Annas high priest, three high priests	wondered, recognized them, nothing to say in opposition	conferred, charged not to teach or speak in Jesus' name

(5:14)	the apostles		multitudes	added to believers	
5:24–26	Peter et al., preaching in Temple, after miraculous release	"	captain of Temple, chief priests, all who heard (in synagogue), the Jews	perplexed, amazed, confounded	brought them peacefully, feared the people
(8:5–12)	Philip proclaims Christ	Samaria	multitudes	hear and are baptized	
9:21–22	Saul proclaimed Jesus	Damascus synagogues	Hellenists	[allowed Saul to preach]	plotted to kill Saul
9:29	Saul preaching boldly, spoke, disputed against the Hellenists	Jerusalem	[the Jews]	[allowed Saul to preach]	seeking to kill Saul
13:5–8	Saul et al., proclaimed the word of God	Cyprus synagogues	false prophet Bar Jesus magician Elymas	tries to turn proconsul from faith	
13:13–43	Paul et al. enter synagogue, preach from Scripture	synagogue, Antioch of Pisidia	rulers of synagogue, people	invited Peter and companions to preach	beg them to preach next Sabbath
			Jews and *sebomenoi*	follow Paul and Barnabas	
13:44	"	"	whole city [Jews?]	gathered to hear	

Chart 1—*Continued*

	Activity of Christian Preachers	Place	Jewish Participants	Reaction of Jews	Further Reaction
14:1–7	Paul and Barnabas enter synagogue, speak	Iconium synagogue	Jews and Greeks unbelieving Jews	believed stirred up Gentiles	city divided try to stone Paul and Barnabas
17:1–9	Paul argues from Scripture, three weeks	Thessalonica synagogue of the Jews	some the Jews	persuaded were jealous	gathered rabble, set city in uproar, haled Jason
17:10–12	Paul and Silas preach	Jewish synagogue Beroea	these Jews	received word eagerly, examining Scriptures, many believed	
17:17	Paul argued	Athens synagogue, marketplace	Jews and *sebomenoi*		
18:4	Paul argued every Sabbath	Corinth synagogue	Jews and Greeks	persuaded	

18:7–8	Paul went to house of Titius Justus, a *sebomenos*	Corinth	*sebomenos* Crispus, ruler of synagogue, Corinthians [Jews?], the Jews	[welcomes Peter] believed in the Lord believed and were baptized, asked Peter to stay longer
18:19–20	Paul went to synagogue, argued with Jews	Ephesus synagogue		
18:24–28	Apollos speaks boldly, confutes	"	the Jews	
19:8–10	Paul enters synagogue, speaks and argues for three months	"	some Jews and Greeks	were stubborn and disbelieved, spoke evil of the Way, heard the Word
(21:20)	Paul meets with James	Jerusalem	zealous for the Law	thousands believed
28:17–25	Paul calls together the Jewish leaders, testifies to kingdom of God, trying to convince them about Jesus from law and prophets	Rome	local leaders of the Jews	have no letters or reports against Paul, want to hear Paul and about "sect," appoint a day for Paul to speak

Pharisees, showed them more sympathy than the Sadducees or the priests.

The second type of reference—the majority within this category—is of a different type and follows a distinct pattern. As Paul and other Christian preachers move out into the diaspora in the 40s and 50s, the drama takes a different form. Paul and others are allowed or encouraged to speak in the synagogue. Those in the synagogue listen, often with eager interest, some debating the Scriptures. Paul stays a long time (14:3), perhaps as long as three weeks (17:2) or three months (19:8), preaching on successive Sabbaths (18:4). They invite Paul to stay longer (18:20). Some of the hearers are persuaded while others are not (14:1; 17:4, 12; 18:4, 8; 19:10; 28:24). In some cases, Paul's success causes "the Jews" to become jealous or angry and stir up feeling against him (14:2, 19; 17:5, 13; 19:9). The main treatment of these examples will be under charts 3 and 4, but even here we note that in them Luke makes a shift and labels the opponents of Paul and the Christian preachers as "the Jews," as if to imply that those who invited him to speak in the synagogue, begged him to return, and were persuaded by him were not Jews.

Luke can be deliberately ambiguous in labeling those who hear Paul, saying "they," "some," or "the people," when the setting is clearly the synagogue. In some examples, it seems there are Jews and Greeks, or Greek women in the synagogue. The *sebomenoi*[20] tend to be included with the Jews and not contrasted with them. At other times Acts states pointedly that Paul went to a *Jewish* synagogue or a synagogue *of the Jews*. In some cases, although Paul does not meet with total success in the Jewish community, he is allowed to continue preaching unhindered, for as long as two years (19:10; 28:30). Even the plots against Paul do not come to fruition until much time has elapsed; presumably he continued preaching in the interim (9:23; 14:3).

How likely is it that Paul and others were invited, welcomed, or allowed to preach in various diaspora synagogues? Paul himself never says so. He alludes many times to visiting churches, but never synagogues. We know, however, that he underwent synagogue discipline five times. If his statement that he became as a Jew to the Jews (1 Cor 9:20) is taken at all literally, it means he would have spent some time in the synagogue as he tried to win Jews.

Were itinerant preachers generally encouraged in diaspora synagogues of the first century? A Jewish traveler would be likely to head for the synagogue or Jewish quarter of a foreign city. The first century Theodotus inscription shows that the synagogue could function as a hostel for travelers.[21] Later rabbinic evidence suggests that well-known preachers would draw crowds from afar.[22] To put these two pieces of evidence together and conclude that Paul received a welcome and invitation to speak in the local synagogue whenever he arrived in a new city requires some acrobatics. The politically precarious situation of the Jews in some places suggests that a preacher of a politically questionable new group might not have been welcome.

The last example of positive interest in Paul's preaching appears in the closing scene in 28:24.[23] The previous two examples appear several chapters earlier, in chapters 23 and 19. This may reflect dwindling acceptance of Paul's message by Jews in the diaspora after the mid-50s. It is consonant with Paul's statements in Romans 9–11, written in the late 50s, where he judges the mission to the Jews a failure.

The theme of Jewish curiosity and interest may serve Luke's theological intent. Perhaps he wants to make clear that the Jews had a chance to hear the gospel and refused it. Perhaps he means to legitimate Paul and show that he is justified in turning to the Gentiles. The problem is that reaction to Paul is mixed. The pattern is one of a bifurcated Jewish response. Some Jews are persuaded. Even a casual reader can see that Paul and other Christian preachers have considerable success. Acts attests to literally thousands of Jews in Judea who become believers even before Paul's mission. The acceptance and rejection of Paul's message are often simultaneous in the first twenty chapters. Even in the very last scene in Rome, some Jews are convinced by Paul (28:24). Scholars who argue that Acts is the story of the "Gentilization" of Christianity must reckon with the "large islands of acceptance which jut out in the midst of opposition."[24] Acceptance of Paul's message among Jews may have dwindled but it never completely died out.

According to Pervo, the bifurcation of the crowd in its reaction to Christian heroes is a literary convention.[25] Some accept the hero, but the excitable crowd stands ever ready to turn violent. This theme of interest and mixed Jewish response seems to serve neither a theme of Israel's hard-heartedness that leads to the transfer of the promise of salvation to the Gentiles (as argued by Sanders and Conzelmann) nor Jervell's argument that Acts chronicles a successful Jewish mission, since the mission is only a partial success.

There is nothing essentially implausible in the response of neutrality and interest (and acceptance) toward Christianity among Jews. We lack significant external evidence to corroborate or contradict this picture. Although I have noted that such a portrayal could serve either a literary convention or a theological tendency, we cannot rule out historicity. I will combine the materials in this group and the next in order to chart the favorable response to Christianity reported by Luke and perhaps to discover a sequence in Jewish reactions to Christians.

GENERAL TOLERANCE

Another type of Jewish reaction in Acts overlaps with the first (note that 28:21–25 appears on both chart 1 and chart 2). This type shows a general tolerance of Christians, apparently on the grounds of fairness and justice. Unlike the previous group of examples, the Jews here are not curious about the Christians, and exhibit no real interest in Christianity, but are motivated by a desire to keep peace (19:33–34), be fair (23:9), or serve their own laws (5:34–39; 23:9). We see no evidence that the Jewish hearers are converted by the apostles or that their sympathy arises from a belief in the correctness of the Christian position. The Jewish hearers are particularized—twice given names or identified as scribes, Pharisees, or local leaders. Only once does the general label "the Jews" appear. Luke is unique among the New Testament authors in showing the Pharisees as particularly sympathetic to the Christians (5:34–39; 23:9; see also *Ant.* 20.4.1 §§ 197–203).

Every example in this category shows Christians as part of the larger Jewish group. This is not surprising in 5:34–39, which depicts Christians in the 30s before the Sanhedrin in Jerusalem. Yet even as late as 58 or so, Paul comes under the jurisdiction of the Sanhedrin in Jerusalem and is defended by some scribes. In both cases, the Christians are caught in the crossfire in an intra-Jewish struggle between Pharisees and Sadducees. In Ephesus in the

Chart 2—Group B: General Tolerance

	Activity of Christians	Place	Jewish Participants	Reaction of Jews	Further Reaction
5:34–39	on trial before Sanhedrin	Jerusalem	Pharisee Gamaliel	warns council to be careful with apostles, leave them alone	
			high priest, Sadducees		heed Gamliel's advice, charge apostles not to preach, beat them and release them
19:33–34	preaching (riot over loss to silversmiths)	Ephesus	the Jews	put forward Alexander	
			Alexander	defends the Christians before the people	
23:6–9	Paul on trial before Sanhedrin	Jerusalem	some scribes of the Pharisee's party	contend they find nothing wrong in Paul	
28:21–25	Paul calls together the (see chart 1) local Jewish leaders	Rome	leaders of the Jews	say they have received no negative reports about Paul, desire to hear him, appoint a day for him to speak, come to hear him	some convinced, others disbelieve, disagree among themselves

mid-50s a Jew named Alexander attempts to defend Christian practice before an angry Gentile mob.[26] In the final chapter of Acts, Roman leaders agree to meet with Paul, set a time for him to preach, and hear his preaching. No Jerusalem officials have sent any reports to Rome against Paul.

How reliable are these references to Jewish tolerance? Gamaliel's speech in 5:34–39 contains at least one error in chronology. Gamaliel the Elder, supposedly speaking in the mid-30s, mentions Theudas. If he means the same Theudas mentioned by Josephus (*Ant.* 20.5.1 §§ 97–99), he led his followers later, in the mid-40s, when Fadus was procurator. Nor is it likely that Luke would have had access to the words of Gamaliel's speech fifty years later. More likely Luke followed the conventions of Hellenistic writers of his time who freely fashioned the speeches of their characters. Perhaps Gamaliel was remembered by Christians as someone who counseled tolerance. Alternatively, Gamaliel in Acts is meant to typify some early Pharisaic responses to Christians.

Luke's portrayal of the Pharisees as sympathetic to Christians may fit in with his intent to portray Christianity as being in accord with Judaism. Even the Pharisees, the most respectable group, find nothing in Christianity to which to object. Perhaps Luke is reflecting his own post-70 situation, where the Pharisees are the *only* group left to appeal to. Some of the Pharisees may have been acceptable to the Roman government as quietists. Brawley's suggestion that the Pharisees are an intermediate group "on the brink of faith"[27] lacks evidence. If Luke wants to make this point he is overly subtle.

The type of the fair-minded and tolerant Jew echoes in two other examples. Justin's Trypho is a Gamaliel-like character, anxious to give Christianity a fair hearing but ultimately unpersuaded. Josephus reports of the "fair-minded ones" who protested the execution of James (*Ant.* 20.9.1 § 201).

The notion of a division between the Pharisees and Sadducees rings true and finds support in Josephus and the Gospels. Furthermore, the shared belief in resurrection makes it more likely that Pharisees would be sympathetic to Christians. As Sanders notes, "when non-Christian Pharisees appear in Acts, they always take the part of the church."[28] Luke emphasizes the wedge between the Pharisees and Sadducees, and attributes much of the troubles of the past to the Sadducees, claiming the Pharisees as supportive of Christians. The Pharisees defend the Christians in the Jerusalem Sanhedrin in the 30s, and take Paul's part when he comes before the same body in the mid-50s.

Note that this category contains only a few references. Sensible, tolerant responses from reasonable people do not make nearly as good reading as villianous behavior. Although there are only a few references, they are spaced evenly throughout Acts, the last one appearing in chapter 28. The theme of Jewish tolerance is a minor one in Acts, but it never totally disappears.

Again, it is difficult to evaluate Luke's picture of certain Jews, particularly Pharisees, as promoting tolerance toward Christians and a "hands-off" attitude. On the one hand, it suits the Lukan theme of Christianity as the true Judaism since it shows Christian ideas as unobjectionable to respectable Jews. Yet Luke does not make this a major theme. Were he creating these scenes to make a point, we would expect more examples and expect them to be drawn in bolder colors. In 19:33–34, for example, the reader can only guess at Alexander's position. Further, the division between the Pharisees and the Sadducees is supported by external evidence. Josephus also provides at least one example of Jews in the 30s who protest the unjust execution of James. These examples of Jewish tolerance from the mid-30s through the 50s in Jerusalem and Rome are plausible, though few in number.

Summary of Favorable Jewish Response to Christians

A combination of the material in this group and the previous one allows us to chart favorable Jewish response to Christians (see chart 6). The sequence shows that in the early days, crowds in Jerusalem are curious and amazed by the miracles and words of early Christian preachers. Thousands of Jews in Judea and Samaria actually believe and are baptized. Certain groups such as the priests and Sadducees in the Sanhedrin oppose Christians. They deal with them as members of the Jewish community, warning them and disciplining them. At least one Pharisee defends the Christians and counsels tolerance.

As the Christian mission moves into the diaspora in the 40s and 50s, Luke reports that Paul is regularly welcomed into synagogues and invited to preach by local Jews. Many of them are convinced by Paul's words. This pattern ends in chapter 19 with Paul in Ephesus, and would appear to be the end of positive Jewish response. In chapter 23, however, Paul is in Jerusalem before the Sanhedrin, and again, some Pharisees argue in his favor. The final chapter shows Jewish leaders in Rome interested in Paul's words, and some even convinced by them. Even those who are unpersuaded do nothing to oppose him. He continues preaching there for two years, "quite openly and unhindered."

These final two examples prevent us from charting a simple chronological course of dwindling favorable Jewish response to Christians. The bulk of references appear in chapter 19 or earlier and represent the period from the 30s to the early 50s. Yet even at Paul's meeting with the Jerusalem Sanhedrin in the late 50s, Luke portrays Pharisees as friendly to Christians. Shortly after, at the end of his career in Rome, Jews in leadership positions are interested in Paul's views, and in some cases, persuaded by him.

PLOTS AGAINST CHRISTIAN PREACHERS, SPONTANEOUS VIOLENCE

In this group, a large number of references show Christian preachers as the victims of individual plots or spontaneous violence by Jews in certain cities (see chart 3). With the exception of the people who dispute with Stephen in Jerusalem and the Sanhedrin, Jewish participants are labeled as "the Jews" or Jews from a certain place. Paul is usually the victim. The attacks seem sudden and capricious, drawing on popular hysteria. They seem to trail Paul throughout his career, appearing consistently throughout Acts.

Several elements make up the reactions of Jews to Christians in this group: (1) plots; (2) inciting crowds to violence; (3) seizing Paul, beating him or trying to kill him; (4) verbal abuse. How credible are these four elements?

Plots

The references to plots (6:9–14; 9:23–25; 20:3, 19; 23:12–27) follow a distinct pattern. With one exception (6:11–13)[29] "the Jews" are the culprits and the plot fails. Those who plot against Paul are inevitably foiled.

A successful plot, at least in its initial stages, is by definition a secret, so examples in the sources are not abundant. Paul says he narrowly escaped in Damascus, but does not implicate the Jews (2 Cor 11:32). The danger from his own people (2 Cor 11:26) could encompass a wide variety of actions. Paul's exposure to synagogue discipline, although it involved some preparation, is not presented as a conspiracy because it represents a public proceeding, not a secret or underhanded action. We face the same problems of interpretation here that we mentioned in reference to the words "discipline" and "persecution"; one person's plan or measured procedure could be interpreted by another as a plot.

Jesus is the victim of Jewish plotting in the Gospel (11:54; 19:47; 20:20, 26; 22:4–6; cf. Mark 3:6; 11:18; 12:13; Matt 22:15; John 11:53). Yet other early materials do not present Jewish plotting as a usual method of dealing with Christians or Christian missionaries. Luke may have wanted to parallel Paul's experiences with those of Jesus. Further, he may have wanted to contribute to his heroic portrayal of Paul by adding elements of suspense and intrigue.

Similar devices of conspiracy, propitious events, and narrow escapes are conventional. Joseph is accused by Potiphar's wife and imprisoned, but rescued when Pharoah's cupbearer suddenly recalls his ability to interpret dreams. *Joseph and Asenath* contains the same elements of a narrowly averted ambush as Acts 23:12–35. Theatrical elements include the production of Lysias's letter and direct speech.[30] Artapanus embroiders his story of Moses by adding various conspiracies against him.[31] That Paul faced opposition is certain, for he says so himself. That it was sometimes planned is likely. But I would attribute the elements of conspiracy and intrigue to Luke's dramatic technique.

Crowd Violence

The element of crowd violence represents one part of the dual reaction to Paul's preaching in Asia Minor and Greece. As I noted in group A (neutral curiosity), a cleavage often occurs in the group responding to Christian preaching (14:2–5; 17:5–9). Some of the Jewish hearers clearly do believe, but Luke separates them from the group that does not believe and he labels the latter "the Jews." The specific complaint of these Jews against Paul or the others is rarely made clear (21:27 is exceptional).

Chart 3—Group C: Plots, Spontaneous Violence

	Activity of Christians	Place	Jewish Participants	Reaction of Jews	Further Reaction
6:8–14	Stephen performs signs	Jerusalem	synagogue of Freedmen, Cyrenians, Alexandrians, those from Cilicia, Asia	arose and disputed with Stephen	secretly instigated men, stirred up the people, scribes, and elders, brought Stephen to Sanhedrin, set up false witnesses
7:54–58	Stephen's speech	Jerusalem	Sanhedrin	enraged, rushed upon Stephen, cast him out, and stoned him	
9:23–25	Paul's preaching	Damascus	the Jews	plotted to kill Paul	
11:19	——	——	[Jews—assume from 7:54–58]	persecution arose, scattered Christians	
12:11	rescued from prison	Jerusalem	the Jewish people	expecting (Peter's death)	

13:45, 50	Paul and Barnabas preach	Antioch of Pisidia	the Jews	filled with jealousy, contradicted Paul's words, reviled him, incited women, stirred up persecution, drove out Paul and Barnabas
14:2–5	Paul and Barnabas enter synagogue and speak	Iconium synagogue	Jews (and Greeks)	believed
			unbelieving Jews	stirred up Gentiles, poisoned them against brethren and stoned them
14:19	preaching	Lystra	Jews from Antioch and Iconium	persuaded the people, stoned Paul, dragged him out of the city
17:13	—	Beroea	Jews of Thessalonica	came to Beroea, inciting the crowds
20:3	Paul traveling, giving encouragement	Greece	the Jews	made a plot against Paul
20:19	Paul relating his travels to elders	Ephesus	the Jews in Asia	plotted against Paul

Chart 3—*Continued*

	Activity of Christians	Place	Jewish Participants	Reaction of Jews	Further Reaction
21:27–32	Paul purifying himself	Jerusalem (Temple)	Jews from Asia	stirred up crowd, laid hands on Paul, accused him of defiling Temple; the city people ran together, seized Paul, dragged him from Temple, trying to kill him, beat him	
22:22	Paul defends himself	Jerusalem	they	listened, cried out he ought not live, waved garments, threw dust	
22:30			the Jews	accused him	
23:12–27	Paul	Jerusalem	the Jews (40+)	made a plot, bound by oath to kill Paul, tried to enlist chief priests	

v 20			the Jews	agreed to ask tribune to bring Paul (ambush)
v 27		Jerusalem (letter from tribune to gov. Felix)	the Jews	seized Paul, were about to kill him
24:18	Paul defends himself	Caesarea (re: Jerusalem)	some Jews from Asia	——
26:21	Paul before Agrippa	Caesarea (re: Jerusalem)	the Jews	seized Paul in Temple, tried to kill him

References where the reaction is only verbal:

2:13, 15	Pentecost, speak in many tongues	Jerusalem	other Jews from every nation	mock apostles, assume they are drunk
18:5–6	Paul argued every Sabbath	Corinth synagogue	the Jews	opposed and reviled him
19:9	Paul spoke for three months	Ephesus synagogue	some	were stubborn and disbelieved, speaking evil of the Way

No one would dispute the reality of mob violence in the ancient world, particularly between Jews and Gentiles. Philo recounts anti-Jewish riots in Alexandria (*Flaccus* 7.44–47; 8.55). Josephus reports the same incidents in Alexandria (*J. W.* 2.18.7 § 487, §§ 489–92 and *Ant.* 18.8.1 § 257; 19.5.2 § 278, § 284) as well as incidents in Antioch and elsewhere (*J. W.* 2.13.7 §§ 266–70; 2.14.4 § 284; 2.14.5 §§ 289–92; 2.18.5 §§ 477–78). Often these writers describe the incidents as the Gentile populace rising up against the Jews. Jewish Christians might well have suffered from some of this anti-Jewish feeling, for some apparently did not distinguish them from other Jews (Acts 16:20). Paul mentions being stoned (2 Cor 11:25), but we cannot know if a group of Jews attacked him or a gentile crowd attacked him as an itinerant Jewish preacher with subversive ideas. Similarly the countless beatings he endured could have come from any quarter. 2 Corinthians 11:23–29 is comprehensive about the dangers Paul faced from all sides—Jews, Gentiles, Romans, even natural disasters. Thus we cannot necessarily attribute the stoning or beatings (except the thirty-nine lashes) to the Jews.

As a literary convention, the image of the excitable crowd, ready to ignite at any moment, features regularly in persecution literature.[32] The Jews and the urban rabble represent an ever-present potential for violence. Luke may have simply used this literary convention.

I would assign limited historicity to these traditions. Possibly Paul and other Christian preachers did occasionally arouse mob violence. Luke probably knew stories from various locales of crowd unrest. Whether the Jewish component of the crowds was as great as Luke suggests is doubtful. In at least one case, he admits that the anti-Christian actions included some gentile involvement (14:2–5). It would not be in Jewish best interest to promote civil unrest, which could result in their expulsion (Suetonius *Claudius* 25.4).

Beatings and Seizures

The number of times Paul is seized, beaten, or nearly killed in Acts is phenomenal. In Stephen's case they succeed in killing him, but Paul always shrugs it off and is soon preaching again. As Pervo notes, this is likely an aspect of Luke's lionizing of Paul.

Paul himself, however, says he was frequently imprisoned, received countless beatings, and was often near death (2 Cor 11:23).

At least some of these incidents probably involved Jews because Paul cites his own people as one source of danger. As with earlier materials, historical reliability is uncertain. The information here fits the literary convention of the sage whose sufferings magnify his strength of character and fits Luke's heroic image of Paul.[33] Yet there is nothing essentially improbable in the notion that some Jews in certain diaspora cities rose up against Christian preachers in the 40s and 50s and attempted to eject them from the community.

Verbal Abuse

The reference to the skeptics at Pentecost (2:13, 15) merely serves to heighten the effect and represents a stock response. Miraculous events are always attended by some scoffers. This is not in the realm of history.

If we admit the possibility of physical violence against Christian missionaries in the diaspora, the notion of verbal abuse requires no justification. The final two references to verbal abuse (18:5–6; 19:9) are curious, however. Paul is reviled in Corinth, but this hostility does not stop him from continuing to speak in the synagogue every Sabbath. In Ephesus, those who speak evil of the Way do not prevent Paul from speaking publicly for three months. The verbal abuse apparently had little effect and seems another version of the dual reaction to Paul. No doubt many of his hearers had little use for Paul's preaching, but the effect of their critiques is apparently negligible.

I will combine the examples from this group and the next group to chart unfavorable responses by Jews to Christians as reported in Acts.

ATTEMPTS TO USE OFFICIAL CHANNELS TO CENSURE OR PUNISH CHRISTIAN PREACHERS

Although this set of examples chronicles a series of hostile reactions by Jews to Christian preaching, it differs from the previous category in several ways. First, these accounts do not generally show the divided response we saw in groups A and C, where some of the hearers are persuaded by Christian preaching while others are not. Here the picture is unfailingly negative. Second, while a certain amount of lynch justice may be at work here, there is an attempt to use official channels—Jewish or Roman—to censure or

Chart 4—Group D: Use of Official Channels

	Activity of Christians	Place	Jewish Participants	Reaction of Jews	Further Reaction
4:2–3	Peter and John speak to the people	Jerusalem (Temple) Sol.portico	priests, captain of Temple, Sadducees	annoyed by teaching and proclaiming in Jesus' resurrection	arrested Peter and John, put them in custody
4:17–21	"	"	rulers, elders, scribes, Annas high priest, Caiaphas, John, and Alexander	decide to warn apostles to speak no more in Jesus' name	charge apostles not to speak or teach at all in Jesus' name
5:17–18	healing and exorcisms	"	high priest and all with him, i.e. Sadducees	rose up, filled with jealousy, arrested and imprisoned them	
5:33–40	Peter responds to question by proclaiming Jesus	Jerusalem Sanhedrin	high priest, all with him, council, senate of Israel	enraged, wanted to kill them	took Gamaliel's advice, beat them and charged them not to speak in Jesus' name
6:8–14	Stephen performs signs	Jerusalem	synagogue of Freedmen and others	brought him before Sanhedrin	
8:1	———	"	———	persecution arose; all but apostles scattered about Judea and Samaria	

Reference		Location	Actor	Description	
8:1–3	—	—	Saul	ravaged the church, entered houses, dragged off and imprisoned men and women	
9:1–2	—	Jerusalem	Saul	breathing threats and murder, asked for letters from high priest to synagogue of Damascus, to bring those of the Way bound to Jerusalem	got letters from high priest to bring brethren
9:21	—	Damascus (re: events in Jerusalem)	Saul	made havoc in Jerusalem, brought them (those of the Way) bound before chief priests	
12:1–3	—	—	Herod the king / (the Jews / Herod	killed James, brother of John / were pleased) / arrested Peter	
22:4	—	—	Saul (own statement)	persecuted the Way to death, binding and delivering to prison	
22:30	Paul unbound	Jerusalem	the Jews	accused Paul	
26:9–11	Paul before Agrippa	Caesarea (re: Jerusalem)	Saul	opposed Jesus of Nazareth, shut up saints in prison by authority of chief priests, cast vote against Christians when put to death	

67

Chart 4—*Continued*

Attempts to involve the Roman authorities:

	Activity of Christians	Place	Jewish Participants	Reaction of Jews	Further Reaction
12:1–3	—	Jerusalem	Herod the king	killed James, brother of John	
			the Jews	were pleased	
			Herod		arrested Peter
12:11	Peter's statement	"	the Jewish people	expected the death of Peter	
17:5–9	Paul argues from Scripture; cf. chart 3	Thessalonica synagogue	the Jews	drag Jason and brethren before city authorities, accuse them of acting against Caesar	
18:12–17	Paul's preaching	Corinth	the Jews	made a united attack on Paul, brought him before tribunal, accused him of persuading others to worship contrary to law	(Jews?) seized and beat Sosthenes

21:11	(prophecy of Agabus)	Caesarea (re: Jerusalem)	the Jews at Jerusalem	shall bind the man who owns this girdle (Paul) and deliver him to the Gentiles
24:1–9		Caesarea	high priest Ananias, elders, spokesmen	laid case against Paul before governor, charged him as ringleader, agitator
			the Jews	join in the charge, affirm it is so
24:27	———	"	the Jews	are done a favor when Felix leaves Paul in prison
25:2–3	———	Jerusalem	chief priests and principal men of the Jews	informed against Paul to Festus, urged him to send Paul to Jerusalem, planned an ambush to kill him
25:7	———	Caesarea	the Jews who had gone down from Jerusalem	stood about Paul, bringing many serious charges which they could not prove

Chart 4—Continued

	Activity of Christians	Place	Jewish Participants	Reaction of Jews	Further Reaction
25:13–19	(Festus puts Paul's case before Agrippa)	Caesarea	chief priests and elders of the Jews	gave information about Paul, asking for sentence against him	
			the accusers	stood up, charged him, had certain points of dispute about their own superstition and about one Jesus, dead, whom Paul asserted to be alive	
			the whole Jewish people	petitioned Festus, shouting Paul ought not live any longer	
26:2, 7	(Paul before Agrippa)	Caesarea	the Jews	made accusations because of the "hope in the promise made to our fathers"	

punish the Christians. Third, the victims vary. Paul is the usual victim of plots and mob violence in the previous group of references. Here the unfortunate are the apostles, Stephen, the church at Jerusalem (after Stephen's death), the unnamed targets of Paul's early fervor, James, Peter, and the saints. Last, the perpetrators vary. In the early days, opposition to Christians in Jerusalem comes from priests in the Temple or parties within the Sanhedrin. Saul persecutes the church and brings Christians to Jerusalem. Herod is also guilty of executing James the brother of John and arresting Peter, which supposedly pleases the Jews. After Christian preaching moves into the diaspora, the culprits are nearly always labeled "the Jews." These Jews who oppose Paul and others rely exclusively on local Roman officials to deal with the Christians. No longer do they employ local, internal Jewish councils or legal structures to contain the Christians. At the end of Paul's career, Jews from Jerusalem petition the Roman governor to release Paul to them, but without success.

This group, then, encompasses three kinds of references: Jews use Jewish legal channels to deal with Christians, Herod executes one Christian leader and imprisons another to placate the Jews, and Jews in the diaspora (and in Jerusalem) in the 40s and 50s rely on Roman judicial structures to control Christians.

Use of Jewish Legal Channels

In these references, the Jewish authorities try to control Christians by warnings, beatings, or imprisonment. Acts implies that Paul acted as an emissary of the high priests or Sanhedrin when he persecuted the Way (8:1–3; 9:1–2, 21; 22:5).

How likely is it that the Sadducees, high priests, and Sanhedrin arraigned themselves against Christians? At the time of Luke's writing, the Jerusalem Sanhedrin no longer existed.[34] The relative competence of the Sanhedrin in the diaspora communities before 70 would depend on the attitude of those communities toward the Sanhedrin. An agent of the Jerusalem Sanhedrin might be authoritative for some diaspora Jewish groups. Acts 28:21 implies that at least in Rome letters from Jerusalem were customary.

The Sanhedrin clearly enjoyed some authority in Jerusalem before 70. Josephus and the Gospels report Sadducean rivalry with other sects within and without the Sanhedrin and disputes over resurrection. The Sanhedrin arrests Peter and John who proclaim resurrection in Jesus. A possible clue to what worried some of the Sanhedrin appears in Acts 5:28, "You are determined to bring this man's blood on us"—an oblique reference to civil unrest and Roman reprisal. Similarly, in Philippi, Christian preachers appeared to outsiders as nothing more than rabble-rousing Jews (16:20). In the 30s in Jerusalem (and no doubt in other places at various times) Christians were viewed by Jews in authority as an internal problem, and an ear was always cocked toward Rome.

Although the question of the Sanhedrin's competence is not settled, there is no evidence that the Sanhedrin had its own prisons, as Acts implies, though it may have had temporary "holding cells." More likely the reference to prisons means the Sanhedrin handed people over to the Romans for imprisonment.

I have noted that the account of Stephen's trial (6:8–14) combines elements of lynch justice and elements of a Sanhedrin trial. The lynch mob aspect is more likely to be historical in Stephen's case, while the judicial proceeding is likely to be the Lukan overlay. Several aspects of the Sanhedrin trial are part of the Synoptic tradition of Jesus' trial and death: the false witnesses, the high priest's question, the Son of Man vision, and the dying prayer. Luke probably applies these traditions to Stephen to consciously parallel the first martyr's death with Jesus' death.[35] Yet the action of the council also fits with reports about other Christians in Acts. Paul claims he brought members of the Way before the Sanhedrin, Peter and others appear before the council more than once, and Paul himself is accused by its members. Luke may have included a Sanhedrin trial for Stephen because he views these actions as typical of early measures against Christians.

Another very different sort of action by a Jewish authority against a Christian appears in 12:1–3. Herod Agrippa I kills James and arrests Peter, which is said to have pleased the Jews. While these actions are not out of character, no external evidence of his career from Roman historians corroborates them. Agrippa went through the motions of piety to placate his Jewish subjects, but he is chiefly remembered for his extravagance.[36] Herod is a handy character, since he is both a Jew and an official of the Roman government. The Jews whom he tries to please actually do nothing and are only guilty by implication. In this reference, as in 12:11 and 24:27, a peculiar sympathy arises between the Roman officials and the Jews, where the former is anxious to please the latter.

Use of Roman Legal Channels

Incidents in Paul's career set in the 40s and early 50s show Jews in the diaspora accusing Christians before the local Roman authorities. No attempt to curb Christians comes from the local Jewish council nor from any synagogue authorities. In the mid-50s, Jews from Jerusalem go to Caesarea to accuse Paul before the Roman governor.

How likely is it that the Jews tried to get Christians in trouble with the Roman authorities? Jews no doubt had varying relations with the secular authorities in different places. They relied on the Romans to keep peace and protect them from the locals. The Jews could ill afford unrest that might lead to expulsions. They would be anxious to dissociate themselves from a politically suspect group.

The status of Christians relative to Rome is shaky. Luke is writing after Nero's persecution of Christians in Rome, probably during the reign of Domitian. Persecutions of Christians are attributed to Domitian (see the section of this study on Revelation, p. 99). By the time of Trajan, some kind of method for identifying and executing Christians is already in place and may hark back to Domitian's reign. Perhaps storm clouds were already gathering in Luke's time and Christians were already suspect. Many scholars argue that Luke is consciously recommending Christianity to Rome and emphasizing its political harmlessness.[37] In support of this contention, note how often Luke paints the Roman authorities as neutral or benevolent to Christians (17:8–9; 18:12–17; 21:32, 35; 24:22–23; 25:14–18).

Thus the Romans in Acts are surprisingly passive and the Jews are unable to get them even mildly excited about these Christian troublemakers. The limited persecutions of Christians in the 60s (Suetonius, *Nero* 16.2; Tacitus, *Ann.* 15.44.2–8) show that at least in Rome the emperor was not indifferent to Christians. Whether Romans were already suspicious of them a decade earlier in Palestine or other places is unclear. At least one example from the 60s shows Jewish leaders handing over an itinerant prophet, Jesus bar

Ananias, and asking Roman help to control him (*J. W.* 6.5.3. § 302–3). Similarly, Jewish authorities in Alexandria advised the people to hand over the *Sicarii* to the Romans (*J. W.* 7.10.1 §§ 409–19) and Jews in Cyrene tried to turn in a leader of the *Sicarii* (*J. W.* 7.11.1 §§ 437–50). Whether they attempted similar actions with Paul and others during his missionary career a decade or two earlier, we do not know. Luke, of course, writes in the 90s, when Christians have already suffered under Nero (and probably also under Domitian). He may have hoped to prevent further persecution by minimizing the Roman role in anti-Christian actions and shifting some of the blame to the Jews.

Many of the examples in this group draw a deliberate parallel between the suffering of the apostles and Jesus' own suffering at the hands of the Jews in the gospel narrative (Acts 21:11; Mark 10:33, 15:1; Acts 17:6-7; Luke 23:2; Acts 22:22, 25:4, Luke 23:18; Acts 25:25; Luke 23:15). This conspicuous parallelism throws some doubt on the historicity of every detail. Also, the references to Saul's actions against the church before his call may be meant to heighten the contrast between his present and former life and underline the intensity of the change.

To summarize, the examples in this group remain in the realm of the possible. We simply lack external evidence for the period 30–50 to inform specific issues in our material. Jewish officials might very well have warned, arrested, or punished Christian preachers, or sent letters about Christians to the Jewish community of a diaspora city. At least one case of Jews turning a troublemaker over to a local Roman authority occurs in the 60s.

Yet the picture of discipline by the Sanhedrin and Jewish invocation of Roman help also serves Luke's literary aim to parallel the suffering of later Christians with the suffering of Jesus. Further, the portrayal of the Jews as goads to Roman discipline of Christians may serve a Lukan theme of Christian political harmlessness. Thus we cannot make a clear judgment of historicity or nonhistoricity.

Interestingly, much of this material suggests that Jews initially considered Christians an internal problem, to be cleared up among themselves if possible. Should these efforts have failed, then a public dissociation of themselves from Christians might have been necessary as well as an invitation to the Romans to intervene.

Summary of Unfavorable Jewish Response to Christians

Combining the material from groups C and D allows us to chart unfavorable Jewish response to Christians reported in Acts (see chart 6).

The examples of Jewish response to Christians in the earliest days in Jerusalem show Christians as still part of the Jewish community. Predictably, some Jews from other cities ridicule those who speak in tongues. The Temple priests and the Sadducees in particular are annoyed by Christian preachers. The Sanhedrin assembles and hears witnesses against Stephen (which we take to reflect customary action, not a genuine recollection of Stephen's death). The Sanhedrin seizes, warns, and punishes Peter and John, but the Pharisee Gamaliel prevents them from further action. Saul is reported as bringing members of the Way to the chief priests for trial. All three sets of judicial actions set in the early 30s are attempts by Jews to deal with Christians within their own Jewish legal system.

Stephen's death is the first example of a mob action against Christians. The subsequent scattering of some Christians and movement of the mission to Samaria and out into the diaspora witnesses a change in Jewish reaction. Beginning at Damascus in the late 30s–early 40s, two things happen. First, certain Jews (and sometimes Gentiles, 14:2–5) in diaspora cities react to Christian preaching with anger and, at times, spontaneous violence. Second, Jews begin to invoke Roman aid in getting rid of the Christians. "The Way" seems to no longer be an internal Jewish matter. The goal of these Jews is not to warn or discipline Christian preachers but to drive them away or eliminate them. Herod, both a Roman official and a Jew, kills James, the brother of John and imprisons Peter. We do not know why he did so, but Luke says the Jews approved of his actions. In several places Luke implies that Roman officials acted against Christians because they wanted to please or placate Jews (12:1–3, 12; 24:27). Whether accurate or not, these examples show that Luke sees Jews as no longer acting directly against Christians, but relying on the power of Rome to carry out anti-Christian actions. Christians have become a problem external to the Jewish community. This scenario is repeated in many gentile cities, at least up to about 58, when Jews from Jerusalem again had to rely on Roman officials to deal with the troublesome Paul. The Romans, it seems, would not release him.

Interestingly, no Jews in Rome troubled Paul at the end of his career. Those who disliked his message simply walked away disagreeing among themselves. Possibly since Paul was already in Roman custody, they had no further power or desire to implicate him. Possibly it was late enough in time that Roman Jews were less fearful that Roman officials would fail to distinguish them from the Christians. Perhaps they were preoccupied with their own difficulties, having experienced an expulsion in the not too distant past (49 C.E.). In this final scene some Jews reject Paul's message, but otherwise reaction is surprisingly mild.

COMPETITION WITH CHRISTIANS IN THE REALM OF MAGIC

Only two references make up this group (13:6–12; 19:11–20). The first involves a Jewish prophet or magician[38] competing with Paul and Barnabas for the attention of the gentile pro-consul Sergius Paulus. The second involves some exorcists attempting to control evil spirits using Jesus' name. They show inferior control compared to the heroes of Acts.

How likely is it that Jewish practitioners of magic or exorcists viewed Christian proselytizers as magicians? We have no external first century evidence, although some later materials support the idea that nonbelievers thought of Jesus as a magician.[39] Ramsay suggests that Christians too were considered magicians and accused of similar crimes, nocturnal meetings, hidden crimes, and unnatural acts.[40] Luke therefore includes these incidents to refute an accusation that Christians engage in magic. Since we have no first-century evidence about the attitudes of Jewish magicians or exorcists, we have no way of verifying (or disproving) what Acts reports.[41]

The seven sons in Acts 19:14 seem to be a different group than the itinerants of the previous verse. The number, status, and Jewish identity heighten the story's effect. Not one person, but even *seven* people cannot do what Paul alone does.[42] Nor are they seven ordinary people, rather sons of the high priest. The Jewishness of these seven competitors may be mentioned simply because people of Luke's day considered Jews consummate magicians, not necessarily

Chart 5—Group E: Competing Magicians

	Activity of Christians	Place	Jewish Participants	Reaction of Jews
13:6–12	Barnabas and Saul, proclaim the word of God	Cyprus, synagogues of the Jews	magician, false prophet Bar-Jesus (Elymas)	opposed Paul and Barnabas, tried to prevent proconsul Sergius Paulus from hearing Barnabas and Paul
19:13–19	healing the sick	Ephesus	itinerant Jewish exorcists	tried to quell evil spirits using Jesus' name
			seven sons of high priest Sceva	"
			many who were now believers (Jews and Greeks of v. 17?)	came, confessing and divulging magic practices

because Luke wants to implicate all Jews.[43] In some early texts Jews are viewed as typical magicians.[44] This is probably the function they play in these incidents.

Luke's overall message in these stories seems to be that Christian faith and the use of magic are antithetical. In Acts 19:19, for example, both Jewish and Gentile believers forswear magic. The competition between Paul and other magicians represents a theatrical touch and allows Paul to demonstrate his superior powers. No other Christians or missionaries are treated this way, which further suggests that skill in the realm of spirits is part of the portrait of Paul, not a statement about Christians as a group or Jewish reaction to them.

These accounts show elements of burlesque,[45] legend, and dramatization. Luke may have had traditions from Cyprus and Ephesus of Paul as a wonder-worker which he has shaped. The tradition about Bar-Jesus is probably not entirely invented. If Luke had invented it, he probably would not have named the false prophet "son of Jesus." Luke presents these traditions as part of his lionizing of Paul. The literary elements here appeal to popular tastes and function to round out the portrait of Paul as a hero. That these magicians are Jews heightens the effect, since Jews were considered gifted magicians. These incidents also hint at jealousy that some Jews felt toward Christians because of their exorcisms and healings (Acts 5:17–18). The story also reflects an ancient milieu where magicians competed for the attention and financial support of the masses.

Observations

In summary, I have identified at least five different categories (and several subcategories) of the portrayal of Jewish reactions to Christians in Acts. The reactions to which I have attributed some historicity are tabulated on chart 6, grouped according to favorable and unfavorable reactions. I have not included on this chart our final category, where Jewish magicians compete with Christians, since the two incidents recorded do not yield significant information on how Jews reacted to Christians. The examples range from extreme hostility to fair-minded generosity. The broad range of the portrayals of Acts explains in part why such radically different theories of Lukan theology have emerged.

Looking at all the Acts material at once yields several observations. First, the most obvious one is that there are more unfavorable Jewish reactions to Christians than favorable ones. Further, the unfavorable response appears quite consistently throughout the book. There are no real gaps or long periods of time where there is no negative Jewish reaction. These points are crucial to those who debate Luke's views of Jews and Judaism and argue whether or not Luke held out hope for a further Jewish mission.

Second, Acts is not simple in its portrayal of Jews. If we include the conversions in Judea and Samaria as part of Acts' picture of favorable response, then the picture is weighted much more heavily at the beginning of the Christian mission in Judea. Opposition to Christianity in the Diaspora increased with the passage of time. Yet some interest and tolerance toward Christians never totally died out. Though there are no massive conversions of Jews to Christianity in gentile cities, at least some Jews are persuaded in Diaspora synagogues. Even in the final meeting between Paul and the Jewish leaders in Rome, some are persuaded by him. Acts really does not present a consistent pattern of initial acceptance of Christian preachers in Judea and increasing rejection in the diaspora as time advances.

The positive reaction by Jews to Christian preaching generally ends at 19:10, which refers to Ephesus in the early 50s. In 20:21 Paul speaks of testifying to Jews and Greeks, but refers to an earlier period. After this point, however, there is some positive response when the Pharisaic scribes defend Paul in the Sanhedrin (23:6–9) and when the Roman Jews show interest in Paul's views (28:21–25). Certain segments in the community, it seems, never totally rejected Christians.

Negative Jewish response to Christians appears among some groups from the very beginning in Jerusalem. Sadducees and priests oppose Christians throughout. Pharisees are always depicted as friendly to Christians. Thus negative and positive reactions appear alongside one another from the outset. Generally the unfavorable responses increase and the favorable ones decrease. It follows that as Christianity defined itself more clearly and became better understood, problems of belief and practice arose to strain relations with other Jews and the gap between the groups widened.

In the 30s in Jerusalem, negative reaction to Christians was

Chart 6—Jewish Response to Christians in Acts

Chaps.	1	2	3	4	5	6	7	8	9	10	11	12	13	14	15	16	17	18	19	20	21	22	23	24	25	26	27	28
Favorable Response																												
Jerusalem	b	b		b	b																		t					
Samaria	c	c	c	c	ct																							
Damascus								b	c																			
Cyprus													c															
Antioch											c		c															
Iconium														c														
Thessalonica																	c											
Beroea																	c											
Athens																												
Corinth																		cb										
Ephesus																		cc	ct									
Rome																												bct

80

Chaps.	1	2	3	4	5	6	7	8	9	10	11	12	13	14	15	16	17	18	19	20	21	22	23	24	25	26	27	28
Unfavorable Response																												
Jerusalem	m			oo	oo	mm	oo	oo	o		m	mo									mro	om	mm	rr	rr	r	ro	m
Damascus					o				m																			
Antioch													m															
Iconium														m														
Lystra														m														
Beroea																	m											
Greece																				m								
Ephesus																			m	m								
Corinth																		mr										
Thess																	r											

b = believe in Jesus   t = tolerance   o = official action

c = curiosity   m = mob violence   r = appeal to Roman authorities

note: some accusations against Paul are made at Caesarea, but involve Jews from Jerusalem and refer to events in Jerusalem, so are classified under Jerusalem on this chart.

81

generally expressed through Jewish legal channels. With the exception of the action against Stephen (which is partially portrayed as a legal maneuver and partially as a lynching), mob actions only take place in the diaspora. As Christian preachers moved into the diaspora, any legal action took the form of enlisting Roman help in limiting Christian influence. In part, this procedure must reflect the fact that Jews outside Palestine had less power, and that the Romans had less tolerance of civil unrest among Jews anywhere as the war of 66–70 approached. After Paul's arrest in 58, even the Jews in Jerusalem were forced to rely on the Romans to curb and eliminate a leading Christian. When the Romans fail to release him to the Sanhedrin, the Jews petition the governor.

Many of these reactions can be understood as attempts to deal with the presence of Christians as an internal issue. Some Jews counsel tolerance of these eccentrics, some talk against them. Feeling against these troublemakers occasionally turns violent. The Sanhedrin or local gerousia tries to contain them with warnings, threats, or discipline. Perhaps it is only as a last resort, when Christians pose a threat to their own stability, that some Jews invoke Roman help in dealing with the Christians. I have cited other instances where Jewish troublemakers became such a problem that other Jews handed them over to the Romans.

We should guard against oversimplicity in our evaluation of Acts' portrayal of Jews' attitudes toward Christians. Themes of Jewish acceptance and rejection appear side by side for a good part of the work. While unfavorable response represents the greater share of the material and there is a basic increase in negative Jewish response, certain positive portrayals appear as late as chapter 23 and the final chapter.

CHAPTER FOUR

The Gospel of John

The Gospel of John portrays Jewish reactions to followers of Jesus in unique and explicit ways. Most scholars fix the date of the Gospel's final composition at 90–100 C.E.[1] The traditional provenance of the Gospel in Ephesus (Irenaeus *Adv. Haer.* 3.1–2) cannot be proven or disproven, but the Gospel appears early in Asia and other sources associate Ephesus with Jewish hostility (Rev 2:9; 3:9; Acts 18:24–28; 19:8–20). Most scholars accept the idea that the Gospel is the product of an anonymous evangelist and a secondary redactor of the Johannine school.[2]

JEWISH REACTIONS TO JESUS

In treating the Synoptic Gospels, I excluded references to Jewish reactions to Jesus and mainly treated examples of Jewish reactions to his followers. In the Gospel of John, the two strands are particularly difficult to separate, for the following reasons: (1) The Gospel makes an explicit equation of the persecution of Jesus and the persecution of his followers (15:18–20). Suffering persecution is an essential part of discipleship. (2) The figure of Jesus is highly symbolic. John contrasts Jesus with the Judaism of his time, and portrays him as the replacement of Jewish institutions (2:14–21; 4:21–26; 5:16–17, 39, 45–47; 8:53–58). Jesus distances himself from Judaism by phrases like "you Jews" or "your Law" (8:17; 10:34) or "their Law" (15:25). This polarization is an anachronism and reflects later polemics between John's community and the contemporary Jewish community. Jesus' contrast with Judaism does, however, allow him to serve a paradigmatic role for later Christians. John's Jesus is "meta-historical"[3] and emblematic for his followers. (3) It is now axiomatic to say that the Fourth Gospel operates on two levels, reflecting situations that prevailed in the time and place of the Gospel's writing, as well as, or instead of in Jesus' time. J. L. Martyn has won wide acceptance for his conclusion that the gospel is a "two-level drama," functioning on the *einmalig* level of Jesus' day and the level of events in the author's day.[4]

The emblematic character of the Gospel does not necessarily make it less historical. No doubt it is based on its own primitive traditions of Jesus' ministry. The Synoptics, too, show Jesus in conflict with Pharisees, rulers, scribes, and Sadducees. Rather, the way John presents conflict promotes Jesus as the embodiment of the Christian struggling with Jews and Judaism. Yet the Gospel is not an allegory. To assume a simple one-to-one correspondence between the figure of Jesus and Christians in John's church would be naive. Jesus himself is never put out of the synagogue, for example, nor is he ever forced into secrecy out of fear of the Jews. The distinctive treatment of the disciples in John suggests they are particularly good paradigms for Christians of John's community.

Jewish reactions to Jesus range from belief (2:23; 8:31; 11:45; 12:11, 19), to a desire to kill him (5:18; 7:1, 11; 10:31–33; 11:8, 49, 53; 18:14; 19:7). They object to him on several grounds, associating him with demons (7:20; 8:48–52; 10:20) and identifying him as a Samaritan (8:48). The charge of demon-possession may be a Jewish counterclaim to Christian preaching of Jesus' miracles.

As in the Synoptics, Jesus' healing on the Sabbath is a source of his difficulties with other Jews (5:9–18; 9:16). However, two other sources of trouble between Jesus and other Jews are distinctly Johannine. First, there are hints that the Jews fear that Jesus will get them into trouble with the Romans (11:48–50; 18:13–14; 19:12; cf. Acts 5:28). Second, Jesus makes statements in the Gospel that profess his own equality with God (John 5:18; 10:24–25, 33, 38; 19:7). The "I am" sayings seem to profess Jesus' divinity, particularly the absolute uses, where no predicate appears (8:24, 28, 58; 13:19), but also the metaphorical uses (6:35; 8:12;

9:5; 10:7, 9, 11, 14; 11:25; 14:6; 15:1, 5). As Scroggs notes, even the statements that profess Jesus' subordination to the Father have the effect of making Jesus equal to God, since Jesus' will is a mirror image of the Father's.[5] These kinds of references do not appear in the Synoptics. They tell us more about the conflicts at the end of the first century and inform us of one of the primary reasons that Jews of the Johannine community were unacceptable to other Jews—because they professed Jesus' divinity. Such a claim looked to Jews dangerously like ditheism.[6]

The Gospel of Matthew, written in the 80s, hints that claims about Jesus, particularly his resurrection, strained relations between Christians and other Jews. John, writing about a decade later, gives fuller information as to how these claims included claims of Jesus' divinity, claims that came too close to a denial of monotheism for other Jews to tolerate. The belief in Jesus' divinity arose very early. The pre-Pauline hymn preserved in Phil 2:10–11 shows that Christian Jews applied the title *kyrios* to the exalted Jesus, suggesting his equality with God.[7] Before John, however, no sources so explicitly apply the divine terms to Jesus before the resurrection.

A large body of literature devotes itself to the subject of the Gospel of John and its relation to Jews and Judaism.[8] Many studies evaluate John's relative anti-Judaism[9] specifically, his use of the term "the Jews."[10] Most of these works concentrate on the author's theology and assume a connection to events in John's community.

In the Synoptic Gospels, Jews who oppose Jesus or the disciples are normally specified as chief priests, scribes, rulers, Pharisees, or Sadducees. John is remarkable for his generalizing term "the Jews."[11] The attitude of "the Jews" toward followers of Jesus is almost unfailingly negative in John (exceptions are 11:31–46 and 12:11–19). These references are of four types, three of which inform and support one another.

GENERAL PERSECUTION

The first set of examples claim the Jews were causing fear among Jesus' followers (7:13; 19:38; 20:19; see chart 1). John does not say what the Jews were doing, but only that Jesus' followers were forced into some kind of secrecy. Being a disciple of Jesus was the offense, but its exact repercussions are left unstated. Following

Chart 1—General Persecution

	Christian Activity	Place	Jewish Participants	Jewish Activity
7:13	No one spoke of Jesus openly	Jerusalem	the Jews	(source of fear)
19:38	Joseph of Arimathea, a secret disciple of Jesus	"	the Jews	"
20:19	disciples shut the doors	"	the Jews	"
15:18–25	Jesus predicts fate of his followers	"	the world (narrowed to those who claim the Law)	will hate and persecute Jesus' followers

the story of the crucifixion, however, the context implies that the Jews would persecute Jesus' followers just as they persecuted him. One passage, 15:18–25, is included in this group as a general reference to Jewish hatred and persecution of Christians, with no specifics attached. "The Jews" are not named but are part of an antinomy set up between "the world" and those who believe in Jesus. "The world," however, becomes increasingly specific in v. 22 when it recalls those to whom Jesus spoke, but who did not hear him. By v. 25, the world has been narrowed to those who claim the Hebrew Bible as their own, or the Jews. In general, the Gospel uses the expression "the world" to denote any opposition, including, but not limited to, "the Jews."[12]

Thus far the references are too general to evaluate for historicity. At most we can say that some Christians of a Johannine bent felt antagonized by other Jews. The motives or nature of the antagonism remain unspecified.

EXPULSION FROM THE SYNAGOGUE

The second set of examples (9:22; 12:42–43; 16:2–3; see chart 2) supplies a reason for this general fear. The fullest version appears in 9:22, "the Jews had already agreed that anyone who confessed Jesus to be the Messiah would be put out of the synagogue." Martyn notes the elements of a formal agreement or decision made before John's writing, where the confession of Jesus as Messiah results in exclusion from the synagogue.[13] The extreme fearfulness suggests something more serious than a temporary disciplinary exclusion. The basic miracle story in vv. 1–11 is free of polemic and probably represents the evangelist's tradition or source. Vv. 13–41 expand the story in terms of bitter controversy and the unsuccessful mission among Jews. This second strata must come from a later period and reflects the evangelist's struggles in his own church.

Martyn has been particularly influential in advancing the idea that John's statements about exclusion from the synagogue refer to the *Birkat ha-Minim,* or The Blessing against the Heretics, instituted at Yavneh around 85–90 to ferret out and exclude Christians, as part of a basic program of "closing the ranks" and establishing rabbinic orthodoxy after the destruction of the Temple.[14] The form of the *Birkat ha-Minim* discovered in a text in the Cairo Geniza

Chart 2—Expulsion from the Synagogue

	Christian Activity	Place	Jewish Participants	Jewish Activity
9:22	(blind man's parents fear the Jews) anyone confessing Jesus to be Messiah	Jerusalem	the Jews	to be put out of the synagogue
12:42–43	Many authorities did not confess belief in Jesus	"	——————	lest they be put out of the synagogue
16:2–3	Jesus' prediction to his followers	"	they	will put you out of synagogues

reads, "For the apostates let there be no hope. And let the arrogant government be speedily uprooted in our days. Let the *noṣrim* and the *minim* be destroyed in a moment. And let them be blotted out of the Book of Life and not be inscribed together with the righteous. Blessed art thou, O Lord, who humblest the arrogant." The rabbinic reference attributes it to Samuel the Small at Yavneh and implies that anyone who falters in repeating it would be removed (*b.Ber.* 28b). A third piece of the puzzle is supplied by Justin, who complains that Jews curse Christ and Christians in the synagogue (*Dial.* 16.4; 47.4; 96.2; 137.2).

Many scholars reason that the curse on the heretics described in rabbinic literature would be understood as a reference to Christians. A believer in Jesus who worshiped in a synagogue would be unable to repeat this prayer and pronounce a curse on himself. Therefore the worshiper would remove himself from public worship or be removed. This withdrawal would be equivalent to permanent expulsion from the synagogue. Therefore John 9:22 is explicable as an instance of the use of *Birkat ha-Minim* to permanently expel Christians from Jewish worship. This reconstruction that equates the instance of *aposynagōgos* in John with the *Birkat ha-Minim* in rabbinic literature rests on several assumptions:

1. Either the term *noṣrim* is original or *minim* would clearly designate Jews who believe in Jesus.
2. A Christian Jew in a synagogue would identify himself or herself as a heretic.
3. The *Birkat ha-Minim* was widely used in the Yavnean era.
4. The curse of *Birkat ha-Minim* carried with it the practice of expulsion from the synagogue.
5. The rabbis at Yavneh were engaged in "closing the ranks," and were increasingly exclusive and intolerant of divergent elements within the community. They had the power to implement a program of establishing uniformity of practice.
6. *Birkat ha-Minim* was used by other Jews as a tool for ferreting out Christians who remained in the synagogue but did not openly reveal their faith in Jesus.

Recent challenges to this reconstruction have focused on the ambiguity of the term *min*, the question of the originality and identity of the term *noṣrim*, and the question of the power and authority of the Yavnean rabbis.[15]

To consider each point in turn:

1. While *minim* must have included Christian Jews, as evidenced by tannaitic references (*t.Hul.* 2.22, 24; *Qoh. Rab.* 7.26), we do not know if it meant that exclusively. Its frequent and varied use in rabbinic literature suggests it was a "catch-all" term for any group of which the rabbis disapproved.[16]

2. A Jew who believed in Jesus and still worshiped in the local synagogue would be very unlikely to identify with the term "heretic." Quite the contrary, John's usage of Jewish terminology[17] and references to Scripture's witness to Jesus (5:39, 45–47; 8:12; 10:34–39) suggest that members of John's church would have considered themselves part of the "true Israel." "Heretic" is rarely a term one applies to oneself. Particularly if *noṣrim* is absent, the blessing is a generic curse against all who trouble Israel.

3. No one knows if the *Birkat ha-Minim* mentioned in rabbinic literature and attributed to Samuel the Small at Yavneh (*b.Ber.* 28b) is the same version that appears in the Cairo Geniza fragment. The Cairo Geniza version has no particular claim to antiquity or wide usage. It has simply survived. Nor are attributions to early rabbis in rabbinic literature always reliable. In this case no saying of Samuel is preserved, rather the anonymous redactor of the Gemara is describing an incident several centuries after it took place.

4. The *Birkat ha-Minim* expresses a general wish for the destruction of the heretics. There is no mention of their expulsion from the synagogue or the community. One who faltered on it was to be removed (*h'lwhw; b.Ber.* 28b–29a) from the post of praying, not from the synagogue or the community. The step from temporary removal as agent of the congregation to permanent expulsion from the community is the one step in the proposed reconstruction for which we have no evidence. Even Martyn must say the falterer is "*presumably* 'drummed out' of synagogue fellowship."[18] Patristic evidence for cursing Christians in the synagogue does not mention expulsion.

5. The evidence does not necessarily point to the period of the rabbis' settlement at Yavneh after 70 as a time when the rabbis tried to rid the community of heretical elements and attempted to impose a stricter rabbinic orthodoxy. In some ways, S.J.D. Cohen argues, the Yavneans tried to widen the umbrella to include varied elements within the community and to discourage a sectarian

consciousness.[19] The authority of the rabbis at Yavneh was far from absolute. Only diaspora Jews of a rabbinic cast would interest themselves in rulings transmitted from Palestine. In any case, some matters were left to the discretion of individual synagogues. J. Heinemann shows that the Yavneans fixed the primary subject matter of the blessings, but let individual communities determine their form, arrangement and secondary subject matter.[20] Thus *Birkat ha-Minim* might be interpreted in an anti-Christian way by a local group, but would be unlikely as a piece of empire-wide legislation. Heinemann also argues that the blessing was not a new addition to the Eighteen Benedictions, but an expansion and revision of an already existing benediction.

6. *Birkat ha-Minim* would not be a very effective tool in rooting out heretical elements because it would probably apply to less than half of the Jewish population. Only a person who could take on the obligation of *šaliaḥ ṣibu(w)r* or agent of the congregation, and pray aloud on behalf of the group would be required to repeat *Birkat ha-Minim*. Later rabbinic strictures excluded women, slaves, some handicapped persons, and children from this role. If, as seems likely, similar strictures were in effect in the first century, then any of these might believe in Jesus and remain in the synagogue, since he or she would never be asked to be a *šaliaḥ ṣibu(w)r*. From the point of view of the Christian Jews themselves, I have suggested that they would not consider themselves *minim* and would not understand themselves to be cursed. How would a Christian know that the ambiguous term *min* really referred to a believer in Jesus, unless hostilities were in the open? If hostilities were open, there would be no need for a special prayer to expose crypto-Christians.

In summary, I recognize the use of a blessing against the *Minim* in the late first century that in some places included Christians. But I question a link between this blessing and the expulsion of Christians from the synagogue portrayed by the Johannine author.[21] How then do we evaluate John's claim that Jews as a matter of policy expelled from the synagogue other Jews who professed a belief in Jesus?

I cannot locate other references to Jews expelling Christians from synagogues as a result of a previously ordained policy or decree. In the Lukan beatitudes (6:22) Jesus predicts the disciples will be excluded and their names cast out, but who is to cast them out and from where is unstated. Paul, Mark, and Matthew refer to synagogue floggings and all three Synoptics speak of being delivered up to councils. Acts and *Mart. Pol.* relate examples of mob violence against Christians. Justin says that Jews cursed Christ and Christians in the synagogue.[22] But nowhere in Jewish or Christian sources can we find another example of an official decree that excommunicated those who confessed Jesus from the synagogue. John is unique in his claim. Nor does the term *aposynagōgos* have a history as a technical term in Jewish sources.

Some Jewish circles employed expulsion. Temporary and permanent expulsion from the community are punishments stipulated in 1QS. Later rabbinic texts also report the use of several bans ranging from the mild and temporary *nidu(w)y* to the permanent *ḥerem*. Further, some of the general references to persecution in 1 Thess 2:14, the Pauline letters, and Acts could include expulsion.

Certain Christians, probably those who hold a lower Christology than the Johannine author, are still within the synagogue. John clearly disapproves of those he considers "secret believers," who practice Judaism outwardly while believing in Jesus (3:1–2; 7:50; 9:22; 12:42–43; 19:38; 20:19). He may be trying to persuade them to leave the synagogues. One of Jesus' bitterest attacks in the Gospel is reserved for Jews who believe in him. In 8:44 he calls these Jews "children of the devil." What calls forth this angry response? Seemingly it is their reliance on their status as "children of Abraham" (8:33, 39, 53). In other words, John scorns those who understand their belief in Jesus as continuous with patriarchal traditions. Similarly he contrasts disciples of Jesus with disciples of Moses (7:49).

The bitterness of John's attitude toward "the Jews," the antithesis he sets up between Jesus and Judaism, and the references to expulsion suggest that John and his group have been ostracized by some Jews for their confession of Jesus as the Messiah. This is continuous with information from Matthew, and later, Justin, that Christology was a major difficulty between Christian Jews and other Jews. Not all the Christian Jews John knows of have experienced expulsion. Some are still within the synagogue and see no apparent contradiction between traditional attachment to Judaism and faith in Jesus.

The absence of other clear references to expulsion of Christians

from the synagogue and evidence for the power of individual synagogues to determine much of their worship suggests that the expulsion John experienced was a local and limited phenomenon. A
more effective approach for Jews to dissociate themselves from
Christians would be to involve the holders of political power—the
Romans. By the time of the Johannine letters, there are no more
references to Jewish expulsion or persecution. The Johannine community has entirely separated from the broader Jewish group and
from other Christians who maintain ties to that community.

ATTEMPTS TO KILL CHRISTIANS

Two references to attempts to kill followers of Jesus constitute a
third type of Jewish reaction to Christians in the Fourth Gospel
(12:9–11; 16:2–3; see chart 3). The Jews plot against Lazarus not
because he confesses Jesus as Messiah, but because he is living
proof of Jesus' power. Jesus' raising of Lazarus has drawn Jews to
belief in him. Thus the plot against Lazarus is really a plot against
Jesus and an attempt to suppress reports of his raising the dead.
This borders on the issue of Christology, namely, Christians making claims about Jesus and his powers that other Jews found
unacceptable.

In the other example—16:2–3 (also in the previous group)—a
prediction that begins with expulsion from the synagogue ends
with a prediction that Jesus' followers will suffer death. "They will
put you out of synagogues. Indeed an hour is coming when those
who kill you will think that by doing so they are offering worship
to God." The verse makes clear this killing is religiously motivated
and viewed as *latreia,* service to God.[23] The "anyone" could of
course include the Romans. Since Jews in the diaspora lacked the
political power to execute their religious recalcitrants, possibly
Jews might be informers and Romans do the actual killing. Brown
suggests that the appearance in the same verse of the charges of
making Christians *aposynagōgos* and killing them means the actions
are related.[24] In other words, expulsion from the synagogue deprived Christians of the shelter of Judaism and left them vulnera-
ble to the Romans. Christians could no longer rely on Judaism's
right of assembly and exemption from imperial worship and could

Chart 3—Attempts to Kill Christians

	Christian Activity	Place	Jewish Participants	Jewish Activity
12:9–11	Lazarus raised from the dead	Bethany	chief priests	plan to put Lazarus to death
16:2–3	Jesus' prediction to his followers	Jerusalem	whoever	kills you will consider it service to God

Chart 4—Positive Responses

	Christian Activity	Place	Jewish Participants	Jewish Activity
11:19–33	Martha and Mary mourn Lazarus	Bethany	the Jews	console Martha and Mary
12:11–19	Jesus enters	Jerusalem	many Jews	come to believe in Jesus
			the crowd	greets Jesus as King of Israel
			the Pharisees	decide to do nothing in response

be accused of impiety or treason. Jews "kill" Christians, then, by withdrawing the protection of Judaism.

The idea that Jews were in some way responsible for the deaths of Christians finds support in Matthew (23:34); Josephus (*Ant.* 20.9.1 §§ 200–2); Acts (see charts 3 and 4); as well as in later literature (Justin, *Mart. Pol.*). Obviously the idea of Christians suffering death also serves John's themes of persecution and imitation of Jesus.

I would attribute a certain amount of historicity to these two statements, not at the level of Jesus' ministry in the 30s, but at the level of John's composition in the 90s. Johannine Christians feel threatened and fear Jewish ill-feeling against them will lead to their death. The threat is put in such a general way, however, that it could cover anything from spontaneous mob feeling to informing to the Romans. Note that at nearby Smyrna, the author of Revelation complains about the "slander of the synagogue of Satan" as well as alluding to Roman persecution. Given the context of anti-Jewish polemic and persecution in the Fourth Gospel, it is perhaps surprising that there are only two possible references to Jews killing Christians, and very general ones at that.

POSITIVE RESPONSE

Two final examples depart entirely from the other Johannine statements about Jewish reaction to Jesus' followers. In 11:19, 31, 33, the Jews console Mary and Martha at the death of their brother Lazarus. These are clearly Jews who do not believe in Jesus, since it is not until 11:45, after they see Jesus raise Lazarus, that some of them come to believe in him. Similarly, in 12:11–19 a crowd goes out to meet Jesus, waving palm branches and declaring him the king of Israel. Many Jews begin to believe in him. The Pharisees decide they can do nothing to stop this positive response to Jesus. Here again is the bifurcation of the group "the Jews" into those who believe and those who oppose Jesus (vv. 36–37, 45–46), a bifurcation that has characterized Jewish reaction to Jesus in the other Gospels. These examples show, however, that even in the Fourth Gospel, where the statements relating to Jewish treatment of Jesus' followers are more bitter than in the Synoptics, the negativism is not completely unrelieved. It also suggests that Jews who believed in Jesus were still seen as part of the community by some other Jews.

Observations

What information does the Fourth Gospel contribute to the broader question of how Jews who did not believe in Jesus saw Jews who were believers?

1. Some Christians were apparently still attending the synagogue since John finds it necessary to censure them and encourage them to break openly with the synagogue and its traditions. Whether these people were secretive about their belief in Jesus or whether John interprets their presence there as proof that they have not really declared themselves is unclear. These believers probably held a lower Christology than John, one that earned them John's contempt.

2. Some followers of Jesus who are mourners are comforted at the death of their brother by other Jews. Apparently their faith in Jesus does not deprive them of the comfort of at least some part of the larger Jewish community.

3. Some Pharisees decide that they cannot effectively do anything to prevent other Jews from believing in Jesus.

4. Some Jews in John's community are being expelled from the synagogue because they declare that Jesus is the Messiah. These Jews probably hold a high Christology like John's that makes them intolerable to other Jews.

5. Some Jews are doing things that cause fear among Christians and may lead to their death at Roman hands. No reference to anything like synagogue discipline occurs here. The Christians who are subject to these pressures see themselves as completely alienated from Judaism.

The results are mixed. Some Christians are still insiders. They continue to attend the synagogue and want to remain there. Perhaps their lower Christology makes them still acceptable. Johannine Christians, however, have made the break with the synagogue and now suffer the consequences. Probably their higher Christology was interpreted as too close to ditheism and other Jews found this impossible to tolerate. They have been alienated from the larger Jewish community, suffered in some way, and even fear this ill-feeling will lead to their death. The break with Judaism leaves them open to Roman charges that they are an illegal and subversive group. Other Jews see them as outsiders to the Jewish community, as they certainly see themselves.

Thus by the early 90s, in at least one area of Asia Minor, some Jewish Christians made claims about Jesus that drew fire from other Jews. Some other Jewish Christians attempt to remain in the Jewish community, maintaining a low profile, possibly by separating themselves from people like the Johannine Christians.

CHAPTER FIVE

Revelation

I know your affliction and your poverty, even though you are rich. I know the slander on the part of those who say that they are Jews and are not, but are a synagogue of Satan. 2:9

I will make those of the synagogue of Satan who say that they are Jews and are not, but are lying—I will make them come and bow down before your feet, and they will learn that I have loved you. 3:9

Most scholars accept Irenaeus' dating (*Adv. Haer.* 5.30.3) of Revelation in the latter part of Domitian's reign, ca. 90–96 C.E.[1] Many link allusions to martyrdom and refusal to worship "the Beast" to Domitian's persecution of Christians[2] and promotion of the Imperial cult.[3]

The letters to the seven churches in Asia show Asia Minor as Revelation's locale, although the author says he is in exile on Patmos at the actual time of writing. W. Ramsay's archaeological work has verified the author's knowledge of the seven Asian cities mentioned.[4]

Scholars show relative agreement that the author's knowledge of Hebrew Scripture, LXX, and targumic traditions, as well as his closeness to contemporary Jewish apocalyptic thought, signal a Christian of Jewish birth and upbringing.[5]

Revelation's two references to Jews identify them with the same words, "the synagogue of Satan, those who say that they are Jews and are not." The figure of Satan appears in connection with Rome in Revelation (2:13; 13:4),[6] but is also applied to other Christians (2:24), and here, apparently, to Jews. The author associates Satan with his own enemies, no matter who they are. On the level of the cosmic struggle, it is Satan at work against the Christians, and his accusations that cause their death (12:9–11). Both the devil and *blasphēmia* are associated with the synagogue and the Romans, suggesting that the author of Revelation sees the two groups acting in concert in Smyrna and Philadelphia.

The author maintains that this synagogue of Satan is peopled by "those who say that they are Jews but are not." The simplest explanation is that he means they are Jews who do not live up to the name "Jew."[7] Normally "Jew" is not a particular title of honor in early Christian literature. It would be more characteristic of early Christians to say others are not true Israelites, true Hebrews, or true descendants of Abraham (Phil 3:5; Rom 9:6).

The author's use of identical wording for two different situations suggests that "synagogue of Satan" and "those who say that they are Jews and are not" are current slogans. Perhaps they are stereotyped phrases that some Jews apply to the author of Revelation and his kind, "You Christians call yourselves Jews, but you are not." Revelation then turns this phrase back on the people who coined it. In any case, this represents an early hint of a Christian view of themselves as the "true Israel."

The Church at Smyrna

The statement in 2:9 gives us three points of information about the church members at Smyrna. They are suffering tribulation (*thlipsis*).[8] They are poor. Last, they suffer from the "slander" (*blasphēmia*)[9] of the synagogue of Satan. These three parts of the Smyrnean church's trouble may be linked causally. The slander of the Jews could contribute to the tribulation and poverty of the church members. The eventual end of these tripartite sufferings is imprisonment and/or death (v. 10). Satan is at work in the synagogue's slander and the devil empowers those who imprison and kill the Christians; thus the three activities are related, at least in the author's mind, under the rubric of the activity of Satan. The mention of imprisonment rules out the likelihood of the kind of lynch mob actions that appear in Acts. Since a local synagogue would not have the authority to imprison or execute, v. 10 must point to the Roman authorities. What began as a verbal assault from a local synagogue has, in the author's mind, become an actual threat to life and liberty from the Romans.

Something these "false Jews" are saying accompanies the suffering and poverty of the Smyrnean Christians and may lead to Roman punishment. Since the content of this *blasphēmia* is not described, many possibilities present themselves. It may mean simple criticism: "You Christians say you are Jews, but you do not properly observe the Law; you worship a dead criminal or you reflect badly on us with the Romans and the locals." Or, "You engage in bizarre sex practices, overturn the lamp, and practice cannibalism."[10] Or, "You Christians are not loyal subjects of Rome (as we are) and are guilty of *maiestas*.[11] We Jews have the right to practice our ancestral customs (Josephus, *Ant.* 14.10.8 § 213–14) and are exempt from emperor worship, but you Christians can claim no such protection."[12] Alternately, "You Christians are still Jews and should pay the *fiscus Judaicus* like everyone else" (hence the Smyrneans poverty in v. 9). The *fiscus* was apparently expanded by Domitian, possibly to fill his depleted treasury (Suetonius, *Dom.* 8.12.2; Josephus, *War* 7.6.6 § 218).

The coin of Nerva, which cites his revocation of the abuse of the Jewish tax, may contain an allusion to Domitian's use of informers in its enforcement.[13] Dio recalls Domitian as an emperor who encouraged informers regarding both impiety and "living a Jewish life" (*Rom. Hist.* 68.1.1–2).

A combination of factors leads me to think that the Jewish *blasphēmia* in Rev 2:9 refers to Jews implicating Christians to the Romans by casting aspersions on their loyalty to Rome. First, the Romans and the Jews are cited together by the author as agents of Satan. Second, the mention of imprisonment in v. 10 points to a Roman punishment. Third, the Roman presence looms large in Revelation as a whole. Fourth, Domitian is said to have encouraged informers. Last, Domitian showed a fondness for displays of loyalty to himself, the gods, and the empire.

The Church at Philadelphia

In 3:9, we are again confronted with criticism of the "synagogue of Satan" and "those who say that they are Jews, but are not." Here they are accused of lying, but about what we cannot be sure. They may be lying about whether or not they are Jews, or may be guilty of slander against the Christians. The author says little about the Philadelphian Christians, except that they lack power (v. 8) and have endured in a situation where they might have denied Jesus' name. This could refer to the test to which Pliny puts Christians, that they curse Christ and worship the emperor.

Of the "synagogue of Satan" in Philadelphia, we know only that they lie, and the author wants revenge. Strangely enough, Revelation's author does not wish for the destruction of these opponents, but that they will actually worship (*proskyneō*) or bow down before the Christians! As in 2:9, something the local Jews are saying is false, here in the context of Christian powerlessness, endurance, and temptation to deny the name.[14] The author never says exactly what these steadfast Christians endured, nor why they had to endure it. Was it torture, martyrdom, or the lure of wealth and accommodation to Rome? Unlike the remarks to the Smyrneans, where further suffering seems certain, v. 10 assures the Philadelphia Christians that they will be spared subsequent trial. The situations in Smyrna and Philadelphia may, of course, not be the same. Perhaps they are only yoked in the author's mind by the theme of Jewish troublemaking. It is intriguing to note that Smyrna and Philadelphia are the only churches that are fully faithful and suffering as a result.[15] Is it a coincidence that these are two places of "the synagogue of Satan"?

In 3:7–8, Christ is the one who holds the key of David, an allusion to Isa 22:22: the one who holds the king's key decides who has access to the king. Christ also maintains the open door, which no one may shut. Collins understands these verses as responses to expulsion of Christians from the synagogue.[16] Some kind of exclusion or separation seems to be in the background here, but it may be physical or psychological. Christians themselves may have withdrawn from the larger Jewish group and now reassure themselves that they have access to God through Christ, now that they no longer have access as members of the people of Israel.

How reliable are these two references in Revelation to friction between some Jews and some Christians in two Asian cities? They are verbal assaults, possibly connected to troubles with Rome. Evidence for Jews in the region of Smyrna exists from early times, though there are no records about Jews in Smyrna itself in the first century.[17] Ignatius reports Judaizers in Smyrna and Philadelphia, twenty years after Revelation, which suggests that some groups still struggled with the relation of Christianity and Judaism and the question of who genuinely inherits Israel's promise. By the time of *Mart. Pol.,* sixty years after Revelation, at least some Christians see Jews in Smyrna as habitual persecutors of Christians. Both elements appear in an incipient form in Rev 2:9 and 3:9.

Persecution by Jews, even in the form of salacious gossip, is not a major theme in Revelation. The author sets his sights on Rome. She is the prime enemy and locus of evil—the beast, the harlot, and the new Babylon, whether because of persecution or the lure of luxury and accommodation. Therefore the two references to Jews in Revelation seem relatively trustworthy, tucked away in letters to the churches and not put in to round out a picture of Jews as persecutors of Christians.

Nor is the author motivated by a simple anti-Judaism. The worst thing he can say is that they say they are Jews and really are not—a remarkably tame critique. He does not indulge in any of the more common anti-Jewish charges of the ancients. Quite likely the phrase is a commonplace bandied about and used by any group of Jews against any other group they disliked. Since I can discover no serious ulterior motive for these two charges and find they mesh with later materials, I judge them to be trustworthy. Their precise meaning is, however, illusive.

Blasphēmia and lies may refer to a whole range of verbal activities by Jews, from nasty remarks within the Jewish community to informing to the Romans. In Smyrna I suspect some connection between Jewish slander and Roman imprisonment since the devil or Satan is at work in both activities. The reference is less clear in 3:9 but suggests friction and that Christians no longer rely on membership in the larger Jewish community. Some sort of exclusion or pulling apart of the two (or more) communities is taking place.

The ambiguity of the references makes it difficult to address the question of how other Jews saw Christians. Neither slander nor lies automatically implies that these Jews saw Christians as outsiders. The author of Revelation saw himself as an outsider to the "synagogue of Satan," but possibly other Christians were relatively at home there. Perhaps he wants to discourage these Christians from further synagogue attendance by disparaging their neighbors, those who say they are Jews and are not. Nor do the references tell us where the impetus is for the struggle and the separation of some Christians from other Jews. Is it mainly Jewish activity or Christian withdrawal? These questions remain open.

CHAPTER SIX

Josephus

About this time there lived Jesus, a wise man, if indeed one ought to call him a man. For he was a doer of wonderful deeds, was a teacher of such people as accept the truth with pleasure, and won over many Jews and Greeks. He was the Messiah. When Pilate, heeding the principal men among us, had ordered him to be crucified, those who had loved him in the first place did not cease. On the third day he appeared to them alive again, for the prophets of God foretold these and myriad other marvelous things about him. And even now the tribe of Christians, named after him has not failed. (*Ant.* 18.3.3 §§ 63–64)

Being just such a one, Ananus thought he had a convenient opportunity, since Festus had died and Albinus was still on the way. He convened the judges of the Sanhedrin and brought before them a man named James, the brother of Jesus, who was called Christ, and certain others. Accusing them of transgressing the Law, he delivered them up to be stoned. But those who seemed to be the most reasonable ones in the city and the most punctilious about the Law became indignant at this, and secretly sent a message to the king, that Ananus not do such things any more. For he had not even been right in doing the first thing. Certain of them also met Albinus on his way from Alexandria and informed him that Ananus did not have the authority to convene the Sanhedrin without his consent. (*Ant.* 20.9.1 §§ 200–2)[1]

The only direct testimony from a non-Christian Jew about his view of believers in Jesus comes from the historian Josephus.

Josephus wrote *Antiquities* in Rome in 93–94 C.E. under the patronage of the Flavians, where he lived after the surrender at Jotapata.[2]

THE *TESTIMONIUM FLAVIANUM*

Two references to Jesus, one to James, and one to Christians appear in *Ant.* 18.3.3. §§ 63–64 and 20.9.1. §§ 197–203. The former, the so-called *Testimonium Flavianum* (henceforth *TF*), has evoked a voluminous scholarly literature. As early as the sixteenth century, some wondered about its authenticity.[3] L. Feldman, P. Winter, Z. Baras, and J. Meier have published summaries of the problem and I need not duplicate their work.[4] I maintain with Feldman, against Winter, that in spite of the many difficulties with the text, the burden of proof rests on those who declare it a forgery, not on those who declare it genuine.[5] The style and vocabulary are Josephan. Certain parts are not what one would expect from a Christian forger (e.g. Jesus as a mere "wise man"). Further, Origen's complaint that Josephus does not accept Jesus (*Contra Celsum* I. 47; *Comm. Matt.* X, 17, 29) would not make sense if Josephus never mentioned him. The truth seems to lie in the direction of neither a total rejection nor a total acceptance of the text as it now stands. The most reasonable explanation seems to be that *TF* is at base a Josephan text that has been reworked by Christian censors who both added and deleted material.[6] Such a hypothesis solves the most problems and meets the weightier arguments on both sides—the arguments in favor that point to *some* Josephan reference to Jesus, and those against which suggest it could not have been in this precise form. By far the most popular view—this idea of a reworked Josephan passage—is expressed in some form by Eisler, Thackeray, Feldman, Vermes, Bammel, Baras, and Meier. *TF,* with a few alterations, sounds like something that probably came from the pen of Josephus.

Following is the received text minus the probable Christian interpolations, with one emendation.[7] The translation is my own and tends to literalism:

> About this time lived Jesus,[8] a wise man,[9] For he was a doer of wonderful deeds, a teacher of those who accept the unusual[10] with

pleasure,[11] and won over[12] many Jews and many of the Greeks.[13] When Pilate, heeding the principal men among us, had ordered him to be crucified, those who had loved him in the first place did not cease.[14] On the third day he appeared to them alive again,[15] for the prophets of God foretold these and a myriad of other marvelous things about him. And even now, the tribe[16] of Christians,[17] named after him, has not failed.[18]

Originally there may have been more material in *TF*, but if so, it is now lost and neither the Slavonic Josephus, the Arabic *TF*, nor the Syriac traditions behind it can recover it. We can see what was added far more safely than speculate about what was removed.

What information does this Josephan nucleus yield? 1. Josephus had heard of Jesus and the bare facts of his death. 2. He saw him primarily as a wonder-worker. 3. In Josephus' eyes, Jesus' primary appeal to his followers was as a miracle-worker, a view that corresponds to various pictures of Jesus in later rabbinic and pagan literature, as well as certain gospel traditions.[19] The fulfillment of the prophets' prediction sounds as if Josephus is quoting believers, or it may be partly interpolated. 4. Josephus sees Jesus as a "wise man" (*sophos anēr*), a positive attribution that implies cleverness and craft, sometimes knowledge.[20] 5. Josephus is impressed by Jesus' continued popularity and the tenacity of his followers. While "tribe" is an odd way to describe Christians, it does not necessarily carry negative connotations, like "gaggle" or "brood." Still, Josephus chooses a strange word to describe a group that is not bound together by race or blood relationships and it is curious that he does not use *hairesis* or "fifth philosophy" or another more appropriate term. Removing the probable Christian additions reveals a neutral, somewhat positive picture of Jesus. Christians themselves come off as politically harmless, perhaps too credulous, addicted to wonder-working and tenacious in their belief. Nothing else in Josephus contradicts this reference. The notion of some Jews as neutral and tolerant toward believers in Jesus coincides with similar portrayals in Acts (see charts 1 and 2), although these portrayals are often overshadowed by the more graphic and numerous references to persecution.

THE DEATH OF JAMES
(*ANTIQUITIES* 20.9.1. §§ 197-203)

In spite of certain problems, few question the authenticity of
this passage. The primary reason for its general acceptance is that
one assumes a Christian interpolation would praise James more.[21]

What are the possible reasons for the anger over Annas' execution of James by "the most reasonable ones in the city and the
most punctilious about the Law?" 1. They admired James and/or
considered him innocent. Of all the various early Christian person-
alities, James would be the most likely to have the respect of certain Jews who did not share his belief in Jesus, since he promoted
law-observance. Note that in Acts, when the Hellenists are persecuted and driven out, James remains in Jerusalem. 2. These law-
observers (Pharisees?) may have been concerned about the power of
the high priest, a Sadducee, being given free rein. One way to keep
him in check would be to appeal to the Roman government. Perhaps they feared that if Ananus were given a free hand and began
executing his enemies, they would be his next targets. They probably had more to fear from a rash high priest than a Roman procurator.[22] 3. They may have feared that Annas' illegal convening of
the Sanhedrin would bring Roman reprisals from which they
would also suffer. Rome might remove whatever power the
Sanhedrin had left and they would give up even more self-rule.
Two or three of these reasons may have combined to motivate the
law-observers.

What does this passage tell us about Jews' reaction to Christians, or in this case a leading Jewish Christian? Merely that they
were angered by James's summary execution and the high-
handedness of Annas, who convened the Sanhedrin illegally. These
reasonable and law-observant people, possibly Pharisees,[23] took
steps that resulted in the deposition of Annas. We can assume they
had a modicum of sympathy for James, although there are many
possible reasons for their anger at his execution. Had they totally
disapproved of him, they would probably have been unmoved by
even his unjust execution. Their message to Agrippa must have en-
tailed some risk or they would not have done it in secret.

Relative to the larger topic of this study, this passage yields the
information that a Jewish historian, writing in the late first cen-

tury under Roman patronage, could speak of a Jewish leader of the Christians in a neutral or possibly sympathetic tone. Furthermore, it reports that a party of Jews who sound very much like the Pharisees were offended at his execution and appealed to the Roman government to depose an opportunistic high priest.

How did Josephus view Christians? They seem to still be Jews as far as he is concerned. Both *TF* and the reference to James are in the context of Jews in Jerusalem as victims of political outrages. Josephus, who has no use for political rebels, does not portray Christians in that light and seems to display a certain amount of tolerance if not sympathy for them. The reference to James' death implies that he considers Christians worthy of Roman protection.

Furthermore, Josephus provides evidence of at least one body of Jews in Jerusalem who take umbrage at mistreatment of a Christian leader and seek official redress, at some risk to themselves. Whether they were motivated by genuine sympathy for James or self-serving interests (*particularly* if they were concerned about their own group), they must have thought of James as somehow part of their community. His unjust execution apparently stirred concern about their own well-being and made them take up his cause as their own.

CHAPTER SEVEN

The Martyrdom of Polycarp

A number of statements in the Apostolic Fathers relate to Christian attempts to define themselves over and against Biblical Israel and Judaism: *Barnabas* and *2 Clement* respond to people who would continue to assign some special status to Biblical Israel. Ignatius' *Magnesians* and *Philadelphians* and the *Didache* discourage Christians from adopting Jewish practices. Only one work—the *Martyrdom of Polycarp*—makes note of Jews reacting to Christians.

> When this had been said by the herald, the entire mob of pagans and Jews living in Smyrna shouted out in uncontrollable rage: Here is the schoolmaster of impiety[1]—the father of the Christians—the destroyer of our gods—the one who teaches many not to sacrifice or to worship. (12.2)
>
> These things happened with great speed, more quickly than it takes to tell: the mob swiftly collected wood and sticks from workshops and baths, and the Jews (as is their custom) zealously helped them with this. (13.1)
>
> But the jealous and envious one who resists the race of the righteous, when he saw the greatness of his martyrdom . . . took care that not even his poor body should be taken away by us, though many wanted to do this and have fellowship with his holy flesh. Therefore he put forward Niketas, the father of Herod, and the brother of Alce, to ask the governor not to give up his body, "lest," he said, "they abandon the crucified and begin to worship this man." And these things [they said? so adds Eusebius] at the provocation and urging of the Jews, who watched when we were about to take it from the fire. (17.1–2)

And so, when the centurion noticed the conflict caused by the Jews, he put the body in the middle and burned it, as is their custom. (18.1)

The *Martyrdom of Polycarp*, an account of the arrest, questioning, and execution of the elderly Smyrnean bishop, was composed at the earliest about 155–56,[2] probably by an eyewitness at Smyrna (15.1) within a year of the event (18.3).

The issue of the integrity of the text is thornier. Since *Mart. Pol.* 1.1a—2.1 is so clearly imitating the Passion of Jesus, H. von Campenhausen has assumed that these parallel elements entered the text later.[3] Yet the imitation theme need not signal a later intrusion. It would be surprising if a mid–second-century writer, who wants to tell the story of a Christian martyr and who also knows the basic narrative of the Passion, would write only a simple account and not note the obvious parallels to Jesus' death, in the manner of Matt 10:17–23; 24:9; John 15:20; 1 Thess 2:14. All of Christian antiquity, notes Delehaye, was suffused with the idea of the individual's suffering as a reflection of Jesus' suffering.[4]

REFERENCES TO JEWS IN THE *MARTYRDOM OF POLYCARP* 12.2 AND 13.1

Some inscriptions attest to a Jewish community in Smyrna on good terms with the Roman government.[5] They indicate that in some matters, Jews relied on the local government to protect their rights, freely used public archives and facilities, participated in civic affairs, and did not shrink from contributing to imperial projects. Although most of these inscriptions postdate *Mart. Pol.*, they do afford support for its picture of pagan-Jewish cooperation.

Mart. Pol.'s first major reference to Jews in 12.2 follows the herald's announcement in the stadium that Polycarp confessed to his Christianity. Parkes and Schoedel have argued that it is highly unlikely that Jews, monotheists exempt from emperor worship, would have said the words attributed to them there.[6] Yet the saying is a collective. The pagans might have said, "our gods," and the Jews "our God." Nor is it impossible for Jews to have been part of the crowd in the stadium. The argument of I. Abrahams, that Jews could not possibly have been in the arena or gathering wood on the Sabbath (7.1; 8.1) assumes that all the Jews of Smyrna were "law-observant."[7] Though we cannot assume that, the fact that it was on the Sabbath probably rules out any official organized opposition.[8] The author probably would have emphasized the role of the Jewish leaders had there been a glimmer of historicity to the accusation against Jewish officials, since it would serve the imitation theme. Yet he makes no such mention. The character of Jewish participation in 12.2, then, is best described as spontaneous actions by individuals, acting as part of a "lynch mob."

The image of Jews caught up in the fever of mob violence also controls the reference in 13.1. This describes the gathering of wood to burn Polycarp, fulfilling his vision that he would be burnt alive (5.2; 12.3).[9] The curious *hos ethos autois* suggests some long-standing antagonism. The author sees Jews as regular participants in anti-Christian actions. If we accept the possibility of Jews in the roaring crowd in 12.2, we must also consider that they might have continued along with the actions against Polycarp. Interestingly, lighting a fire and gathering wood are the only two specific actions forbidden on the Sabbath by the Torah. Clearly these would be Jews with no pretense to piety.

There is nothing essentially contradictory or unlikely in the idea that individual Jews joined in a mob action against Polycarp. Similar references appear in Acts. *Mart. Pol.* is probably more realistic, however, in that Jews are not the main culprits, but part of a pagan mob. The author may be underlining the totality of opposition to Polycarp. Both Gentile and Jew—that is, the whole world—is arraigned against him.

Does the feature of the Jews as persecutors constitute a literary motif? The martyr-act became a highly conventional and stylized genre and certain elements are predictable. Fishel notes twenty-four aspects of the stereotyped schema of Jewish and Christian martyr-acts, such as the victim's foreknowledge of death, the martyrdom's occurrence on a special day like the Sabbath or Passover, or the angelic appearance of the martyr.[10] *Mart. Pol.* reflects virtually all of these aspects. Some features are borrowed from Hellenistic *martyria*, deaths of Stoics or Cynics, or Jewish versions of the same, such as 4 Maccabees. *Mart. Pol.* is really the earliest of the Christian martyr stories, and it both borrows from earlier forms and helps to fix the types for later Christian acts.

The element of Jewish participation in the martyrdom of Christians is not a regular feature of martyr-acts. Obviously it would not appear in the early Jewish and pagan versions of the genre. Even the later Christian *martyria,* however, do not often portray Jews as culprits in the death of Christians.[11] This is surprising considering the abundant New Testament material to suggest it. In fact, a few of the Christian martyr stories say that these martyrs were buried in Jewish cemeteries, which would require the approval of the Jewish community.[12] Although these legends are of doubtful reliability, they show that, on a literary level, Christians attributed some generosity to Jews in dealings with Christians. *Mart. Pol.,* then, does not include the Jews as persecutors in its account to serve a literary convention of the martyr-acts.

Any stereotype in the portrayal of Jews as persecuting Christians in *Mart. Pol.* would involve an imitation of Jesus' suffering as presented in the Gospels. *Mart. Pol.* is quite explicit that Polycarp is an imitator of Jesus and fellow participant in his sufferings (1.1–2; 6.2; 14.2; 19.1). Yet the Jews in 12.2 and 13.1 bear little similarity to the Jews in the Gospels. No leaders act in an official capacity. Polycarp is betrayed and executed by Gentiles. Jews are part of an angry crowd, but the crowd is predominantly Gentile. The gathering of wood by the Jews in *Mart. Pol.* has no close counterpart in the Gospels. The poverty of the parallelism is a point for veracity.[13] A fabricator would have done a better job and made the parallels more distinct. While *Mart. Pol.* in general shows many deliberate parallels to the Passion, the particulars of Jewish involvement in 12.2 and 13.1 do not seem to arise from conscious imitation.

REFERENCES TO JEWS IN THE *MARTYRDOM OF POLYCARP* 17.2 AND 18.1

The next reference (17.2) shows a shift in subjects. Initially, the devil is the subject who incites Nicetes, Herod's father, to petition the governor not to give up Polycarp's body. By 18.1, the Jews are the main instigators. The association of the Jews and the devil is not new, nor is the notion of the devil acting through a human agent. Von Campenhausen argues, however, that the reference in 17.2 fits badly with the syntax of the surrounding material, and is probably interpolated.[14] In fact Eusebius adds "they said" (*eipon*)

which makes the sentence flow more smoothly. Von Campenhausen suspects the reference in 18.1–2 is also a later interpolation,
since the cult of relic-worship is a later development and would be
unexpected in a mid–second-century document.[15] Verse 18.1 also
shows some confused syntax: "And so, when the centurion noticed
the conflict caused by the Jews, he put the body out before everyone and had it cremated, as is their custom." According to whose
custom is the body cremated? It sounds as if he means Jewish custom, but we have no ancient examples of Jews who practiced cre-
mation rather than burial. Presumably he means pagan custom, but
the grammar is ambiguous.

These latter two references show a closer imitation of New Testament material. The notion of the Jews as plotters and as contentious is a theme in the Gospels and Acts. So is the docility of the
Roman officials who do the Jews' bidding out of fear or a desire to
please them. The Jews' request that the Christians should not have
Polycarp's body lest they begin to worship him clearly echoes Matt
27:64 and *Gos. Pet.* 8.30. The statement in 17.2 is curious; the
Jews would have no real reason to care whether or not Christians
venerated a martyr's relics or even claimed his resurrection. The
Romans, however, were disturbed by the appearance of a new su-
perstition. If Jews said the words attributed to them here, their
goal would clearly be to harass the Christians by jeopardizing their
relations with the Romans.

Observations

I accept the probability that the author reports accurately the actions of the Jews in 12.2 and 13.1. These references show that
some Christians viewed Jews as violently opposed to Christians
and influential with the Romans. Inscriptions from Smyrna confirm cordial relations between some Jews and their Roman governors. I am less sure about the historicity of the references in 17.2
and 18.1. The confused syntax, presence of the imitation theme,
and the anachronism of relic-worship in such an early work invite
suspicion.

When I judge Jewish attitudes toward Christians in these references, for once it is clear that Christians are viewed as outsiders.
There is no question of any synagogue discipline or a negative reflection on the Jewish community relative to Rome. Polycarp and

the one who informed on him are Gentiles. The hostility of the Jews is difficult to understand, but Simon is no doubt right that it is limited in time and space.[16] Since the martyrdom takes place on the Sabbath, and since we doubt the historicity of the statements in 17.2 and 18.1, I assume this is not part of official or organized Jewish persecution of Christians, but a brief skirmish. One thing that is clear, however, is that by 155–60, at least in Smyrna, Jews saw Christians as distinct from their own community.

CHAPTER EIGHT

The Gospel of Peter

The fragmentary passion narrative *Gos. Pet.,* discovered at Akhmîm a century ago, shares certain elements with the canonical passion narratives, but also departs from them in significant ways. Some propose *Gos. Pet.*'s dependence, literary or otherwise, on the canonical Gospels[1] (which I shall simply call "Gospels" in this discussion), while others conclude it is completely independent.[2] Within this latter group, some maintain that an early stratum of *Gos. Pet.* was used by the Gospels.[3] In my judgment the verbal similarities between *Gos. Pet.* and the canonical Gospels are not striking enough to support a theory of literary dependence in either direction. *Gos. Pet.* shares elements with all four canonical Gospels, however, which begs for explanation.[4] A convenient answer is that the author of *Gos. Pet.* knew the canonical Gospels, though perhaps only from memory or in an oral form. Brown suggests that *Gos. Pet.* is a popular harmonization;[5] its core material is from the canonical Gospels and certain popular, imaginative elements are added. This is a useful working hypothesis, but the reader should know that the relationship of the Gospels and *Gos. Pet.* is highly disputed.

The final redaction of *Gos. Pet.* is normally dated around 110–50.[6] Its reference to Rhossus has led most scholars to argue for Syria as the place of origin for *Gos. Pet.*

Virtually no scholar argues for the historicity of the narrative as it stands.[7] It contains many implausibilities (e.g. the Jewish crowd crucifies Jesus) and mistakes (e.g. the Feast of Unleavened Bread lasts only three days). The author seems to know little about Palestine in the 30s (e.g., Pilate needs to ask permission from Herod). Furthermore, *Gos. Pet.* presents an elaborate apologetic to "prove" the resurrection (the Jewish and Roman witnesses; Peter's claim as an eyewitness) that seems contrived. Although the bulk of *Gos. Pet.* is material shared with the Gospels, the sequence and character of the material are confused. Imaginative elements such as the centurion's name and miraculous features such as the speaking cross are no doubt details added to liven a popular story.

The historical utility of *Gos. Pet.* for this study lies not in illuminating events, but in allowing us to hear the voices of second-century popular apologetic. It gives a glimpse of how some Christians, lacking the reserve of the canonical authors, saw Jews. By extension, it reveals points of dissension in Jewish-Christian debate.

Gos. Pet. portrays the Jews in two ways. They are responsible for Jesus' death, and they pose a threat to his followers. The work assigns total culpability for Jesus' death to the Jews. Pilate withdraws early from the trial, leaving Herod the Jewish king and his judges to give the orders for Jesus' death and to deliver him to the people. A number of pronouns follow, the antecedent for which can only be the Jewish crowd. This has the effect of replacing the Roman soldiers with the Jewish mob, so that every act that the Roman soldiers perform in the canonical accounts, the Jewish crowd performs in *Gos. Pet.,* including the scourging, mockery, dividing of Jesus' garments and casting lots, crucifixion, offering a drink of gall and vinegar, taking the body down and handing it over to Joseph. The Romans reenter the scene only to supply a centurion and soldiers to watch the sepulchre at the request of the scribes, Pharisees, and elders (8.31). The Jewish crowd's guilt is underlined by the statement of the wrongdoer crucified with Jesus, "This man who has become the savior of all men, what wrong has he done you?" The remorse of the Jews after Jesus' death also heightens their responsibility (7.25, 28).

As in the canonical Gospels, Jesus' suffering in *Gos. Pet.* is doubtless exemplary for his followers. Aspects of his role such as silence under suffering and supernatural events at his death, also appear in early Jewish martyr accounts and the martyrologies of the second century and later.[8] However, since *Gos. Pet.* precedes the earliest extant Christian martyr-act (except Stephen in Acts), we may not propose a borrowing of motifs from a full-blown Christian literary form.

Our main interest, however, is in the second category of references to Jews in *Gos. Pet.*, namely Jewish reactions to those who confess Jesus. Within this category are three kinds of statements (see charts 1–3).

THE JEWS CAUSE PHYSICAL SUFFERING TO ONE WHO CONFESSES JESUS

But one of the wrongdoers rebuked them, saying, "We are suffering because of the evil which we did, but this one, who has become the savior of men, what harm has he done you?" And they were vexed at him, and ordered that his legs not be broken, so that he might die in torment. (4.13–14)

This first example is provisional since the language of the Greek does not make clear *whose* legs are not broken, the malefactor crucified with Jesus or Jesus himself. The anger of the Jewish crowd is obviously directed against the criminal for confessing Jesus, but the next step might have been either to withhold the *crurifragium* from the criminal and prolong his suffering, or to withhold it from Jesus out of anger that he has made yet another follower. The breaking of the legs was supposedly an act of mercy done to hasten death.[9]

The ambiguity of characters could simply reflect the author's confusion, since he shows confusion on other issues. Yet the shifting of characters may be deliberate. If the author of *Gos. Pet.* has a tradition that Jesus' legs were not broken (cf. John 19:33, there because he is already dead), but also wants to paint the Jews as vengeful and arrayed against Jesus' followers, the lack of clarity would serve his purpose. It also illustrates the kind of overlay of Jesus' sufferings and those of his followers that is apparent in the canonical Gospels. The shuffling of characters and ambiguity is typical of *Gos. Pet.* elsewhere (see discussion of 11.47–48 below). The malefactor is the more probable object of the Jews' cruelty, since the previous sentence refers to an exchange between him and the crowd. Thus, we have a likely example of the Jews inflicting

Chart 1—The Jews Cause Suffering to One Who Confesses Jesus

	"Christian" Activity	Jewish Characters	Jewish Reaction
4.13–14	malefactor rebukes crowd for crucifying an innocent man, the savior of all men	the crowd	withholds the *crurifragium*

Chart 2—The Jews Appeal to the Romans

	"Christian" Activity	Jewish Characters	Jewish Reaction
8.29–30	——	scribes, Pharisees, elders	request a centurion, soldiers to watch tomb, join them in the watch
11.47–48	——	"all" (elders?)	entreat Pilate to prevent soldiers' report of the resurrection

suffering, albeit by omission, on one who confesses belief in Jesus as Savior.

The reproof of one criminal against the other in Luke (23:39–41) becomes in Gos. Pet. a reproof against the Jewish crowd. The failure to employ the crurifragium (explained in John as unnecessary), is in Gos. Pet. an example of Jewish malice toward Jesus' followers. Two traditions that also appear in canonical Gospels are thus reworked to tarnish the image of the Jews. Their content is not particularly useful to us, but does reveal the author's ill will toward the Jews. Similar revision of traditional material to focus blame on the Jews appears elsewhere in Gos. Pet. (1.1; 5.15–18; 6.21–23; 8.28–30; 11.45–48).

THE JEWS APPEAL TO THE ROMANS TO HELP PREVENT THEFT OF JESUS' BODY

They were afraid and came to Pilate entreating him and saying, "Give us soldiers that we may guard his tomb for three days, lest his disciples come and steal him, and the people assume that he rose from the dead and do us harm." (8.29–30)

Then they all came to him (Pilate), entreating him and calling upon him to order the centurion and the soldiers not to tell anyone. "For it is better," they said, "that we be guilty of the greatest sin before God, than to fall into the hands of the people of the Jews and be stoned." (11.47–48)

In these examples the scribes, Pharisees, and elders approach Pilate and ask him to provide soldiers to guard the sepulchre to prevent the disciples from stealing the body, and presumably trumpeting the resurrection. The broad outlines of the tale are paralleled in Matt 27:62–66. Gos. Pet's version differs because the request for a guard comes in response to the Jewish people already recognizing Jesus' righteousness (8.28). Pilate accedes and sends the centurion Petronius and soldiers. The elders and scribes accompany the Romans to the sepulchre and stay there, "pitching a tent" and keeping watch (8.32). Their securing of the tomb, stated simply in Matthew (27:66) as "they set a stone," is embellished by the addition of seven seals (cf. Rev 5:1) in Gos. Pet. (8.33). Gos. Pet. makes it clear that the unbelieving Jews actually witnessed the resurrection and have no excuse for their unbelief.

Chart 3—Jesus' Followers Fear the Jews

	"Christian" Activity	Jewish Characters	Jewish Reaction
7.26–27	mourned, hid	the Jews, elders, priests	sought the disciples as evildoers, incendiaries
12.50–52	Mary Magdalene does not remain at the tomb on Friday, goes early on Sunday	(for fear of) the Jews	were inflamed with wrath

In 11.44–45, the company hastens to Pilate to report the event of the resurrection, admitting "In truth he was the Son of God," yet in v. 47 "all" come to Pilate begging him to command the soldiers to say nothing of what they saw, explicitly preferring sin to falling into the hands of the Jewish crowd and being stoned. Here it is not the Christians, but the Jewish leaders who, recognizing the resurrection, fear "the Jews." This wedge between the Jewish people and their leaders, also evident in 8.28, seems to be the result of replacing the Romans, whose fear of the excitable crowd appears in the canonical Gospels, with the Jews in *Gos. Pet.* The strange result is the picture of the Jews fearing the reaction of the Jews. In Matt 28:11–15, the Jews bribe the soldiers to say the body was stolen, thus combining elements which are separate in *Gos. Pet.*— the rumor of the disciples' theft of the body and the attempts to hush up the soldiers.

The point *Gos. Pet.* makes in 11.47–48 is that the Jews' conscious and deliberate denial of Jesus leaves no excuse for their unbelief. Here they fear stoning, which could mean a lynch mob of the sort that attacked Stephen. Perhaps *Gos. Pet.* is purposely imitating the account of Stephen's death in Acts. In later Jewish tradition Jesus was said to have been stoned (and hung *b.Sanh.* 43a). Stoning was the normal punishment for blasphemy, a crime which ironically suits the "greatest sin" mentioned in 11.48 (Lev 24:16; John 10:33; Acts 7:57–58; *m.Sanh.* 7.4; 9.3).

Gos. Pet. fleshes out the details of Jewish involvement, where Matthew is more circumspect. In *Gos. Pet.* Jews actually roll the stone to seal up the tomb on Friday, pitch a tent, and watch for three days with a guard. This is "failsafe apologetic,"[10] since the Jews and the guards do not leave the tomb for a moment, then witness and attest to the resurrection. The overall effect of the seals, Roman presence, Jewish presence, crowds, etc., is to forestall Jewish objections to the reality of the resurrection, as well as to underline Jewish unbelief. Both *Gos. Pet.* and Matt 28:11–15 suggest that the resurrection was a major point to which Jews objected. John 20:15 also hints that someone may be claiming that Jesus' body was removed from the tomb.

There is an inconsistency and shifting of characters in this sequence characteristic of *Gos. Pet.* Initially the Jewish leaders are part of the company of the centurion keeping watch at the tomb.

But when the company hastens to Pilate to report the resurrection, the Jews seem to be missing, because later a group of Jews comes to Pilate to ask his help in suppressing the report. They seem ready to accept the truth of the report, so they must have been part of the initial group witnessing the resurrection (11.48). Where were they in the interval? They fear falling into the hands of the Jewish people, but are they not "the Jews"? *Gos. Pet.* does not make clear why the leaders fear the people. Is it because the leaders know now that Jesus is the Son of God and the people will be angry because they do not believe it, or will they be angry because they do believe in him and know the leaders helped perpetrate his death? We cannot press *Gos. Pet.* too hard for consistency, but should recognize that the fuzziness and shifting of characters always seem to result in darkening the Jewish role.

JESUS' FOLLOWERS FEAR THE JEWS

But I mourned with my fellows, and, wounded in spirit, we hid. For we were sought after by them as evildoers and as those who wanted to burn the Temple. (7.26–27)

Early on the Lord's day, Mary Magdalene, a disciple of the Lord, who, fearing the Jews who were inflamed with anger, had not done at the sepulchre of the Lord the things which women were accustomed to do for their dead loved ones, took her friends with her and came to the sepulchre where he was placed. And they feared lest the Jews see them, and said, "If on the day he was crucified we could not weep and mourn, we can do so now at his sepulchre." (12.50–52)

These two references have in common the theme of intense fear of the Jews. The first case (7.26–27) contains the only hint we have in ancient literature that Jews blamed Christians for wanting to destroy the Temple. Swete and Vaganay suggest that an anti-Temple stance by Christians could be inferred from the words of their master (Mark 14:58; 15:29; Matt 26:61; cf. Acts 6:13–14).[11] Incendiarism may have continued to be a typical charge against Christians after Nero (Tacitus, *Annals* 15.44). Jews may have resented the idea extant in early Christian literature that the calamity of 70 was really a punishment on the Jews for the crime of killing

Jesus (Justin, *1 Apol.* 35, 38, 40, 47, *Dial.* 108; possibly 1 Thess 2:16 see pp. 16–19) and in some way tried to parry the charge by implicating Christians.

The other example, 12.50-52, is similar to the Gospel of John (20:19) because Jesus' followers are motivated by "fear of the Jews." As in the Synoptics, the women do not stay at the sepulchre. In the Synoptics, however, it is because the Sabbath is approaching. Here Mary Magdalene and her friends leave because of fear of the Jews. In the Synoptics, the women visit the tomb early on the third day, although no motive is stated. In *Gos. Pet.* they go early because they fear the Jews will see them. *Gos. Pet.* may be a conflation of the traditions of leaving the tomb on Friday and the early Sunday visit from the Synoptics, and the "fear of the Jews" from John. Here is another example where the ambiguity and rearrangement of characters and events serve to shift blame to the Jews.

Whatever the ambiguities, the point of the two examples in this category is the intense fear of the Jews. Polemic between Jews and Christians has perhaps risen to a point where some Christians are in danger. The nature of the danger, however, is unclear.

For the purposes of this study, I have already discounted *Gos. Pet.* as direct testimony to events surrounding the Passion and placed it in the milieu of second-century Jewish-Christian polemic. *Gos. Pet.* testifies to traditions about the Jews and their treatment of Jesus' followers that are generally found in the canonical Gospels as well, but paints them with bolder, simpler strokes. Does the author paint the Jews so negatively because he and his fellow Christians fear actual violence? Or is he merely guilty of anti-Jewish acrimony and puts the Jews in the worst possible light? Many of the texts I have examined and accorded some historicity corroborate the idea that Christians had something to fear from the Jews (Rev 2:9; 3:9; *Mart. Pol.* 12.2; 13.1; see also Justin Martyr below pp. 142–44). While *Gos. Pet.* is theatrical and indulges in some of the conventions that characterize martyr acts, I do not discount its evidence. The fact that it uses traditional material but reworks it in such a way that it always implicates the Jews cannot be accidental. Nor can I ignore the fact that it presents an airtight argument to prove the reality of the resurrection.

Gos. Pet. thus provides evidence of hostility between Jews and

Christians that made the Christians fearful. The usual range of possibilities presents itself. Perhaps it was only a war of words. Perhaps it was a war of words that escalated into violence. Perhaps Jews feared the local populace or the Roman government would associate them with these troublemakers and wanted to distance themselves from Christians. One thing is clear: the resurrection represented a major point of controversy between Jews and Christians. Some Jews argue that Jesus' body was actually stolen, while *Gos. Pet.* parries with an account that shows that it is impossible.

Christians hardly appear as any kind of insiders to the Jewish community in *Gos. Pet.* From the author's point of view, Christ and Christians are the victims of the Jews. Perhaps "the Jews as persecutors" is a fixed literary type in *Gos. Pet.* and does not reflect an actual historical relationship.

The implication of continued Jewish-Christian polemic is intriguing, however. Why does the author bring reams of proof for the resurrection? Whom did he hope to convince? He may not have been totally cut off from the Jewish community if they were still arguing this point. While he characterizes himself as an outsider, perhaps other Jews still considered these Christians and their claims worth fighting about.

CHAPTER NINE

The Christian Apologists

The apologists recommend Christianity to several audiences. To the pagans they present it as the ideal philosophy. To the Roman government Christians portray themselves as an innocent and law-abiding group. To Jews and Jewish Christians they claim to be the inheritors of the promises of the Hebrew Bible—the "true Israel." To gentile Christians they are also the legitimate successors to biblical Israel, minus the restraints of the ritual law. In every case, the apologists are promoting Christianity's legitimacy before a yet-to-be-convinced audience. Christianity's legitimacy hinges in part on the fulfillment of prophecy and the promises to biblical Israel. Naturally, the continued existence of Jews and Judaism unaffected and unconvinced by Christianity calls for explanation.

THE *EPISTLE TO DIOGNETUS*

Among the apologists of the early second century who discuss Judaism, only the *Epistle to Diognetus* (henceforth *Diogn.*) and Justin talk about Jewish treatment of Christians. *Diogn.* contains one pertinent passage:

> They [Christians] are warred against (*polemoō*) by the Jews as foreigners and are persecuted (*diokō*) by the Greeks, and those who hate them cannot say the cause of their enmity. (5.17)

While no consensus exists, a significant number of scholars

place *Diogn.* in the mid–second century,[1] mainly because of its similarity to other second-century apologists, in particular the *Apology of Aristides* (ca. 125).

The author remains anonymous in spite of attempts to link him to various ancient figures. The text is similarly unyielding as to place of origin. It belongs to a place of pagan-Christian discourse, but little more can be said.

The reference above makes a general statement that Jews "war against" the Christians, while the Greeks persecute them. The verb *polemoō* is easy to translate, but hard to define. Obviously, the author is being figurative. He cannot mean that Jews go out with armies to engage in military conflict. As with the term "persecution," "war against" can mask a whole range of activities, from verbal criticism to physical assault. The context implies both sorts of threats, verbal and physical. In v. 14, someone speaks ill of or slanders (*blasphemeō*) the Christians, a verbal assault (cf. Rev 2:9). However, Christians are put to death according to v. 12 and "punished" (*kolazō;* lit. "cut off" or "maimed") in v. 16, which implies a physical threat. The reason for the antagonism of the Jews or the persecution by the Greeks is not explained, nor is it clear how organized or sustained was either form of hostility. The mention of the Greeks and Jews in the same sentence need not mean the two are acting in alliance against the Christians, as Frend suggests,[2] but only that the author sees both sets of enemies in the same light.

The reference to Jewish and Greek hostility toward Christians in v. 17 comes at the end of a series of paradoxes—"they [Christians] love all men and are persecuted by all men" (v. 11); "they are poor and make many rich" (v. 13); "they are insulted and render honor" (15b). Verse 17 departs from the form, however. We expect to hear of the Christian behavior which contrasts with the ill-treatment they receive, something like "They are warred against . . . but they show love to all." Instead, the persecutors—the Jews and Greeks—become the subject: "those who hate them cannot say the cause of their enmity." The author revises the form to say that the hatred is baseless and to emphasize Christian harmlessness, which hints that someone is saying Christians are dangerous. The claim that neither group could identify the cause of their hatred hardly seems plausible, but makes for good apologetic because it emphasizes the irrational nature of the hostility.

The author says Christians are warred against as (*hos*) "another tribe."[3] In Acts 10:28 the same word (*allophyloi*) clearly means "Gentiles." The Christians see themselves as separate from Jews in *Diogn.* (1; 3.1–3; 4.1, 6), but also from the world as a whole. They are eternal sojourners, "in the world, but not of the world" (6.3). Verse 5.17 implies that, according to the apologist, Jews too saw the Christians as outsiders. While he shows some faint appreciation of their former connection, now the break is complete and absolute.

The author of *Diogn.*, while showing no great appreciation for Judaism nor assigning Israel any role in the plan of salvation, grudgingly allows that Jews are superior to pagans because they do not worship idols but the one God of the Universe (3.2). However, their manner of worship and fussiness about food, Sabbath-observance, and other ritual matters are entirely ridiculous (*katagelastos*, 4.1; cf. 4.5–6). The author betrays no deep knowledge or understanding of Judaism and is probably a Gentile. Pagan worship is the real target of this work and it is largely concerned with answering pagan charges about Christianity.

There is no particular reason to discount the historicity of this reference. The author does not seem to insert v. 17 to fulfill a literary form, and in fact departs from the paradox form to make his point. He has already made the point that Christians are persecuted by all men (5.11) and suffer unfairly (5.12, 14–16). The notion of Jewish opposition to Christians adds little to his theological point. *Mart. Pol.* and *Apoc. Pet.* and parts of Justin's *Dialogue with Trypho* corroborate the possibility of Christians suffering at Jewish hands in the mid–second century.

Specifics elude the reader. The context mentions both verbal and physical suffering, and Jews may be implicated in one or both of these. What is most useful is the information that Jews viewed these Christians not as Jews, but as members of "another tribe."

JUSTIN'S *FIRST APOLOGY* AND *DIALOGUE WITH TRYPHO*

Justin's remarks about Jewish treatment of Christians are plentiful and often strikingly specific. Many of his charges become standard in the anti-Jewish polemic of successive church writers, either because of Justin's influence or because they enjoyed a wide currency.

The *First Apology* (henceforth *1 Apol.*), which presents Christianity as the true philosophy, is designated for a gentile Roman audience, including the emperor and the Roman people. It was probably composed around 151-55 C.E. The *Dialogue with Trypho* (henceforth *Dial.*), cast in the form of a polemic with an educated Jew, probably dates from 155-60.[4] Scholars propose various audiences for the *Dial.*—Jewish, pagan, Jewish *and* pagan, Jewish Christian, and gentile Christian. Justin seems to be operating on many fronts simultaneously and therefore singling out one audience is probably unwise.

1 Apol. contains a few of the same charges that appear in *Dial.*—Jews do not understand their own prophets and mistreat Christians. One specific passage says Christians are singled out for punishment by Bar Kochba. The main focus of *1 Apol.*, however, is not the relationship of Christians to Judaism, but to paganism.

Justin, according to his own testimony, grew up in Flavia Neapolis, a city of Samaria in Palestine (*1 Apol.* 1.1). According to later church tradition, he spent time in Rome, founding a school there. From there he may well have written *1 Apol.* and *Dial.* Justin also traveled widely, so pinpointing the place of composition is not too helpful in assigning a locale to certain traditions.

Justin provides two kinds of information—indirect and direct—about Jewish reactions to Christians. First is the picture he draws of Trypho, a courteous and eminently reasonable gentleman who shows a keen interest in Christian ideas, although he is ultimately not persuaded by Justin. Much of the image of Trypho probably stems from the conventions of the dialogue form. There is considerable debate over gradations of historicity in the *Dial.*, whether Trypho was a real person[5] or fictional,[6] whether *Dial.* is a record or memory of a real debate[7] or stylized fiction, and whether Justin knows or presents an accurate picture of second-century Judaism.[8] It is helpful to realize that Justin really presents not a dialogue, but a monologue. Whether the impetus for his writing comes from historical elements or not, his hand is uppermost in composing the work. Whether Trypho existed or not, we are reading Justin's view of how an intellectual Jew would react to an argument for Christianity based on reason.

Chart 1—Group A: Jews Are Curious, Respectful toward Christians

	Jewish Characters	Jewish Reaction to Christians
8.3–4	Trypho	applauds some of Justin's remarks, recommends Plato, the Commandments
9.2	Trypho	agrees to go off with Justin to avoid his raucous friends
10.1	Trypho	rejects anti-Christian slander of cannibalism, sexual promiscuity, reads, admires the gospel, asks Justin to explain nonobservance of the commandments
58.2	Trypho	compliments Justin for his rhetorical facility
87–90	Trypho	claims Justin is persuasive, but asks for proof that Scripture refers to Jesus
118.5	Trypho	expresses pleasure at Justin's words
142.1, 3	Trypho	expresses pleasure at their meeting, wishes they could meet again, asks that he and his companions be remembered as friends, wishes Justin a safe journey

Chart 2—Group B: Jews and Christians Disagree over Scripture

	Jewish Characters	Jewish Reaction to Christians
8.3–4	Trypho	claims Christians deceived by false words, follow disreputable men, invent a Christ, Trypho recommends the commandments
10.1	Trypho	thinks Christians believe something false and do not observe the Law
67.2	Trypho	says Christians who tell of strange phenomena are in danger of talking foolishness like the Greeks
71.2—73.6	the Jews	have removed passages from Scripture which prove Christ is God
79.1	Trypho	says Justin's interpretations are contrivances, blasphemies
115.6	you Jews (Justin to Trypho)	light on small, petty contradictions, ignore larger, intelligible speech, falsify the truth

Chart 3—Group C: Jews Attack Christians Verbally

	Jewish Characters	Jewish Reaction to Christians
1 Apol. 49.6	Jews who did not recognize Christ	say slanderous things against those who confess Christ
8.3; 9.2	Trypho's companions	laugh at Justin's remarks
16.4; 93.4; 95.4; 96.2; 108.3; 123.6; 133.6	you (Jews; Justin to Trypho)	curse Christians (in synagogue, 16.4; 96.2)
47.4	some of the seed of Abraham, who live according to the Law, and do not believe in Christ	anathematize Christ
137.2	archisynagogoi	teach the Jews to scoff at Christ after the prayers
17.1; 108.2	you (Jews; Justin to Trypho)	sent out men from Jerusalem to warn of the godless sect of the Christians
108.2	you	claim the disciples stole Jesus' body from the tomb, then claimed his resurrection and ascension
117.3	you	cause Christians "to put on filthy things"

Chart 4—Group D: The Jews Hate Christians

	Jewish Characters	Jewish Reaction to Christians
1 Apol. 36.3	the Jews	hate those who say Christ has come
16.4	you	reject Christians
35.7; 39.1; 133.6; 136.2	you	hate us (Christians)

Chart 5—Group E: Jews Murder, Wish to Murder, or Physically Harm Christians

	Jewish Characters	Jewish Reaction to Christians
1 Apol. 31.6	they	kill and punish us when they have the power
	Barchochebas	ordered that Christians only (suffer) terrible punishments unless they deny Jesus Christ
35.7	(Jews implied)	Christians are killed by friends
16.4	you	lay hands on Christians when you have the power
95.4	you	curse Christians, put them to death when they can
96.2	you	curse Christians in the synagogue, other nations carry it out, put Christians to death
110.5	you and all other men	as much as in their power, drive out Christians from their property, the world permits no Christian to live
26.1	sons of Abraham	persecute Christ
122.2	proselytes	wish to torture and kill Christians
133.6; 136.2	you	murder (and hate and curse) Christians as often as you can

Chart 6—Group F: Jewish Teachers Discourage Dealings with Christians

	Jewish Characters	Jewish Reaction to Christians
9.1	teachers	persuade people like Trypho (that Scripture does not testify to Christ)
38.1	teachers	made a law that Jews should not associate with Christians nor converse about Scripture
137.2	archisynagogoi	teach people to scoff at Christ in synagogue

The same reasoning applies to the second kind of reference, where Justin talks directly about what Jews say and do about Christians. Most of the charges he makes cannot be proven or refuted because few contemporary parallels exist. They show what Justin thinks or wants his readers to think Jews are doing. Many of these charges resound in later church writers. Justin's apparent sensitivity to Jewish allegations against Christians is telling, however, since it suggests that certain controversial issues were still very much alive between Jews and Christians, despite the fact that Christianity was already largely Gentile in membership and hardly still part of Judaism.

At times Justin parallels Christian suffering at Jewish hands with a picture of Jesus' victimization by the Jews (*Dial.* 16.4; 17.1; 93.4; 108.2–3; 133.6; henceforth all references are to *Dial.* unless otherwise noted). Occasionally he calls contemporary persecution or cursing of Christians "persecuting Christ" (26.1), "cursing Christ" (133.6), or "anathematizing Christ" (47.4). A reference to Jesus' suffering does not accompany every example of Christian suffering, nor the reverse. Justin's primary point is that the Jews killed Jesus or handed him over to be killed (*1 Apol.* 35.6; 38.7–8; 40.6; *Dial.* 16.4; 17.1; 32.2; 93.4; 103.2; 104.1; 133.6). Justin is the first to propose explicitly that the destruction of Jerusalem in 70 is punishment on the Jews for rejecting and/or killing Christ (*1 Apol.* 32.4-6; 47–49; 53.2-3; *Dial.* 25.5; 26.1; 108.3), although the theme is implicit in New Testament references to Jewish guilt (Matt 27:25) and predictions of impending disaster (Luke 19:42-44; 21:5-6, 20–24; 23:28-31; Matt 23:37-39; 24:2; Mark 13:2). The idea that 70 is a punishment for Jewish rejection of Jesus takes deep root in church literature. It represents a Christian understanding of a Deuteronomic theme that suffering and destruction are God's punishment for the sins of the Jews and a call for reform.

JEWS AS CURIOUS AND RESPECTFUL TOWARD CHRISTIANS

The examples in this group show Trypho as the soul of courteousness throughout the exchange in *Dial.* He compliments Justin as a rhetor (58.2), approves of some of his remarks (8.3), and agrees to go off with Justin to avoid some of his own raucous companions (9.2-3). He says he has read the gospel carefully and admires it (10.2), but finds its precepts too wonderful to keep. Trypho is surprised at the content of Christian belief and claims this is the bone of contention (10.2–3). He utterly rejects pagan claims that Christians engaged in cannibalism or sexual orgies (*Dial.* 10.2; cf. *1 Apol.* 26.6–7; 29.2).[9]

In disagreeing with Justin over the meaning of Scripture Trypho is surprisingly deferential, asking only for information (87.1). He seems open to persuasion, but finds the cross a genuine obstacle to Jewish belief (89.2; 90.1), reminiscent of a picture to which Paul alludes (1 Cor 1:18–23). Trypho gently needles Justin for his long-windedness (118.5). At the end of the conversation, Trypho expresses pleasure at the meeting, wishes they could meet again to search the Scriptures, bids him a safe journey, and asks that Justin consider him and his companions friends (142.1). Although unpersuaded by Justin, Trypho emerges as the ultimate "live and let live" type, conceding that Christ may be fine for Gentiles, but unnecessary for Jews (64.1). How ironic that in spite of the many charges Justin makes against Jews that they hate, kill, and traduce the Christians, the picture he presents of Trypho could not be more affable or sympathetic. His behavior contradicts outright some of Justin's complaints.

Is Trypho a real person? Certainly he receives nothing like equal time and we barely hear any of his own arguments. He is primarily a "straight man" for Justin to promote his views. He is the same sort of meager character as the interlocutors of Socrates in Plato's *Dialogues.* His remarks show a formal character. Trypho follows a pattern of acknowledging the truth of Justin's words and then asking for further explanation or clarification (save 9.2), similar to the way Menon responds to Socrates in their discussion of virtue or the way Socrates' companions respond to him in *The Republic.* Justin employs the form of the dialogue, a favored form by writers of the "Second Sophistic" period who mimicked the conventions of the Golden Age of Greek rhetoric.[10] Thus Trypho's courtesy and lack of defense of his own views may be more an aspect of the dialogue form than an indication of how an individual Jew responded to Justin.[11]

An assumption of the dialogue form is that the author composed much of the material. Diogenes Laertius, who considered Plato the greatest practitioner of the dialogue form (*Plato* 3.48) reports a tradition that "on hearing Plato read the *Lysis,* Socrates exclaimed, 'By Heracles, what a number of lies this young man is telling about me!' For he has included in the dialogue much that Socrates never said" (*Plato* 3.35). Thus while Trypho might have existed (as did Socrates) and the original impetus for the composition of *Dialogue with Trypho* might have been an actual conversation, we can assume that Trypho's words are largely put in his mouth by Justin.

What is useful about Trypho for our purposes are the points that he defines as problematic between Jews and Christians, understanding of Scripture, Christology, and law-observance. Justin's Trypho provides a window into second-century debates between Jews and Christians, whether or not he ever existed.

JEWS DISAGREE WITH CHRISTIAN VIEWS OF SCRIPTURE

Another group of references portray Trypho (and whomever the "we" he uses includes) puzzled at Christian understanding of Scripture. The Christians believe something untrue, an unknown Christ (8.4) which they have invented for themselves. Even more mysterious is their failure to observe the commandments (10.3). Although they profess to be pious, Christians flagrantly ignore the observance of festivals, the Sabbath, and circumcision. Piety and keeping the commandments are apparently synonymous for Trypho, and he invites Justin to defend his approach of piety without observance. Curiously, Trypho characterizes the gospel as "precepts too wonderful to be kept." Is he tweaking Justin for using something like Paul's argument that the Law is good, but impossible to observe in its entirety (Rom 7:12-25) and reversing it to apply to the gospel?

As the dialogue wears on, the wrangling over the status of the Law and its meaning becomes more heated. Trypho calls the notion that Jesus' identity as the Christ is proven from Scripture "strange phenomena" and warns Justin against "talking foolishly like the Greeks" (67.2). Justin and Trypho spar over the present role of the Law. Justin concludes that it is temporary and remedial, given only because of Jewish obstinacy, to keep the sinfulness of the Jews in check (chaps. 18-22). After one of Justin's "proofs" that Scripture witnesses to Christ and that Christians have replaced the Jews as "Israel," Trypho departs from his customary courtliness and becomes angry. He accuses Justin of presenting expositions that are "mere contrivances, even blasphemies" (79.1). So at best, Christians are wrongheaded in their belief that Jesus is the Messiah of the Hebrew Scriptures and that the ritual Law need no longer be observed. At worst, these beliefs border on blasphemy. For his part, Justin accuses Jews of removing passages from Scripture (chaps. 71–73) and of being too contentious and petty, lighting on minor contradictions (115.6).

How likely is it that in Justin's time, Jews and gentile Christians like Justin are still (or again) debating the status of the Law? Were the two issues at stake in *Dial.*—Scripture's witness to Jesus and observance of the commandments—still viable controversies? Or is *Dial.*, as Harnack argued, a mere rhetorical exercise?

K. Katz has shown that *Dial.* conforms to the style of the dialogue imitated in the period of the Second Sophistic. It is not a mere aping of forms, however. Justin does not systematically set out a series of Jewish objections and then refute them as he would in an artificial exercise. Often he fails to give the specifics of the objections (e.g. 17.1). Or he states the accusation and never does refute it (e.g. 108.2—the disciples' theft of Jesus' body).[12]

Furthermore, *Dial.* does not seem to have been written primarily to convert Jews. Were that the case, we could expect Trypho to be ultimately persuaded or admit the superiority of Justin's arguments. Yet Justin leaves Trypho and his friends still unconvinced and prays for their conversion (142.2, 3). Nor is *Dial.* an anti-Jewish diatribe, intended simply to attack Judaism and its rites. Justin battles Marcionite thinking which denigrates the Law and strips it of all authority (35.6). He requires the Law to retain its authority because it witnesses to Jesus and the truth of Christianity. Justin attributes a certain limited validity to Judaism and even tolerates Jewish Christians, saying those who believe in Christ and practice the Law (including Gentiles who are persuaded by Jewish Christians) will probably be saved (46.2, 4). Thus if *Dial.* is written neither to condemn nor convert Jews, yet takes up Jewish objections to Christianity at length, it must be that these objections are still under debate.

Justin is anxious to prove the validity of Christ and Christianity from Scripture, but must justify freedom from literal observance of the commandments.[13] He must attribute authority to the Bible because Jesus' divinity is proven from it. But the Bible also proclaims Israel's special status and the obligation to keep the command-ments. Justin solves the problem by appropriating Israel's role in salvation history for Christians, proclaiming Christians the "true Israel" (11.5; 123.6–9; 135.3). This idea of Israel forfeiting her special status and losing it to Christians appears earlier, in Matthew's Gospel (21:43), but Justin is the first to use the term "true Israel" (although John 1:47 uses "true Israelite"). Justin uses allegory to underline Scripture's proof of Jesus' status as well as to justify Christian freedom from the Law. He also attributes to the commandments a temporary, remedial function for Jews alone (chaps. 18–22). Justin, unlike Paul, does not face the problem of God's apparent revocation of divine promises to the Jews.

Jewish observance of the law for Justin means circumcision in particular, the Sabbath, new moons and feasts, food laws, and (for-merly) sacrifices (8.3; 10.1, 3, 4; 16.3; 18.2; chaps. 18–22). All of these laws are biblical and could have been gleaned by anyone who read the LXX. They do, however, represent a summary of what ancient writers considered the distinctive practices of the Jews.

The other area of dispute revolves around three Christian claims about Jesus.[14] Aside from general claims that Scripture predicts Jesus, the most frequently cited point of debate is Jesus' crucifix-ion. The argument that one who is crucified is cursed by God (Deut 21:23) and therefore could be neither the Christ nor God is attributed to Trypho and his people in five places (10.3; 32.1; 38.1; 89.1; 90.1). Justin goes to greater lengths to refute this charge than any other and marshals verse after verse to prove that Scripture foretold Jesus' death on the cross (32.2; chaps. 89–90; 94–99; 105–108).

A second area of debate is apparently the understanding of Isaiah 7:14 (*Dial.* 43.8; 66.2; 67.1; 71.2—73.6; 77–78; 84.1). Trypho argues that it reads "Behold, the young woman shall con-ceive and bear a son," and refers to Hezekiah (67). Justin employs the belief in a virgin birth to intepret it "Behold the virgin shall conceive, and bear a son," and applies it to Jesus. While the differ-ence is explicable as a difference between the Hebrew MT and the Greek LXX, the issue is not so easily resolved. Justin devotes so much space to his proofs of the virgin birth that it must have been a live point of debate between Jews and Christians.

A third controversial issue is the Christian claim of Jesus' resurrection. Justin, like the author of *Gos. Pet.* (and by implication, Matthew), insists that the *Jews* know Jesus rose from the dead, but choose to deny it (17.1). Justin uses Scripture to prove the resurrection (32.3–6; 106–108). He repeats the charge found in Matthew and *Gos. Pet.* that Jews say the disciples stole Jesus' body from the tomb (108.2).

The debate over Scripture centers on Christian freedom from the Scriptural commandments and Christian claims about Jesus' birth, death, and resurrection. This information helps us understand Justin's complaints about Jews' verbal attacks on Christians as outlined in chart 3 (above, p. 131), and may furnish some of the particular substance of these attacks.

Justin clearly is not and never was an insider to Judaism. Nor is there any hint that Christians are viewed as simply a recalcitrant or eccentric group within Judaism. Trypho couches all his complaints as "we" versus "you." Yet Justin goes to great lengths to refute Jewish objections to Christianity. At least three major issues are alive and still being thrashed out. Jews and Christians, though separate, still vigorously debate one another's claims, thus implying some social contact in Justin's time or the recent past.

JEWS ATTACK CHRISTIANS VERBALLY

If Jews and Christians were engaging in learned polemic and sparring over Scripture, there was no doubt a popular, less erudite side to the battle as well, in the form of slander and verbal abuse. The largest body of references to Jewish treatment of Christians in Justin's works consists of verbal attacks on Christians. Many are direct attacks, ridicule, or cursing. Many more are indirect slander directed to a third party with negative repercussions on the Christians.

Trypho's companions are an example of direct ridicule. They greet Justin's remarks with laughter, although Trypho himself is courteous (8.3). Their behavior is so offensive that Justin begins to leave (9.2). They lack any real substance as characters, however, but serve mainly as a literary device, acting as foils for the seemly Trypho.

In several places, Justin cites Jews as slandering Christians to someone else. The same people who slandered Jesus "say slanderous things against those who confess him" (*1 Apol.* 49.6). Some support for this accusation appears in *Mart. Pol.* 17.2 (contemporary with *Dial.*), which alludes to Jews implicating Christians to the Romans as a politically dangerous cult. Justin alludes elsewhere to Jewish powerlessness, which suggests that slandering Christians to those in power may be the only available approach to defeat them (16.4; 95.4; 96.2).

The statements in 137.2 and 47.4 refer to Jews scoffing at (*episkōptō,* to mock) or anathematizing Christ, the former after their prayers in the synagogue, at the instruction of the *archisynagōgoi,* leaders of the synagogue. Possibly cursing Christ is a traditional formula repeated by Jews for certain reasons (1 Cor 12:3; Mark 14:71; Matt 26:74), just as it is a formula to test political innocence in Trajan's era (Pliny, *Letters* 10.96.6). Yet Justin may simply be stating a general complaint about Jewish unbelief and contentiousness.

Justin claims that Jews sent emissaries out from Jerusalem to warn other Jewish communities against the godless sect (*hairesis*) of the Christians (17.1; 108.2). They are energetic in publishing bitter, unjust things against the Christians, just as they slander Jesus. The terms "lawless" and "godless" characterize the *hairesis* of the Christians in Jewish eyes, according to Justin. Stanton[15] maintains that this language may actually come from Jewish anti-Christian propaganda, for several reasons: Justin does not simply set out an artificial list of Jewish allegations in order to refute them, since he never does deal with some of them. Nor does he elsewhere ever use *hairesis* to mean Christianity per se. The Gospels never use the terms "godless" or "lawless," so Justin did not inherit the phrasing from them.

The terms "lawless" and "godless" could equally well describe Jewish or Roman views of Christians. "Godless" harks back to the "atheism" charged against the Christians for their failure to worship the emperor or the *divi.* Jews also thought the whole concept of Jesus as divine was blasphemous, says Justin. Likewise, "lawless" could refer to Roman wariness of Christian loyalty to the state. Jews curse the Christians but others carry out the curse (96.2). This could mean the Jews slandering Christians to the Romans, perhaps like the slander by the "synagogue of Satan" in Rev 2:9.

Yet it may also cover Jewish disapproval of Christian failure to observe the Law. In either case, the sending of emissaries implies that Christians were viewed as a threat to Jewish communities. They may have been a threat for external reasons, namely that they upset the stability of the Jewish community and threatened its position with the Roman government or the locals. Or Christians may have been a threat for internal reasons, peddling theologically unacceptable ideas and competing for gentile converts.

The only example of Jews sending out emissaries to combat the Christians is Acts' depiction of Paul's early persecution of the Way a century before Justin (Acts 9:1; 22:5; 26:12). Paul, in his letters, never says he was an agent of anyone else. Tannaitic materials do report that emissaries were sent from Yavneh to inform diaspora communities on liturgical questions (*m.Roš Haš.* 1.4). Other matters decided at Yavneh such as the final fixing of the calendar and the final fixing of the canon would affect diaspora Jewry and have to be communicated to them. As S. Katz points out, the Tannaim were travelers and could have also brought unofficial, popular criticism of Christians to different communities.[16] Thus, the structures were in place for communication about various matters, including the sect of the Christians, although Justin's claim has no direct corroboration.

Dial. 108.2 includes a reference to the Jewish allegation that the disciples stole Jesus' body from the tomb, also found in Matt 28:13–15 and *Gos. Pet.* 8.29–30. The idea that Jews were the source of this rumor clearly has a certain durability and currency, but Jewish involvement in the empty tomb events does not appear in any early Jewish sources such as Josephus or the tannaitic materials. The allegation that the disciples stole the body is an aspect of the larger dispute over the nature of Jesus, in particular the reality of the resurrection, to which Justin frequently alludes. Justin never refutes the charge outright, so he did not include it simply to dispute it.

In a number of places Justin alleges that Jews curse Christians (*Dial.* 16.4; 93.4; 95.4; 96.2; 108.3; 123.6; 133.6). I have already noted the possibility that cursing or anathematizing Christ is a traditional practice reflected in Paul's statement in 1 Cor 12:3 and Peter's denial (Mark 14:71; Matt 26:74). Twice he says Jews curse them in the synagogues (16.4; 96.2) leading many scholars to conclude that Justin is talking about *Birkat ha-Minim,* the curse against the heretics attributed to the Yavnean period in a third-century text.

Two schools of thought exist on Justin's testimony to *Birkat ha-Minim.* One camp stresses Justin's inaccuracies on other matters, his tendentiousness and inclination for the theme of Jewish persecution of Christians, the absence of unequivocal contemporary evidence for the Jewish cursing of Christians within prayers, and the lack of certainty as to whether *minim* meant Christians exclusively.[17] Some within this group point to this as a purely internal matter, involving a Christian heresy within Judaism of a later period.[18]

The presence of bias on Justin's part does not rule out historicity, however. A second group of scholars takes Justin as supporting evidence for the practice of *Birkat ha-Minim* as a method for expelling Christians from the synagogue and a significant factor in the "break" between Judaism and Christianity.[19] They bolster their arguments with reports from later church writers, Epiphanius, Origen, and Jerome. Once a scholar has established the reality of *Birkat ha-Minim* on other grounds, Justin can provide additional support. However, Justin's references alone cannot prove its existence or utility because he says nothing about expulsion from the synagogue, and cursing never occurs in connection with Jewish prayers in Justin (cf. 137.2). His complaints could refer to general Jewish criticism or name-calling of Christians, and need not imply any accompanying action against them.

For the purposes of this study, I simply note that Justin many times repeats the charge that Jews curse Christians, sometimes in the synagogue, and extends it to cursing Christ himself. He occasionally says that only their powerlessness limits the Jews to verbal imprecations. He says nothing about expulsion or any curse within the prayers. Possibly Christians *felt themselves* cursed within the context of a general malediction against heretics.

Another possibility is that when Justin talks about Jews cursing Christ and Christians he is referring not to Jews cursing Christians outright, but to Jews arguing that Jesus is cursed because of his death on the cross. Justin alludes frequently to the cross as a point of contention between Jews and Christians. The charge of Jews cursing Christ and Christians appears in proximity to Justin's refutation of the problem of the cross (chaps. 93; 95–96; 108; 131–33). The references to Jews anathematizing or cursing Christ may be references to Jews arguing their case that one who dies on a cross is cursed by God (Deut 21:22–23).

The charge of slander or cursing invites a whole range of possible interpretations, from informing to heated polemic to criticism. The charge of slander echoes Rev 2:9, the slander of the synagogue of Satan. In a more general way, material in the Gospels and Acts that speaks of disputes between Jews and Jesus and Jesus' followers supports the idea of verbal insults tossed back and forth at an earlier time.

Possibly Justin read the Gospels and Acts and is merely passing on their material. Verbal abuse is a fairly easy charge to make and really requires no proof. It serves his theme of Jewish persecution as well as his theological point that suffering Christians imitate Jesus' suffering. What is perhaps most interesting are Justin's statements that Jews attack Christians *only* verbally, though (he says) they would wish to do more (see chart 5). In the following set of statements Justin accuses Jews of animosity toward Christians.

JEWS HATE CHRISTIANS

Miscellaneous references speak of Jews hating Christians. For example, *1 Apol.* 36.3 says that because the Jews misunderstood the prophets they did not recognize Christ when he came and crucified him and "even hate us who say that he has come." The same elements appear in 16.4, but there the Jews have slain the prophets, not merely misunderstood them, slain Jesus, and now "reject those who hope in him." *Dial.* 35.7 contains similar elements, Jesus' foreknowledge through prophecy of what would happen to him and "those who believed and confessed him, the Christ." An intriguing phrase appears in this example: "For all that we suffer, *even when killed by friends,* he foretold would take place ... wherefore we pray for you and all other men who hate us." If the friends include the Jews, as seems possible from the context, he insinuates that close relations still should exist between Jews and Christians; somehow things have gone wrong, as in a family feud.

As in other works, the lenses often shift without warning. The image of Jesus' suffering is frequently juxtaposed or superimposed on that of his followers. For example, having already equated prophecy with philosophy, and having "proven" from Psalms that Christ is the subject of prophecy, Justin moves to the present and finds it "not surprising that you hate us who think these things and convict you with good reason of a continual hardness of heart" (39.1). Likewise in 133.6 and 136.2 Jewish hatred (and murder and cursing) of Christians is linked to the Jews killing Jesus. Ultimately the Jews hate and insult God, who sent Jesus.

Hatred of Christians by Jews in Justin's work always appears in tandem with Jewish mistreatment of Jesus. Justin may have been inventing charges so that his work echoes the Passion. Or he may simply have been drawing on obvious parallels to make sense of current Christian suffering. Given the number of complaints he brings against the Jews, I incline to the latter possibility. The charge that Jews hate Christians is nothing more than a variation of the material in charts 3 and 5 that accuses Jews of verbal violence and a desire to kill Christians. Even debates over Scripture (chart 2) can escalate into hatred, as Justin says in 39.1. None of these references carries an implication of violence or anything but verbal polemics. The next set of references treats Justin's charges that Jews actually want to inflict physical harm on Christians.

JEWS WISH TO MURDER OR TORTURE CHRISTIANS

Justin accuses Jews of murdering or torturing Christians in numerous examples. In virtually every case, however, he places the incident in the past or qualifies his statement by alluding to Jewish powerlessness. Jews, he says, kill or punish Christians "when you can," "when you have the power," or "as often as you can." Even the rabid proselytes only "wish to" torture and kill Christians. Justin considers these people less than full-fledged Jews, but blames the Jews for the proselytes' particular virulence against Christians, "for in all things they strive to be like you" (122.2). In 16.4 and 95.4 Justin implies that the Jews would put the Christians to death or lay hands on them if they could. In 110.5 he says that to the extent of their power, Jews and others drive out and kill Christians, suggesting that they do not always have the power to do so. In 96.2 he suggests that they cause others to kill the Christians while the Jews themselves are limited to verbal imprecation.

In 26.1 he cites general persecution of Christ in the present tense, which no doubt means persecution of Christians, but may mean any variety of forms.

The example in *1 Apol.* 31.6, where he claims Bar Kochba persecutes Christians, is thorny, since Justin is the only source for this allegation. One of the Bar Kochba letters warns against the Galileans. Some have assumed that the Galileans threatened there are Christians, but "Galilean" is not normally an early name for Christian, nor is the wording of the letter clear. Why Bar Kochba would single out Christians for his wrath might have to do with their lack of support for his revolt or his judgment that they are not good Jews. Later traditions say that some of his followers thought of Bar Kochba as the Messiah or a semi-divine figure (*y. Ta'an.* 4.8, 68d; *Hist. eccl.* 4.6.2). If so, Christians, as followers of a rival messiah, could not be tolerated. In a situation of siege, anyone not directly loyal to Bar Kochba would probably have been perceived as an enemy. Justin, writing twenty years after the revolt, had information of violence against Christians in the past. He perceived Jews as anxious to kill and hurt Christians. Yet he does not produce a single incident from his own experience that says Jews were presently attacking Christians physically. He qualifies his accusations by noting Jewish powerlessness. Ironically, Justin provides evidence that Jews, at the time of his writing, were not personally killing or attacking Christians, however he might have attributed to them a desire to do so.

THE TEACHERS OF THE JEWS DISCOURAGE DEALINGS WITH CHRISTIANS

Throughout his works Justin uses the terms "the Jews" or "you" in addressing Trypho and generally does not draw distinctions among Jews or Jewish groups. However, in 9.1 and 38.1, Justin blames the teachers of the Jews for misleading the people. In a patronizing tone, he tells Trypho, "I forgive you, for you know not what you say, but are persuaded by teachers who do not understand the Scriptures." Justin may be imitating the Gospels, where the leaders of the Jews are often distinguished from the people and bear a good deal of the blame for opposition to Jesus (102.5; 103.2).

The majority of references to the Jewish teachers say that they misread and misunderstand the Scriptures. In two places Justin accuses them of elevating the requirements of men over the Law of God (48.2, 4; 140.2), an allegation that seems to have been an anti-Pharisaic commonplace.[20]

Justin says that the teachers have gone as far as to make a law that Jews should shun Christians. Trypho says they "made a law that we should not associate with any of you" (38.1). The very fact of the dialogue contradicts this, of course, or suggests it was not regarded very seriously. Similarly, debate over Scripture implies some contact. Justin is caught in a contradiction. He wants to transmit the idea that Jews are forbidden to deal with Christians, but must explain Trypho's participation. He solves the problem by suggesting that Trypho is simply disobeying his teachers. This is not a very satisfactory solution, of course, since a law that is not obeyed by even a respectable character like Trypho has little power.

Two tannaitic references support the idea that Jews forbade association with Christians. In *t.Hul.* 2.20 Jews are forbidden to buy or sell from *minim,* marry them, teach their children a trade, eat their food, drink their wine, or accept their healings. A connection between *minim* and Christians follows in the text. The discussion continues with the famous story of R. Eliezer arrested for *minut* (*t.Hul.* 2.24). When he recalls that he once listened to an interpretation by a disciple of Yeshu ben Pantiri (seemingly a name for Jesus), he judges himself as having transgressed the words of the Torah. Christians might have been shunned by some Jews in some circles for their lack of observance or their unusual ideas. Members of particular Jewish sects like the Essenes or Therapeutae apparently avoided contact with other Jews of a different mold. Yet Justin's own overwhelming evidence for verbal Jewish-Christian polemics and the example of Trypho himself undercut the idea that Jews could not associate with Christians. We cannot know how widely known or closely observed was the stricture against association with *minim.* A certain social withdrawal by some Jews from Christians or discouragement of contact by some leaders might be interpreted by Christians as the result of official legislation.

Looking at the material from Justin as a whole, I interpret it primarily as evidence for continuing verbal controversy between

Jews and Christians. The interpretation of Scripture is the arena of debate. The issues concern (1) Who is the true Israel, the inheritor of the promises to biblical Israel? (2) How are the commandments to be understood, literally or figuratively? How do Christians justify their failure to observe the commandments, if they are indeed the "true Israel"? (3) How is Jesus' status as the Christ and God proved by Scripture? In particular, how is the problem of his death on a cross solved? How is his birth by a virgin and resurrection proved at the bar of Scripture? Justin also alludes to bitter verbal attacks by Jews on Christians and inadvertently supplies evidence that Jews in his day never went beyond the verbal level or indulged in violence.

Why did these debates take place? Justin is himself a Gentile and by the time of his writing, Christianity is largely Gentile. Why is he still arguing with Jews about who is the true Israel and whether or not the commandments should be observed? These do not seem to be issues which would interest the Roman government or the gentile populace in their evaluation of Jews. The debate may represent simply the search for self-understanding and self-definition. Yet it is possible that Jews and Gentiles are competing for gentile converts. Their commonality of origin would actually contribute to the problem and cause each group to present itself to potential gentile converts as the "true Israel." To consider Justin's major themes (the purpose and status of the Law as temporary, remedial, and only for Jews; proselytizing; Christians as the new Israel; Christ as the Messiah of the Hebrew Bible and pre-existent *Logos;* Christianity as the true philosophy; and Gentiles as the inheritors of the promises of the Hebrew Bible), all fit with the idea that Christianity and Judaism are actively competing for gentile converts, as Nilson suggests.[21] One of Justin's unspoken complaints against Judaism may have been its continuing vitality and attractiveness.

CHAPTER TEN

Jewish and Christian Writers after 150 C.E.

Without intending to be exhaustive, I mention here some materials written or redacted after the mid–second century that shed light on the period 30–150.

CELSUS

The church father Origen (ca. 248) records arguments of the pagan Celsus against Christianity outlined in Celsus's work *The True Doctrine*. The work, now lost, was probably composed around 177–80,[1] although no one knows where. Even Origen does not know much about Celsus, whom Chadwick classifies as "an eclectic Platonist." As a pagan, Celsus is an invaluable witness because he promotes neither Judaism nor Christianity.

Celsus presents his attack against Christians in two ways. First, he speaks against it directly as a pagan. Christianity is unwholesome, a menace to Roman society, destroying familial unity, encouraging impiety by discouraging worship of the gods. But in Books 1 and 2 he puts his complaints in the mouth of a Jew and presents supposed Jewish objections to Christianity. Thus Celsus can combine both pagan and Jewish objections to belief in Jesus, although he clearly has little regard for Judaism. He also transmits some of the standard pagan canards against Jews—they are barbarous and descendants of a motley band of slaves. They revere a God and text that show human aspects and are inferior to the timeless verities of Plato.

In Books 4 and 5, Celsus attacks the Jews and Christians together, judging them guilty of the same errors. Their Scripture is a
lot of silly fables, clearly inferior to philosophy. Origen finds himself frequently defending the Jews on these points as a necessary
step in his defense of Christianity. But Jews, says Celsus, at least
have the merit of being traditional. Their customs are peculiar and
their beliefs superstitious, but they are the customs learned from
their forefathers.

Celsus directs against Christians some of the standard pagan accusations against Jews—they are misanthropic (3.14; 8.2), a rag-tag
band of slaves and lowlifes (1.62; 2.44, 46), they alter the Bible to
suit themselves (2.27, cf. Justin who says Jews tamper with the
text), Jesus was a sorcerer, as was Moses (1.26, 28, 38, 68, 71;
2.32; 5.41), their superstitions appeal to the stupid and childish
(4.33, 36, 40–50, 87).

Ironically, Celsus attacks Christian belief partially because of its
Jewish elements and inferior Scripture. But he also attacks Christians for their departure from Judaism, for denying the law of their
fathers (2.1, 3, 4; 5.33). They deny and pervert the Scripture that
they claim proves Jesus' divinity (1.50; 2.28–30). Christians had
their own difficulties with the problem of their allegiance to Judaism and their freedom from it, as we have shown. The letters of
Paul and the book of Acts are some of the earliest attempts to re-
solve this problem; Justin still wrestles with it a century later.

Celsus's Jew centers most of his attack on Jesus. His pedigree is
suspect. The virgin birth is fabricated and in fact Jesus' mother was
an adulteress and his father a Roman soldier named Panthera (1.28,
32, 69). Jesus' origins are humble, not those of a king (1.28, 29).
He went to Egypt and learned the magical arts (1.38). He cannot
be the son of God because he did not act like a god (1.61,
66, 67, 69), but rather fled and hid under duress (2.10, 70) and did
not save himself (2.33–35). His own disciples even betrayed him
(2.11, 12, 20–22, 45). Nor did he vanquish his persecutors after
death (2.35, 63, 67), but only appeared to one woman (2.70). The
resurrection is a fraud, one of a series of stories invented by Jesus'
followers (2.13–16, 25, 54, 57–60).

No doubt some of these accusations reflect genuine Jewish-
Christian debates. Obviously the statements of Celsus's Jew con-
cerning Jesus are pointed toward contemporary believers. Some are

probably charges made by Jews in Celsus's own time while others probably reflect Celsus's own reading of the LXX held up against what he knows about Christian belief. Some of the objections—Jesus being the son of Panthera, for example—show up later in Jewish sources—*t.Hul.* 2.22–23 and *Toledoth Yeshu.*[2]

In addition to the objections Celsus's Jew raises against belief in Jesus, the major part of the evidence, what does he say Jews were saying and doing about Christians?

1. Jews and Christians are quarrelling over Christ, an argument that Celsus considers wholly trivial, fighting over "the shadow of an ass" (3.1–4).[3] The content of this contentiousness may be the kind of Jewish objections against Jesus contained in Book 1. Justin provides additional support that the arguments revolved around interpretation of Scripture. These debates, says Celsus, are silly arguments of crude and illiterate people, "worms and frogs" (4.23, 87). When Christians are in trouble with Jews, they apparently fall back on the claim that they all worship the same God (6.29).

2. Celsus's Jew thinks that Jesus' followers invented tales about his life after the fact such as the story of Herod's tracking him and the virgin birth (1.28; 2.13–16, 25). The Gospel accounts are not only lies, but illogical (2.20–25), violating their own premises (2.74). The believers alter the Gospel three or four times over. Celsus may be referring to the canonical Gospels or to the work of Marcion. Justin accused the Jews of altering their Scripture to suit their views. If debates between Christians and other Jews centered on Jewish Scripture, then a likely standard charge would be that each side altered it for their own purposes. Celsus also accuses the Christians of sophistry, quoting prophecies about Jesus which could in fact apply to almost anyone. This represents another aspect of the charge of manipulating Scripture (1.50; 2.28, 29–31).

Even Jesus' own disciples did not believe him or the stories they made up about him (1.62). They were traitors and conspirators (2.20–22), who denied him (2.45, 58, 74–75).

3. Celsus's Jew says that Jesus' disciples were infamous rabble and lowlife (1.62–65). He only managed to gather ten sailors and tax collectors around him while he was alive (2.46).

4. Celsus's Jew echoes the complaint that Jesus' present-day followers abandoned the law of their fathers (2.1–4; 3.5; 5.33). Al-

though they claim an allegiance to Scripture, in fact they misread and misinterpret it and have abandoned its commandments (cf. Trypho's complaints to Justin).

5. Jews suffer from the Christians and their revolt and introduction of new and subversive ideas into the community (3.1–5). Christians blame the Jews for rejecting Jesus and claim the destruction of 70 C.E. is just punishment for it (4.22).

Celsus, writing about 177–80, confirms several points made in earlier materials:

1. Christians and Jews engage in verbal polemic that centers on claims about Jesus. Jesus' legitimacy and his pedigree are problematic, as the earlier materials suggest. Matthew's infancy narratives may be implicit responses to the charge of illegitimacy. John points to Jesus' ancestry (6:42) and place of origin (7:27, 52) as things to which some Jews objected. Celsus supplies a specific charge, that Jesus was the son of Panthera. Celsus further echoes the idea that Jews dismissed christological claims such as the virgin birth and the resurrection as inventions. Matthew and the *Gospel of Peter* refer to the resurrection as a point that Jews attacked. Justin's Trypho also argues that the disciples invented tales of Jesus' life.

2. Celsus confirms the notion that Jews could not understand the Christian claim to revere Jewish Scripture while abandoning observance of many of her commandments. This supports information in the Synoptics, where some Jews query the disciples' law-observance. In Acts, Paul comes under suspicion of teaching Jews to abandon the Law. Sixty years later, Justin's Trypho is still puzzled by Christians' failure to observe biblical commandments, although they claim the Jewish Scripture as their own.

3. Celsus echoes the idea that the Christians upset the stability of the Jewish community and are viewed as troublemakers. I have noted in earlier materials a political aspect of "the Christian problem" for Jews. In Acts, the Sanhedrin accuses Christian preachers of intending to bring them ruin (5:28). Further, some Jews hale Christians before local authorities. In John 16:1–2, the author makes a connection between Jewish objections to Christians and their death at Roman hands. In Revelation and *Mart. Pol.,* Jews are implicated in a process that involves Roman punishment of Christians.

Celsus seems to have specific information about Christians and not just wild, unsubstantiated prejudices. He is useful as an observer who has no desire to promote either Judaism or Christianity, since he considers both systems inferior to Platonic philosophy.

CHRISTIAN WRITERS

A large number of apparently anti-Jewish remarks in the Church fathers are occasioned by situations that had nothing to do with actual Christian-Jewish relationships. Sometimes severe anti-Jewish polemic carries with it no hint that the author ever knew or had any dealings with any Jews (Ephrem the Syrian is an example). The Church fathers defined their own "Israel theology" for internal consumption.[4] In response to the Marcionite challenge the Church fathers had to "save" the God of the Hebrew Bible, which included affirmation of his promises to biblical Israel, and yet to explain Jewish refusal of Jesus and the legitimation of Christians as the rightful heirs to the covenant. The escape from this dilemma was often through a variety of anti-Jewish interpretations of history.

Similarly, Christian attempts to justify themselves to pagans and refute the charge of being an upstart religion required that Christians "borrow" the antiquity of the Jews. Yet Christians could not claim much success among Jews. This contradiction often provoked an explanation that denigrated Judaism, but also declared Christian separation from Judaism. Tertullian, for example, says, "aside from the question of age, we have nothing to do with the Jews" (*Apol* 21.3). Again, Christian anti-Jewish remarks do not necessarily spring from actual relations with Jews. The development of a standard, highly stylized *Adversus Judaeos* tradition by church writers explains many anti-Jewish motifs. Various themes have become stereotypes—the destruction of the Temple as punishment for Jewish responsibility in Jesus' death, Jewish anathematizing Christ and Christians, or Jews' ignorance and perversion of their own Scripture, and may have nothing to do with actual human relationships. Certain references in later church writers bear consideration, however.

ORIGEN

Origen lived in Caesarea in the first half of the third century, but traveled extensively and wrote prolifically. He is remarkable as a Christian writer who knew Hebrew and studied the Bible with Jews. Much of the scholarly work on Origen has centered on his relative knowledge or use of Jewish exegetical traditions. He displays many themes that are familiar from earlier Christian writers, including Justin—the Jews killed Jesus and the debacle of 70 C.E. is God's punishment on them, Hebrew Scripture testifies to Jesus and Christianity, and Christians are the true Israel. Like *Barn.*, Origen often divides up verses of prophecy and applies the predictions of judgment to the Jews and the predictions of future glory to Christians. Only a few statements here inform our topic.

Origen makes three vague references to Jewish persecution, but does not specify when the persecution took place (*In Rom.* 8.12 [*PG* 14.1199]; *In Ps.* 37 hom. 1.1 [*PG* 12.1321]; *In Jud. hom.* 8.1 [*GCS* 7.509]). Nor does he provide any specifics. "The argument is really theological, not historical," says N. de Lange using the literary motif of Jewish opposition to Christianity.[5] Origen also reports a "Judaizing" tendency. Some of the people who come to hear his homily on Sunday have apparently spent the previous day in synagogue (*In Lev. hom.* 5.8 [*GCS* 6.349.4-5]). Like material in Ignatius and Justin, Origen's disparagement of Judaism is meant to discourage gentile Christians from involvement with Judaism or Jewish practices. Thus it provides more evidence of Judaism's continued attractiveness to some Gentiles and some measure of welcome extended by Jewish communities.

Origen relates two items which, he says, spring from Jewish libel of Christians: the question of Jesus' pedigree and legitimacy, and the accusation that Christians engage in Thyestean feasts, practicing cannibalism and sexual promiscuity. If correct, he then supplies some of the content of various verbal polemics between Jews and believers in Jesus. We have noted that Celsus's Jew accuses Jesus of lacking pedigree. Not only is he of humble stock, but the offspring of an adulterous union between his mother and a Roman soldier ben Pantera (*Contra Celsum* 1.28, 32, 69). In his refutation of these libels, Origen does not deny they were spoken by Jews. A tannaitic report mentions healers who heal in the name of Yeshu ben Pantiri (*t.Hul.* 2.22–24 and the medieval *Toledoth Yeshu* put forth the same accusation). Thus Origen confirms that attacks on Jesus' legitimacy and humble origins were part of early Jewish objections to Christianity. There is nothing strictly from the period before 150 along these lines (save John 8:41), but their appearance in Celsus suggests that not long after 150, Jews in popular circles were employing this jibe against Christian believers.[6]

A second calumny that Origen attributes to Jews is that they hold Thyestean feasts, sacrificing an infant and partaking of its flesh as well as indulging in all manner of sexual licentiousness (*Contra Celsum* 6.27). The charge is not new. What is unusual is the assignment of blame for it to the Jews. Normally it is a pagan charge against Christians or an accusation by one group of Christians against another. Justin, for example, identifies it as a pagan charge (*1 Apol.* 26.6–7; 29.2), and Trypho emphatically denies that Jews think Christians guilty of these crimes (*Dial.* 10.2). John 6:52 reflects Jewish bewilderment at the Eucharist, especially the language of "flesh," but it is unclear if this was translated into a charge of cannibalism in John's community. The absence of this charge as a Jewish calumny in other Christian writers, Justin's definite denial that Jews think this about Christians, as well as its absence in Jewish sources of any period, suggest that Origen is unreliable on this point.[7] He may have conflated two familiar themes—the hostility of the Jews and anti-Christian charges of cannibalism and promiscuity, thereby establishing a link between the two that did not exist in reality.

A third charge that Origen levels at the Jews is that they curse and blaspheme Christ in the synagogue and plot against those who believe in him (*Hom. Ps.* 37 [36]; *Hom.* 2.8 [*PG* 12.1387]; *Hom. Jer.* 10.8.2; 19.12.31; *Matt* 16:3 [*GCS* 10.469]). There are early hints of cursing Christ in Peter's third denial (Mark 14:71) and Paul's statement "No one speaking by the Spirit of God says, 'Jesus is cursed'" (1 Cor 12:3). Yet Origen says nothing that he could not have read in Justin. Further, Origen knows of some Christians attending synagogue on Saturday and Christian worship on Sunday, so the cursing is much more limited than he lets on, or it has ceased by the time he is writing. Whatever other gentile Christians thought, or whatever Jews did, some Christians thought they could profess Jesus and attend synagogue. These Christians could

have been Gentiles who were curious spectators, Gentiles who converted to Judaism, or Jews who became Christians and never
stopped attending synagogue. Evidently they did not feel that they
had to renounce their Christianity to attend the synagogue. A
Christian presence in the synagogue also mitigates against a connection to a formal *Birkat ha-Minim* aimed at ejecting Christians
from the synagogue. These statements provide little more than
confirmation of the notion of verbal polemics that include attacks
on Jesus, his pedigree, and aspects of his life. This material is outlined more thoroughly by Celsus, from whom Origen may have
gotten some or all of his information.

TERTULLIAN

Like Origen, Tertullian's biblical exegesis shows affinities with
Jewish exegesis, but how direct or extensive was Jewish influence
on him is difficult to gauge. Like other church writers, Terullian
wanted to make use of the antiquity of the Jews, but had to explain the failure of Christian proselytism among the Jews. He too
inherited and transmitted (and contributed to) the *Adversus Judaeos*
tradition. The evidence of North African Christianity, says Frend,
shows its closeness to Judaism and Jewish practices as well as hostility between Jews and Christians.[8] A certain rigorism appealed
to African Christians, including Tertullian, so that they seemed to
"outdo" the Jews in stringency. Some apparently observed Sabbath laws and abstained from meat that still contained blood.
Frend calls it "a baptized Judaism."[9] Archaeological evidence
raises the possibility that some Christians remained sufficiently
close to other Jews that they were buried alongside them.[10]
Whatever their fraternal squabbling, the two faced a common
threat from the pagans.

A survey of Tertullian produces two possibly relevant references
to Jewish reactions to Christians. In one, an apostate Jew carries a
caricature of a Christian that includes a picture of a donkey, which
he labeled "Onocoetes," literally "begotten by a donkey," a reference to the god of the Christians (*Ad. Nationes* 1.14). Tertullian
says this happened "not so long ago," which might place it in our
period of study. In connection to this story, Tertullian claims the
Jews are "the seed-plot of all the calumny against us." Yet this

seems a particularly sorry example to bring as proof—one example of ridicule by a person no longer even considered a Jew. Nor does he bring more examples to support his charge. I have noted that some pagans accused both Jews and Christians of worshiping a donkey.

The second accusation is one of general persecution, "Will you plant there both synagogues of the Jews—fountains of persecution—before which the apostles endured the scourge, and heathen assemblages with their own circus, indeed where they readily take up the cry 'Death to the third race'" (*Scorp.* 10.10). With one mention of the apostles and one of contemporary pagan persecution, it becomes difficult to know when Tertullian dates the persecution in the synagogue. It may refer to the early second century. The *Martyrdom of Polycarp,* in the mid–second century, provides a similar juxtaposition of Jewish hostility and pagan persecution.

Yet the evidence Tertullian himself provides of a certain closeness between African Christians and Jews in matters of practice and scriptural interpretation suggests that persecution cannot have been the only mode of Jewish connection to Christians. Perhaps it was not even the prevailing mode. Perhaps there *was* mutual hostility but it was rarely acted upon. In spite of his indictment of the synagogues, it is telling how little material Tertullian actually musters to suggest Jews persecuted Christians.

EUSEBIUS

Eusebius writes in Caesarea at the beginning of the fourth century. He collects and compiles many earlier works. Like many earlier Christian writers, he asserts the antiquity of Christianity on the basis of its connection to Judaism. In his *Demonstratio* he argues that Christianity is the genuine continuation of the religion of the patriarchs, while the reception of the Mosaic Torah and its observance forms an unpleasant and insignificant interlude in history. Eusebius carries forward the inherited *Adversus Judaeos* tradition, including themes such as the destruction of the Temple as punishment for killing Jesus (*Hist. eccl.* 2.6.8) and the Jews as plotters against the Christians (*Hist. eccl.* 3.5.2). Yet he credits Jews with superior knowledge of Scripture (*Praep.* 11.5; 12.1, 4) and admits

the Law had some beneficial effect on the "barbarians," as a preparation for the gospel (*Hist. eccl.* 1.5.1). "Their law," he says, "became famous and spread among all men like a fragrant breeze"
(*Hist. eccl.* 1.2.23).

Eusebius cites several references to Jewish treatment of Christians. He quotes Apolinarius (fl. 177) who writes against the
Montanists, "Is there anyone, good people, of those whose talking began with Montanus and the women, who was persecuted
by Jews or killed by the wicked? Not one. . . . Or was anyone of
the women ever scourged in the synagogue of the Jews or
stoned? Never anywhere" (*Eccl. hist.* 5.16.12). In other words,
some "true" Christians (as opposed to the Montanists) were persecuted by Jews and scourged in synagogues. It is unclear when to
date these persecutions and scourgings suffered by the "true
Christians." If they are contemporary with the Montanists, that is
naturally too late to inform our time period. But they may refer
to treatment suffered by Christians at an earlier stage. The reference does suggest that these women were still considered Jews
and subject to synagogue discipline. Conversely, the Montanists
were free from it.

In his *Praeparatio*, Eusebius reports two features of Jewish complaints against Christians that mesh with material in Justin's *Dial.,
Barn.,* Celsus, and others,

> But the sons of the Hebrews also would find fault with us, that
> being strangers and aliens *we misuse their books, which do not belong to
> us at all,* and because in an impudent and shameless way, as they
> would say, we thrust ourselves in, and try violently to thrust out the
> true family and kindred from their own ancestral rights. (*Praep.* 1.2)

This sounds like the same kind of Jewish-Christian verbal polemic in evidence in Justin and Celsus. Jews and Christians play
tug-of-war with Scripture, each claiming it truly belongs to them
alone. The Jews reject Christian interpretation of Scripture,
namely the exegesis that links the Hebrew Bible to Jesus. Both
sides claim it as their book and claim themselves as the true Israel.

A second Jewish objection to Christians, reports Eusebius,
echoes the complaint of Justin's Trypho,

The most unreasonable thing of all is, that though we do not observe the customs of their Law as they do, but openly break the Law,
we assume to ourselves the better rewards which have been prom-
ised to those who keep the Law. (*Praep.* 1.2)

Jews in Justin's day expressed similar puzzlement that Christians
could claim their rights to Scripture yet ignore the commandments. This, says Trypho, is the main stumbling block to Jews taking Christianity seriously.

Eusebius brings forth no unique information about Jewish treatment of Christians in our period, but confirms the image of some
Christians undergoing synagogue discipline (which they understandably interpret as persecution) and verbal polemic in which
Jews and Christians argued over rights to inherit Scripture and the
relative obligation to do the commandments.

THE RABBIS

The paucity of early material that explicitly reports rabbinic reactions to Christianity is often lamented.[11] Nor is rabbinic literature the ideal source to chart early Jewish attitudes toward
Christianity because the majority of Jews with whom Christians
interacted probably did not feel bound by rabbinic teaching. J.
Lightstone notes how rarely early Christian literature mentions
rabbis.[12] The only person so addressed in the New Testament is
Jesus.[13] Gamaliel is a rabbinic figure, although he is not identified
as one in Acts. Lightstone also argues that Christianity flourished
in areas precisely where the rabbinic movement did not (as far as
we know)—Syria, Asia Minor, Egypt, North Africa, Greece, Italy,
and the islands around the Mediterranean. Indeed in my survey of
early materials, I encountered no rabbis, but rather high priests,
false messiahs, Pharisees, or most often simply "the Jews." The situation for apprehending nonrabbinic Judaism in antiquity, however, is even worse than for rabbinic Judaism. Philo's works, *Sefer
ha-Razim,* some papyrii, inscriptions, and artifacts are all that is
available. None of these mentions Christians or Christianity. In the
end, rabbinic evidence is all that is available.

For the sake of chronological integrity, I limit myself to the earliest strata of materials, the tannaitic literature—Mishnah, Tosefta,

the tannaitic midrashim and some beraitot within the Talmud. At the earliest, these materials were redacted in the early third century—50–75 years after the period of our concern—although they contain some older materials. The early rabbinic material affords two kinds of evidence—incidents that include Christians and references to *minim* and *minut,* "sectarians," and "sectarianism." Most scholars agree that *minim* cannot have been applied exclusively to Jewish Christians, but must have included them at certain junctures. Some *minim,* for example, deny the resurrection and the next world (*m.Ber.* 9.5; *b.Sanh.* 91a), which cannot mean Christians. Most likely the term meant different things to different people at different times. Other equally vague types populate the literature—those who assert there are "two powers in heaven,"[14] or "the Ten tribes,"[15] both seemingly catch-all terms for unacceptable types. Thanks to censorship, the terms "Sadducee" (*ṣidwqy*) or "Samaritan" (*kwty*) sometimes mask references to Christians.

Generally, references to Jesus are not the focus of this study unless they are elements in anti-Christian propaganda. Two points deserve mention. First, Jesus and his followers are portrayed as magicians, confirming Celsus's report. Second, Jesus' legitimacy and pedigree are points of anti-Christian propaganda, which also confirms Celsus. Nothing in rabbinic literature echoes the idea that Jews question the resurrection or claim the disciples stole Jesus' body.

Incidents Involving Christians

Three incidents between rabbinic Jews and Christians appear in tannaitic literature. In the first, R. Eleazar ben Dama is bitten by a snake. A healer named Jacob of Kefar Sama comes to cure him in the name of Yeshu ben Pantiri, but is prevented by Rabbi Ishmael. Ben Dama claimed to have a scriptural proof that the Christian healer was permissible, but died before he could produce it (*t.Ḥul.* 2.22–23). Whether the incident is genuine or not, it shows that some Jews thought of Christians primarily as healers (or magicians) and effective ones at that, and that in certain areas, the two groups maintained sufficient contact to perform healings on one another. Unlike Simon Magus or the seven sons of Sceva in Acts, rabbinic literature does not portray Christian magicians as bumbling and inadequate, but apparently very competent (cf. *y.Šabb.*

14d, where a man saves the grandson of Jehoshua ben Levi from choking by whispering over him in the name of Yeshu ben Pandera).

In a second incident, Rabbi Eliezer is puzzled when arrested for *minut*. Rabbi Akiba reminds him, "Perhaps one of the *minim* said to you a word of *minut* and it pleased you. He replied: By Heaven, you reminded me. Once I was walking in a street of Sepphoris, and chanced upon Jacob of Kefar Sichin and he told me something of *minut* in the name of Yeshu ben Pantiri and it pleased me. And I was arrested for words of *minut* because I transgressed the words of Torah, 'Keep your way far from her and do not draw near to the door of her house'" (*t.Ḥul.* 2.24; cf. *b.Abod.Zar.* 16b–17a where Jacob is identified as a disciple of Jesus the Nazarene). In other words, this story does not portray conversations between Jewish Christians and other Jews as out of the ordinary.

The citation of the verse from Proverbs shows that, in theory, hearing Christian interpretations of Scripture is unacceptable, and contact with Christian teachers should be avoided. In reality, however, their interpretations are close enough to those of other Jews that Rabbi Eliezer enjoyed the one related by Jacob. This situation is reminiscent of the situation in Justin's *Dialogue,* where he says Jews are forbidden social relations with Christians, yet provides varied evidence for contact in his descriptions of their arguments over Scripture.

The third example appears only in the Babylonian Talmud and reflects a later stratum of literature. The characters are Yavneans, however, and its allusions to Matthew show it is a fairly clear reference to Christianity. Imma Shalom and her brother Rabban Gamliel come before a judge, a *philosoph*[16] to divide their inheritance. He had a reputation that he did not accept bribes and they wanted to test him. She bribes him with a golden lamp and he temporarily decides in her favor. Gamliel brings a tradition that where there is a son, the daughter does not inherit. The judge counters Gamliel's verse from the Torah by (supposedly) citing the Evangelium, "A son and a daughter inherit equally."[17] Her brother then bribes the judge with a Libyan ass and the judge decides in favor of Gamliel, paraphrasing Matt 5:17, "I came not to destroy the Law of Moses nor to add to the Law of Moses." She reminds the judge of her gift: "She said to him, 'Let your light shine as a lamp' (Matt 5:16). Rabban Gamliel said to her, 'The ass has come and kicked over the lamp' (*b.Šabb.* 116a)." Again, the actual historicity of the incident is unimportant. It suggests that the rabbis had some rudimentary knowledge of Christianity, that Jews sometimes subjected Christians to ridicule, and that they considered some Christians capable of corruption.[18] To take this incident as anything more than a piece of burlesque is to misread it. We have already seen that the friction between Jews and Christians worked itself out on the vulgar level as well as the intellectual one.

Measures against Minim

The term *minim* sometimes included Christians and measures enacted against *minim* probably affected Christians at some points. The most well-known anti-heretical measure is the *Birkat ha-Minim,* the blessing against the heretics (*b.Ber.* 28b–29a). I have already discussed this material in connection with the Fourth Gospel and Justin. As I have noted, the rabbinic reference merely says that someone who faltered in reciting it was removed from the position of praying on behalf of the community. Whether just for that service or just for that day, no one knows. There is no mention of a permanent exclusion from the community. Nor does it seem to be a formula directed specifically against Christians. The Cairo geniza version that includes *noṣerim* has no special claim to antiquity or reliability. I suspect some people did mean "Christians" when they said the *Birkat ha-Minim,* but when and where is unclear. As anti-heretical measures go, the blessing seems a fairly mild one. It is a general wish for an end to sectarians, apostates, and arrogant governments. Since few people considered themselves "sectarian," most probably dismissed it as pertaining to other people.

The books of the *minim* are judged to be unsacred, even though they contain God's name (*t.Šabb.* 13.5; *t.Yad.* 2.13). This is a relatively theoretical point from the point of view of the *minim* and would not particularly affect their dealings with Jews. I do not interpret the canonization of Scripture that took place in part at Yavneh to be a specifically anti-Christian measure, since a great deal of that process apparently took place much earlier.[19]

A number of rulings discourage dealings with *minim.* A series of prohibitions appears in *t.Ḥul.* 2.20–21, where a Jew is forbidden to eat meat which passed through their hands, drink their wine, sell or buy from them, apprentice their sons, and the like. Their children are *mamzerim* (bastards). Clearly this is an attempt to limit contact with people judged to be *minim*. How successful this ruling was is anyone's guess. These *minim* were not officially drummed out of the community in any way, but the Rabbis promoted a certain social withdrawal from them. Similarly, a mishnah forbids variation in dress or liturgy that steers too close to *minut* (*m.Meg.* 4.8, 9). Again, these attempts to contain and discourage *minut* through informal social means were not responses solely to Christianity, but must have sometimes been precipitated by the perceived threat of Christian ideas.

The denigration of their books, the malediction against them, and the attempt to limit social intercourse with them show that the early Rabbis harbored no great respect for *minim*. But they cannot be total outsiders either. Furthermore, a low-level social ostracism could only be recommended if there is considerable contact. These *minim* were not rabbinic Jews but did not seem to be complete apostates either. The Rabbis confronted various forms of sectarianism, including Jewish Christianity, with a haphazard set of rulings, but they did not apparently confront Christianity in any systematic manner.

OBSERVATIONS

These later materials confirm certain aspects of our pre-150 texts. They afford a glimpse of some of the content of verbal anti-Christian propaganda that is so frequently alluded to in our materials. With the exception of Eusebius' reference to scourging, which is difficult to date; Tertullian's label of synagogues as "fountains of persecution," a label we found suspect; and the rabbinic reference to an economic boycott, all of these later materials show hostilities played out on the level of verbal polemic and propaganda. This data confirms the trend discovered for references in materials from about 100 C.E. and later. In these later works, Jewish objections continue to center on christological claims, Christian failure to observe the Law, and relations with Rome. In christological debates, Jesus' human aspects are worthless—his origin, legitimacy, and pedigree. Yet equally problematic are claims of his divinity—he did not act like a god, his disciples betrayed him, he failed to vanquish his enemies. Furthermore, Jews objected to the Christian claim to adhere to Scripture since they failed to observe many of the commandments.

Finally, two references seem to allude to Jewish troubles with Rome caused by Christians. Rabbi Eliezer is tried by the Romans because he is suspected of *minut*. Celsus claims that Christians "trouble" the Jewish community, which may be an oblique reference to difficulties with Rome. Troubles with Rome appear to be less of an issue in these later materials, however, probably because more Roman officials distinguished Christians from Jews by this time. Some Christians, however, are not judged by Jews to be total outsiders to the Jewish community and are subject to synagogue discipline and certain attempts to limit their social contact with other Jews.[20]

PART TWO

Major Trends

CHAPTER ELEVEN

Major Trends Detected

What are the major trends and peculiarities in the literature we have surveyed? Several points emerge. First, division and classification of materials on the basis of geography are not useful or even possible. Frequently the provenance of a work is unknown, or even if known tells us little. An author may grow up in one place, study in another, and write in a third. He or his teachers may be travelers, garnering traditions from various places. Further, materials from the two most frequently identified locales—Syria-Palestine and Asia Minor—show the whole range of reactions, from tolerance to persecution.

A more serious problem of the materials is the inability, in most cases, to distinguish between Jewish Christians and gentile Christians. Justin's many statements about Jewish treatment of Christians, for example, do not mention the ethnic origin or practices of those Christians. Context is not always trustworthy, either, since a gentile Christian like Justin (or possibly Luke) may be passing on a memory of an original interaction between Jewish Christians and other Jews, but use it as ammunition in a battle between subsequent Jews and gentile Christians. From the point of view of the Christian authors, the relative Jewish or gentile origin of individuals pales beside their identity as Christians, so is often unspecified. For the Jews whose reactions I attempt to track, however, surely a world of difference separated Jews who believed in Jesus from Gentiles who did.

TOLERANCE

A rarely noted trend emerges from examination of the materials. Some Jews seemingly took a relatively tolerant view of Jews who believed in Jesus. Josephus, writing in the 90s, knew something of Jesus and the Christians and was not highly critical of them. The *Testimonium Flavianum,* minus the probable interpolations, evinces a Jew with certain limited information about Christians. At worst he sees them as gullible and overly fond of wonder-working. Possibly he is sympathetic to Jesus as a victim of Pilate's clumsy misman-agement of Judean affairs. In the second reference to Christians, James is clearly seen as a victim of political high-handedness. Josephus approves of the actions of "the reasonable ones" who are offended at James' execution and take steps to remove his persecu-tor from office. Thus a Jew writing under the reign of Domitian (an alleged persecutor of Christians) lodges no serious complaint against the Christians and even implies that they deserve fairer treatment than they receive. Furthermore, his report provides evi-dence that some Jews defended a Jewish Christian and sought Roman help to avenge his death.

Acts, written about the same time as *Antiquities,* also produces some instances of Jews who promote a policy of "benign neglect" toward Christians. Gamaliel (5:34–39), the Pharisaic scribes (23:6–9), the Roman Jewish leaders (28:21–25), and possibly Alexander at Ephesus (19:33–34) are anxious to give Christians a fair hearing and find them inoffensive. These Jewish figures are not particu-larly partisan toward Christians and remain largely unpersuaded by them (save the "some" who are convinced in 28:24). Yet these Jews do not think Christians should be harassed, nor deprived of the same opportunities and benefit of the doubt enjoyed by other Jews. While the scenes are composed and show some mistakes, these Jewish characters are not totally suspect. They do not serve a clear Lukan *Tendenz,* and the relative scarcity of these kinds of characters suggests Luke did not invent them to make an obvious point.

The many Jews in Acts who are curious about Paul and regu-larly welcome him into the synagogue serve certain literary and theological purposes and are historically suspect. Yet even they must have had a few real counterparts. Paul could not claim sorrow over the failure of the Jewish mission (Romans 9–11) had no Jews ever heard him or other Christian preachers. Some Jews must have given them sufficient hearing to decide to refuse them. Acts also leaves the impression that thousands of Jews in Jerusalem believed in Jesus. The numbers may be exaggerated, but some Jews must have become believers or there would not have been any anti-Christian measures in Judea. Thus some number of Jews must have been well disposed to hearing Christian preaching in the early days.

These materials from the end of the first century (which describe events from the 30s and 40s) project no sense that Christians were anything other than Jews with ideas unpopular in some other segments of the Jewish community. Even in the Fourth Gospel—a work not calculated to flatter the Jews—the Jews who comfort Martha and Mary (John 11:19) do not treat the women any differently than other Jews.

In one community in North Africa, as late as the second or third century, Jews may have allowed believers in Jesus to be buried with their fellow Jews.[1] Certain elements within these communities must have promoted a policy of laissez-faire and evenhanded treatment of Christians.

The next example of Jewish tolerance does not arise until Justin's Trypho fifty to sixty years later. By that time, Jews and Christians seem to view one another across a divide. They must explain basic points of their own faiths to one another. They are distinct groups and the issues are no longer disputes between Jews, but questions of who inherits and rightly understands Scripture as a whole—Jews or Christians? Trypho himself may be more conventional than real, and Jews and Christians are already separate groups, but his character in the *Dial.* shows that even as late as 155–60, a Christian could at least imagine a Jew giving him a fair hearing.

These examples of fair-mindedness and tolerance are few in number. Speculation about what is not there is always risky. Yet I wonder, for several reasons, if this trend is not underrepresented in ancient literature. First, the responses of sensible, tolerant people do not make for dramatic reading. They are not newsworthy. Negative events are often more interesting and unusual. Second, these examples of tolerance do not make a pressured minority feel better.

If suffering persecution is a requirement of true followers of Jesus and affords them a special status, as some Christian writers assert (John 15:18–20; Revelation) it would not do to remind Christians that they were once relatively acceptable. Last, these examples would not serve the needs of later Christian writers locked in polemic with Jews, nor those struggling with the question of Israel's general refusal of the Christian message and its implication for Christian identity and claim to Scripture. If Jews are sensible and fair-minded, their refusal of Christianity becomes more problematic than if they are hard-hearted, vicious, and ignorant of their own Scripture.

How widespread was this attitude of Jewish acceptance of Christians is impossible to know. Perhaps it was the majority view. Perhaps it was the exception. Yet these few examples that survive allow us to hear the quiet voice of toleration amidst the din of voices that claim Jews were sources of persecution.

PHYSICAL ATTACKS

More frequent in early literature is the claim that Jews in some way threatened the physical well-being of Christians. Many of the categories within this group of references overlap. The account of Stephen's death, for example, belongs in three of the groups— "Early Judean Persecution," "Spontaneous Violence," and "Murder."

Early Judean Persecution

Jews are frequently charged with posing a physical threat to Christians. The particulars of many of these charges are masked by the word "persecution," a term that implies sympathy with the recipients of the action and judgment on those who mete it out; it says nothing of what the latter group did, thought it was doing, or hoped to accomplish. When Paul, for example, says that he persecuted the early church, he speaks in retrospect as a believer. At the time he no doubt thought he was safeguarding his form of Judaism. The term "persecution" could stand for anything from harassment to judicial flogging to mob violence.

One of the earliest examples of Jews reacting violently to a believer in Jesus is the stoning of Stephen (Acts 7:57–60). Originally this event was probably a mob action, which Luke reworks to appear as a judicial proceeding.[2] The scattering of the church after Stephen's death leaves the Jerusalem apostles untouched, suggesting that Stephen and the Hellenists are persecuted for some reason other than the specific proclamation of Jesus. Surely the Jerusalem apostles also proclaimed Jesus. Most likely Stephen and those like him were too liberal in their attitude to the Law, since he is accused of speaking against Moses and against the Law (6:11–13). His attitude toward the Temple is particularly problematic (6:13). Paul, too, may be in danger from the "unbelievers in Judea" (Rom 15:31) because he is not stringent enough in his law-observance. The author of 1 Thess 2:14–16 claims the churches in Judea suffered something from the Jews. Verse 16 offers a clue that preaching to the Gentiles is problematic in Thessalonica, and this may be the problem in Judea as well. Perhaps Christians were preaching to Gentiles and accepting them into their community or joining them in table fellowship without demanding circumcision. These three examples are vague but suggest Jews reacted to Christians in Judea negatively, the Christians saw this as persecution, and law-observance was at the heart of the problem.

Judicial Flogging

Paul points to his own experience—"Five times I have received from the Jews the forty minus one" (2 Cor 11:24), that is, the penalty of flogging imposed by a Jewish court for a variety of offenses. What Paul calls persecution is, from the point of view of the Jews administering it, a religiously motivated discipline meant to bring a recalcitrant member into line with the rest of the community. Even Paul, when he speaks of his former "persecution" of the church, implies that it was part of his zeal for his ancestral traditions (Gal 1:13–14) and his righteousness under the Law (Phil 3:6). He thought he was disciplining wayward members of his own group, promoting law-observance, and safeguarding his ancestral traditions—that is, Torah. Failure to require circumcison of gentile converts was a major complaint against Paul (Gal 5:11) and others (Gal 6:12) from some quarter, either Jewish or Jewish Christian. Perhaps the troublesome Jews in 1 Thess 2:16 who obstructed the gentile mission were flogging Christian preachers for this same offense.

The notion of Christians subject to judicial flogging occurs

some forty years later in Matthew's Gospel (10:17), "They will
... flog you in their synagogues." Matthew revises the pre-
compositional tradition that appears in Mark (13:9), which uses
the more colloquial *darēsō*, and employs the more technical
mastigoō. Mark's version takes place in the synagogue and could
mean either a spontaneous crowd beating or a legal punishment,
but Matthew's version clearly implies the latter. Both Matthew
and Mark coordinate the beatings with deliverance up to councils
(sanhedrins), suggesting a judicial context. Neither Gospel mentions the crime for which Christians are punished. Circumcision
does not seem to be the issue by this later time. The issues are
broader and, at least for Matthew, the hostilities deeper. Yet both
references suggest that Christians in these communities are still
seen by other Jews as subject to the strictures and punishments of
the broader Jewish community. As late as the 90s then, Christians
are still seen as Jews in some places, and some Jews are determined to keep them so.[3]

The Gospel authors, of course, saw things differently. A chasm
separates them from those in "their synagogues." Luke has no reference to floggings in his Gospel, but includes the traditions of
Christians delivered up to synagogues (21:12). He even alters a Q
saying to include "synagogues" (12:11). In Acts, however, he includes Paul's recollection of beatings he administered to Christians
in the synagogue (22:19) as well as the case of Peter and the apostles beaten by the Sanhedrin and released (5:40). The latter qualifies as a clear case of a punishment handed down by a judicial
authority.

Spontaneous Violence

Alongside these traces of Jewish discipline meted out to Christians are suggestions of less orderly reactions. I have already mentioned Stephen as a victim of an angry mob. The author of 1 Thess
2:14–16 says the Jews drove them out. Needless to say, some of
Paul's references to his own persecution could indicate spontaneous
violence as readily as orderly discipline.

The primary examples of Christians suffering from spontaneous
Jewish crowds are in Acts, where Jews react to Paul's preaching.
With the exception of Stephen's case, Paul is always the victim (he
is joined by Barnabas in one place), the perpetrators are always "the

Jews," and the attempts to kill and injure Paul are always unsuccessful. They beat him in 21:30–32, but with no apparent ill effects. He is still ready to make a major address. Many elements of plot, intrigue, and narrow escape are conventional. They are also a reflection of the victim's perspective. Just as one person's prosecution is another's persecution, one person's plan and orderly procedure could be interpreted by the victim as a plot.

It is possible that Jews engaged in spontaneous, angry reactions to Christians. Such cases are probably not as common as Luke implies, however, since no example of a definite mob action by Jews against Christians occurs again until *Mart. Pol.* (ca. 155), where the Jews are part of a gentile pagan mob (although these actions are cited as customary). Possibly *Diogn.*, written about the same time, refers to similar actions, when it notes that Jews war against the Christians while Greeks persecute them.

Some Jews in the diaspora must have hoped to maintain a low profile, especially after the war of 115–17. Mob violence could easily get out of hand and backfire. The Jews hale Paul before Gallio in Acts 18:12–17, for instance, but the crowd turns around and beats Sosthenes—the ruler of the synagogue. An attack by Jews on what pagans would perceive as one of their own could easily erupt into a scene where the gentile populace attacked the Jews. Nero singled out Christians in Rome, but other pagans probably would not have distinguished Jews who believed in Jesus from other Jews in certain places. Witness Acts 16:20, where Paul and Silas are identified as "Jews disturbing our city." Jews were no strangers to expulsions as punishments for civil unrest (*Ant.* 18.3.5 §§ 81–84; Suetonius, *Tiberius* 36; *Claudius* 25.4; Dio Cassius, *Rom. Hist.* 57.18.5a; Tacitus, *Ann.* 2.85) or to anti-Jewish riots. Perhaps the Jewish element in spontaneous anti-Christian actions was less significant than it appears in Acts, since the evidence for it outside of Acts is minimal.

Murder

A more specific charge that Jews actually murdered Christians appears in a few instances. The high priest Ananus kills James, but according to Josephus, his action is highly unpopular with other Jews. In contrast, Herod's murder of James, the brother of John (Acts 12:1–3), is reported to please the Jews. Stephen's death appears to be the result of an unruly crowd. John 16:2–3 predicts that expulsion from the synagogue will be followed by religiously motivated killings. Who does the actual killing—Jews, pagans, or Romans—is unclear. Justin offers a variety of charges that Jews kill Christians. He accuses Bar Kochba (*1 Apol.* 31.6) of ordering cruel punishments, which might include death. Justin always tempers these charges with statements of Jewish powerlessness. Most telling is the statement in *Dial.* 96.2, "you curse Christians in your synagogues, and other nations carry out the curse, putting to death those who simply confess themselves to be Christians."

Indeed, what is frequently hard to discern is whether Jews are seen as actual killers or part of a process that results in the deaths of Christians. If Jews are mere contributors to threats against Christians, their role could be manifold—informing, slander, failure to offer the protection of the Jewish community, and the like. The high priest Ananus, clearly responsible for James' death, manipulates circumstances in the vacuum created by a procurator's death. Neither Herod nor Ananus are rank-and-file Jews or meant to represent the entire community. Although Jews are often accused of plots or a desire to kill Christians in Christian literature throughout this time period, the evidence of their doing so *directly* is singularly limited.

A large body of references seems to fall into the category of physical acts against Christians, but is simply unclear. From Paul's many uses of the term "persecution," to "fear of the Jews" as a determinant in John and *Gos. Pet.,* to the claim of *Diogn.* that Jews "war against" Christians, the possibilities are numerous, ranging from social ostracism to physical assault. Some sort of physical threat is implied, but possibly the interpretation of the sufferers dramatizes the threat.

Interestingly, the few identifiable claims of Jewish *actions* against Christians before 150 seem to be intra-communal, Jews acting against other Jews who professed Jesus. Synagogue discipline implies a hope for repentance of the wayward member. The few examples of violence, such as the death of Stephen and the death of James, have the character of internecine strife. The first cases where Jews seem to act against Christians as foreigners appear in sources written 150 or later, *Mart. Pol.* and *Diogn.*

Use of Official Channels

An intermediate category between physical activity against Christians and verbal response is the attempt to use official channels to deal with the Christians.

Accusations before Jewish Authorities

According to Acts, the Sanhedrin made various attempts to control the Christians, through detentions (4:2–3; 5:17–18), warnings (4:17–21; 5:40), and beatings (5:40; 22:19). The method (as distinct from content) of the accusations against Stephen before the Sanhedrin (6:8–13) probably does not reflect the historical event, but may reflect typical practice against Christians. Certain matters are clearly internal problems. Disputes over resurrection (4:2–3, 33; 23:7–8) are conflicts between the Pharisees and Sadducees, hardly of interest to non-Jews. Nor would jealousy over healings and exorcisms (5:15–18) concern those outside the community.

In some cases, however, the Sanhedrin apparently worried about how Christians would reflect on the rest of the Jews vis-à-vis Rome. In 5:28, for example, they chide the apostles, "You have filled Jerusalem with your teaching and you intend to bring this man's blood upon us." Paul is also accused before the Sanhedrin (22:30—23:9), but in the end the Romans refuse to release him to the council. The Sanhedrin depended on Roman goodwill to exercise its authority and any Jews who threatened communal stability might have threatened the further function of the Sanhedrin or local diaspora councils. Perhaps this is also the reason Ananus executed James.

The remainder of references to the Sanhedrin's actions against Christians relates to the persecution after Stephen's death and the commission of Saul to deal with members of the Way. I suggest the scattering of the Hellenists relates to their liberalism in law-observance. Likewise Saul's commission, if at all historical, relates to law-observance, since he associates his persecution of the church with zealousness for his father's traditions and righteousness under the Law. Christian jibes at the "tradition of the elders" suggest disputes over particular laws. Christians pose a threat because they are still within the community and are viewed as undermining certain authority. Of course the liberal attitude toward law-observance stems from belief in Jesus' authority.

Christians are also delivered up to local "sanhedrins," according to the Synoptics, in conjunction with floggings in the synagogue (Mark 13:9; Matt 10:17–18). Luke reports that Christians will be delivered up to synagogues (12:11; 21:12). Similar to the references to Christians before the great Sanhedrin, these texts reflect attempts to deal with Christians as internal Jewish matters.

The Gospel of John reports that at some point Jews expelled Christians from the synagogue because they professed Jesus to be the Messiah (9:22; 12:42–43; 16:2–3). In John's area at least, Christians are no longer an internal disciplinary problem, nor is law-observance at issue. Expulsion of Christians from the synagogue was probably very limited. Jews possessed no widespread network of authority to enforce such a practice. Furthermore, the charge that Jews expel Christians from the synagogue is not leveled by other ancient writers, even ones who catalogue Jewish actions against Christians (e.g. Justin).

Two charges also appear in *Dial.,* that Jews send emissaries to warn Jewish communities of the Christian *hairesis,* and that Jewish teachers forbid contact with Christians. Since Yavneh and the diaspora communicated with one another, there may have been emissaries, but whether they brought popular, informal criticism, or official warning is unclear. If *hairesis* is the Jews' term, as seems likely, then they think of Christians as a sect of Judaism, though with ideas that are unacceptable or even dangerous to other Jews. Absolute outsiders would be less worrisome and not as likely to provoke warnings.

The other singular reference says Jewish teachers legislated that Jews should avoid Christians. A later rabbinic reference supports this idea, to the extent that the term *minim* includes Christians (*t.Ḥul.* 2.20–21). Perhaps that was the content of the emissaries' message—that Christians should be avoided. Yet the evidence of considerable wrangling over Scripture between Jews and Christians, even after Justin's time, indicates that this legislation was not notably successful. Furthermore, what Justin perceives as Jewish avoidance may have been an outsider's view of informal social withdrawal from Christians, not the result of a legal ruling.

Accusations before Roman Authorities

Many examples in the second half of Acts show Jews accusing Paul and his companions before Roman authorities. Jason appears as a stand-in for Paul. The nature of the charges against Paul (or Jason and others) are acting against Caesar (17:5-9), persuading others to worship contrary to law (18:12-17; whose law is not clear), being an agitator among all the Jews and ringleader of the Nazarenes (24:5). In Festus's words, the Jews' accusations against Paul involve only the proclamation of Jesus risen (25:13-19). Paul's own defense is comprehensive, "I have in no way committed an offense against the law of the Jews, or against the temple, or against the emperor" (25:8).

Paul's statement may offer a clue to the nature of the charges some Jews were making against Christians. While the genuine complaints of the Jews concern the proclamation of Jesus' resurrection by Paul and others (25:13-19; 26:2, 7) and the failure to sufficiently promote Torah-observance (18:12-13), these charges would not be of interest to the Roman government, as Festus and Gallio say (18:14-15; 25:18-19). Therefore the Jews could only accuse Christians of offenses against the Roman state, such as atheism or lack of patriotism—accusations that were sometimes leveled against Jews themselves. Acts 17:7 is telling because it melds the political crime of acting against Caesar with the religious offense of proclamation of Jesus: "They are all acting contrary to the decrees of the emperor, saying that there is another king named Jesus." In other words, what really bothers the Jews—namely, Christians' faith in Jesus' messiahship, divinity, and resurrection—is presented to the Romans as a crime against the Roman state. While the particular scenes are contrived, they give us a taste of the sort of charges made against Christians.

A decade or so later, Revelation's author complains of the "slander of the synagogue of Satan" in Smyrna (2:9). Perhaps this slander is similar to that in Acts—religious complaints couched as political ones to outsiders. Justin's charge that Jews curse Christians but other nations carry it out (96.2) or "you and all other men as much as is in their power, drive out Christians and do not permit them to live" (110.5), also connotes Jews implicating Christians to the Romans. Similarly, his many indictments that the Jews kill Christians *when they can* may refer to Jews slandering Christians to the Romans or informing against them. The *Martyrdom of Polycarp* implies that Jews denounced Christians as subversives.

It is hard to discern how successful the Jews were in landing Christians in trouble with Rome and how great the Jewish role really was in causing problems for Christians. As depicted in Acts, the Romans are peculiarly apathetic about Christians. Both Acts and Justin's *Dial.*—the major sources for these kind of references— are attempting to present the Christian faith as politically harmless, and therefore would have good reason to shift blame for Christian difficulties off the Romans and onto the Jews. Both may exaggerate the Jewish role in political troubles of Christians.

The attempt to involve the secular authorities suggests a certain abandonment of Jewish Christians by Jews. While the Jews were obviously fearful that the Romans would see Christians as part of their community, they themselves were ready to publicly dissociate themselves from those who believed in Jesus and give them over to the government. Perhaps this handing over was a "last resort," when "the Christian problem" proved insoluble and threatened the stability of the larger community. Josephus reports a similar case where the Alexandrian elders decided to hand over the refugee Sicarii to the Romans to ensure the peace of their own community (*J. W.* 7.10.1. §§ 412–415; 6.5.3. §§ 302–303). Whether all Christians were unacceptable to these Jews is unclear. Possibly they only implicated the public rabble-rousers, the preachers, or those who were no longer welcome because of their failure to properly observe the Torah. If the Christians in question were Gentiles, then of course they were never part of the Jewish community.

VERBAL REACTIONS

The greatest number of Jewish reactions to Christians attributed to Jews take place in the verbal arena. Many are in the form of general verbal abuse—cursing, slander, questioning—things which may, from the Jewish point of view, have meant simple criticism and disapproval.

Criticism

In the Synoptics, some Jews criticize the disciples' form of law-observance, and in Matt 10:14, some of the house of Israel do not receive the Twelve. They associate the Master and those of his house with Beelzebul (Matt 10:25b). In Acts Jews make fun of those who speak in tongues as drunkards (2:13–15; a stock response to wonders), revile Paul (18:5–6), and speak evil of the Way (19:9). In Rev 2:9, the "synagogue of Satan" is charged with slander (*blasphēmia*) against the Christians. Justin complains that Jews slander and curse Christians and scoff at Christ. Jewish verbal censure of Christians is a consistent theme throughout our period 30–150, with many categories overlapping.

Disputes over Legal Observance

At an early stage, verbal sparring between Jews who did not accept Jesus and those who did revolved around issues of legal observance. In some pre-compositional traditions in the Synoptic Gospels (pre-70–90s), followers of Jesus suffer censure for their failure to follow certain extra-scriptural commandments— handwashing, fasting, and Sabbath laws. The Jews who followed these laws no doubt invested them with the same authority as scriptural prohibitions and commandments. Jesus' followers apparently did not. The teachings of Jesus allowed them to interpret the law in a different way. Criticism of certain oral traditions as mere human invention was commonplace. To counter this criticism and invest these traditions with authority, the Pharisees attributed them to the "elders." Yet both sides shared the basic assumption that the Jewish Scriptures are authoritative, God's gift to Israel, and the inheritance of all Jews. They share the "root idea" that the Bible belongs to them both and its commandments are binding. For one group, authority to interpret Scripture resides in the "tradition of the elders"; for another authority resides in the words of Jesus. Paul's difficulties, whether over circumcision or table fellowship, are in the class of disagreements over Torah-observance, since they hinge on what Gentiles must do in order to participate in a life of community with Jews. In Acts, Stephen is accused of speaking against the Law and attempting to change Mosaic customs (6:11– 14). Apart from these few references in Paul, the Synoptic Gospels, and Acts, however, there are no more references to legal observance as problematic between Jews and believers in Jesus until Justin. By then, the objections are very different in character.

Possession of Scripture

By the time of Justin's *Dial.*, the issue is not so much how to observe or interpret the Torah, but whose Bible is it? Who rightly understands its meaning, Jews or Christians? Who is the true Israel? Trypho is not upset that Christians do not observe certain extra-scriptural strictures, but that they apparently do not observe the Torah at all. They do not follow the biblical prescriptions of circumcision, Sabbaths, and feasts, but rather allegorize them. A gulf divides Jews and Christians. They can no longer rely on the assumption that everyone means the same thing when they speak of Scripture, as in the early halakic debates.

Apparently the possibility that Scripture might belong to both groups is inadmissible. *Barn.* rails against "those who say the covenant is both theirs and ours" (4.6; 13.1). Only one group can be the true community of God. Whether Jews also felt this was the only choice, we do not know. Trypho seems to say that if Christians only observed the commandments, all would be well (10.1). The covenant could admit Christians, too, if they practiced the commandments. Celsus, some thirty years later, reports that Jews are puzzled that Christians accept the authority of the Hebrew Bible but ignore most of its laws.

Christology

Yet matters are not so simple. Another set of issues clouded relations between Jews and Christians. These were claims about Jesus: a crucified man was the Messiah, he rose from the dead, and he was born of a virgin.

In five places Justin attributes to the Jews the argument that one who is crucified is cursed by God (Deut 21:23) and therefore Jesus could be neither the Messiah nor God (10.3; 32.1; 38.1; 89.1; 90.1). Possibly his claim that Jews curse Christ means that Jews argue that Jesus *is* cursed because of his death on the cross. The notion that some people curse Jesus has some early attestations (Peter's denial; 1 Cor 12:3). Justin also devotes the largest amount of space to showing that Scripture predicted the crucifixion (32.2; 89–90; 94–99; 105–108). Paul's note that Christ crucified is a scandal to the Jews (1 Cor 1:23) suggests that the cross was a major difficulty for Jews as early as the 50s, and probably from the very beginning of the Christian kerygma. Even Paul's interpretation of Deut 21:23 in Gal 3:13 may be relevant. Although in its immediate sense Galatians is responding to the activity of law-observant Christians, Paul may be using a verse bandied about by other Jews who objected to the idea of a crucified messiah. Justin shows the objection never disappeared.

Justin relates a second christological issue that, he says, bothered Jews—namely, the resurrection.[4] The earliest explicit hint of the resurrection as problematic appears in Matt 27:62–65, where the chief priests and Pharisees ask Pilate to guard the sepulchre to prevent the disciples' theft of Jesus' body and subsequent claim of his resurrection. While the scene itself is historically improbable, it suggests that up to the 90s the resurrection was a sore point between believers in Jesus and other Jews. Matthew 28:11–15 makes this quite explicit, for when the chief priests and elders bribe the guard to say Jesus' body was stolen, Matthew tells us "this story is still told among the Jews to this day." Matthew charges Jews of his own time with talking against the resurrection. Less certain is John 20:15, which hints that someone claims Jesus' body was removed from the tomb. The charge that the disciples stole Jesus' body is a Jewish barb in the context of verbal disputes between Jews and believers in Jesus. Floggings and halings before councils in Matthew's day may not have been only for offenses against practice, but for preaching this and other christological claims. The two are not, of course, unrelated. The Gospel of John is quite clear that some Jews expelled Christians from the synagogue because they professed Jesus to be the Messiah.

Some decades later *Gos. Pet.* has a scene similar to the Matthean one, where the scribes, Pharisees, and elders ask for a centurion and soldiers to guard the tomb (8.31). This popular work elaborates considerably on the theme. Jews accompany the soldiers, help seal up the tomb, set seven seals on it, set up a watch, and wait there for three days. All the details contrive to prove that the resurrection took place and that the Jews knew it. Moreover, the Jews intentionally suppress reports of the event, although they admit it happened. No rumor is started by the Jews, as in Matthew, but it does not have to be. The many details of Jewish witness of the resurrection and obstruction of its reports as well as elaborate attempts to forestall any possible Jewish objections to its reality show the resurrection has become a major polemical point between believers

in Jesus and Jews. The more subtle apologetic aspects of the canonical Gospels suggest it was an early problem. Nothing is surprising
in this, for the resurrection is at the heart of Christian belief, yet
nothing in Judaism prepared Jews for a messiah who rose from the
dead.

Justin provides evidence that the resurrection remained problematic—a point Jews could not accept and Christians could not
concede. In *Dial.* 108.2 he transmits the accusation from
Matthew's Gospel, that Jews claim the disciples stole Jesus' body
so they could tout his resurrection. Like the author of *Gos. Pet.,* he
says the Jews really know Jesus rose from the dead, but willfully
deny it (17.1). Furthermore, Justin goes to some lengths to prove
the resurrection from Scripture (32.3-6; 106–108), implying it is
still a live point of debate. Despite the fact that by the time of *Gos.
Pet.* and Justin, Christians and Jews seem to already have a consciousness of themselves as separate from one another, the problem
of the resurrection remains.

Justin mentions the third controversial issue, the interpretation
of Isa 7:14 that asserts Jesus' birth from a virgin. The Matthean
and Lukan infancy narratives suggest that in the 90s some Christians already believed in the virginal conception of Jesus, which affected their interpretation of Isa 7:14,[5] although the New
Testament offers no other examples of this idea. At this stage, virginal conception may be entirely within the realm of Christian
self-definition and working out of their own beliefs and may not
relate to Jewish-Christian polemic. Nothing in Judaism would be
particularly sympathetic to the idea of a virgin birth, however.[6] It
would be a likely candidate to cause dissension within Jewish
groups, and by Justin's time, it has become a full-blown controversy between Jews and Christians. Celsus confirms that Jews objected to this claim. So too, later rabbinic materials that call Jesus
"ben Pantiri" indirectly refute the claim of a virginal conception.

In addition to his attempts to counter these specific objections
to claims about Jesus, Justin spends a good deal of time marshal-
ling Scripture to prove Jesus' messiahship and divinity. The prophets in particular predict his coming and the truth of Christian
belief. Whom is Justin attempting to persuade? Christians, including Jewish Christians, already believed in Jesus and Christianity.
The Romans would be unlikely to be impressed by arguments

based on the Hebrew prophets. The authority of Scripture carries the most weight with Jews. Quite possibly the Jews whom Justin says scoff at Christ and anathematize him are Jews who simply reject the interpretation that Scripture witnesses to Jesus. That Jews are the ones arguing against Christianity from Scripture is indicated by Justin's peculiar accusation that Jews remove passages from Scripture that testify to Christ's equality with God (71.2—73.6). Later, Eusebius reports that Christians are accused by Jews of misusing Scripture. Trypho, for his part, accuses Christians of "inventing" a Christ (8.3–4). Celsus confirms this as a Jewish charge. Justin argues that almost every line of Scripture testifies to Christ and Christianity.

The Gospel of John provides a link between claims of Jesus' resurrection as a controversial point in the 90s, as evidenced in Matthew's Gospel, and full-blown claims of Jesus' divinity in the mid–second century, as shown by Justin. Matthew relates the claim of the virgin birth and resurrection, while John moves closer to explicit claims of Jesus' divinity. The "I am" sayings as well as statements of Jesus' equality with God show that by the end of the first century, some Christians held a very high Christology, which must have rankled Jews.[7] For Jews, these claims would veer too closely to ditheism. Surely the high Christology and the hints of Jewish hostility to Christians in John are not unrelated (Jewish persecution of Jesus is clearly linked to claims of divinity, 5:16–18; 10:33). In Justin's time the controversy is still heated, but the players now include gentile Christians. Post-150 materials confirm the notion that Jews objected to aspects of Jesus' humanity (pedigree, legitimacy) as well as the assertion of his divinity.

Fulfillment citations are nothing new with Justin. Paul and the Gospels show that they were part and parcel of Christian preaching from the beginning. Yet I know of no other place where they are used against Jews to such a striking extent.[8] In Justin the attempts to prove Christianity's legitimacy from Scripture have taken on an intense quality. No longer is the situation one where both sides share the same assumptions about the Bible and argue over the meaning of its verses. Rather it seems to be a fight for control, part of a larger debate over who really inherits God's promise as the true Israel. The notion of the transfer of God's covenant to Christians, implicit already in Matt 21:43 and Rev 2:9 and 3:9, has by Justin's time become explicit. Jews, for their part, continue to maintain their status as biblical Israel and rely on other interpretations of the texts favored by Christians (Isa 7:14, for example, refers to Hezekiah, not Jesus). Trypho objects strenuously to Justin's allegorizing, but the method is known among Jews, such as the extreme allegorizers mentioned by Philo.

OBSERVATIONS

I have illuminated a spectrum of Jewish reactions to Christians in the period after Jesus' death to the mid–second century. No smooth time line emerges that charts the gradual separation of Judaism and Christianity. Chronology alone does not explain things any more than geography does, because the simple passage of time is only one factor in the way people and societies work. Some of the trends uncovered are early, some are late, and some surface here and there on the time line for no clear reason. Jewish attitudes toward Christians (and vice versa) did not follow an inexorable, irreversible process. A law-observant Jewish Christian might have been acceptable to some Jews throughout this entire period. A gentile Christian with no original connection to Israel might be attracted to Judaism and Jewish practices quite late in this period or even later (Origen, John Chrysostom). Neither would fit the picture of an irreversible divergence of the lines marked Judaism and Christianity.

Among the ways in which Jews reacted to Christians, toleration, as indicated in Acts and *Antiquities,* seems to have been real. I noted that this trend may be underrepresented in ancient sources because it is less "newsworthy" or theologically useful.

The vast majority of reactions to Christianity attributed to Jews are negative. With the notable exceptions of *Mart. Pol.* and *Apoc. Pet.,* after 100 C.E. or so, reactions are in the verbal sphere. Nothing like the synagogue discipline mentioned in Paul's letters (2 Cor 11:24–26), Mark (13:9), and Matthew (10:17–18) appears again. Nor is mob violence like that against Paul in Acts a frequent factor in post-100 accounts. Justin, with his many complaints about Jews, never shows spontaneous crowd violence. However Jews may have attacked Christians in the past, he does not say they are doing so now. Below I suggest reasons why.

Materials before 100 generally recount incidents between Jews and Jewish Christians, although in some cases the author reporting it is not clearly a Jew (e.g. Luke). Those flogged in the synagogues (Paul, Synoptics), those who fear expulsion from the synagogue (John), those who are hindered from talking to the Gentiles (1 Thess), those who are defended before the Sanhedrin (Acts), and those who are run out of the synagogue and attacked (Acts) would have to be Jews.

Only a few isolated incidents of Jews attacking Christians appear in materials after 100 c.e. Justin tells us that Bar Kochba punished Christians severely. Jews take part in an angry mob in *Mart. Pol.* These incidents are more dissimilar than similar and do not represent a trend. Nor are they any kind of organized, official, or widespread actions.

In later, post-150 materials the Christians who form one side of the encounter are less clearly Jewish Christians. Polycarp is a Gentile. In *Diogn.,* Jews see the Christians as foreigners, but we do not know how Christians saw themselves. The author is likely a Gentile. Justin is himself a gentile Christian, but often the reader does not know if the incidents he complains about involve Jewish or gentile Christians. It is clear that in his mind the two groups of Jews and Christians are quite distinct, since they must explain themselves to one another.

Scriptural polemic seems to have swelled in importance as Christians and Jews moved further apart. While a variety of Jewish reactions to Christians are reported before 100, none openly involves the question of who rightly possesses the key to Scripture. They argue about *halakah* and the authority of the "tradition of the elders," but these are questions of extra-scriptural practices. At the end of the first century, the Gospel of John alludes to debates over interpretation of Scripture. By the time of Justin, the question of who is right about Scripture is paramount. Questions of Christology, especially Jesus' resurrection, surface before the composition of Matthew (and probably as early as the preaching of the risen Jesus). In Justin, however, they are presented as primarily issues of scriptural interpretation. If he can only prove the resurrection (and the crucifixion and events of Jesus' life) from Scripture, he will have accomplished his purpose. He will have vindicated Christianity's right to Scripture. Celsus, thirty years later, testifies to the importance of scriptural polemics between Jews and Christians.

Why did interpretation of Scripture become the arena where Christians and Jews played out their differences and defined themselves? In part, this reflects the fact that the church became increasingly Gentile, and questions of observance of extra-scriptural traditions or inner-community discipline were no longer relevant. Furthermore, verbal polemics may have been the safest and most available avenue to Jews as they became less politically powerful. While in Judea at an early stage, Jews enjoyed a certain autonomy and degree of self-government under the Romans; as the focus shifted to the diaspora they were more limited in their autonomy and fearful of civil unrest. The displeasure of the local gentile populace had to be kept at bay by maintaining a low profile and relying on Roman justice. Neither the Roman administrators nor local Gentiles would interest themselves in scriptural controversies. Witness the pagan Celsus, who judges these debates to be complete nonsense, "arguments about the shadow of an ass." Thus, disagreements over Scripture might have been the only sensible place to work out their differences.

Much of these polemics are also explicable in terms of competition for gentile converts. We might ask, if Christians no longer saw themselves as under Jewish jurisdiction, why should other Jews care that they claimed the Scriptures as their own? Why not let them go, especially if their group was now largely Gentile? What is the difference if they hold bizarre views? What is the difference between a follower of Jesus and a follower of Mithra? The answer is that Jews themselves needed the Bible for their own proselytizing purposes. They would appeal to the same groups to whom Christians were preaching. Judaism's status and attractiveness to Gentiles are mainly predicated on its special role in history as presented in its Scripture. Should another group usurp its role, claiming to be the true Israel, it loses its strongest lever. For Christians, it is important to claim the antiquity of the scriptural heritage to counter the pagan charge that they are a new, upstart religion.

The question of the extent that Jews in antiquity sought converts is under debate. Some evidence shows, however, that ancient Jews proselytized more than later Jews. Whether because of aggressive missionizing or less formal methods, Judaism exercised an attraction for Gentiles. Jews were expelled from Rome in 139 B.C.E. for promoting their rites to others (Valerius Maximus 1.3.3. epitome of Januarius Nepotianus). The king and queen of Adiabene converted to Judaism after learning Jewish practices and traditions from Jewish merchants (*Ant.* 20.2.3 § 34—20.2.4 § 48). Horace referred to Jewish proselytizing as a commonplace (*Satires* 1.4.140).[9] Matthew is not alone in depicting Jews as anxious for converts (23:15). Any of these writers could be accused of exaggeration, but are they all fabricating this image? Attraction to Judaism, its ethical code, and its practices was a continuing reality and provoked much of the Christian material that proclaimed Christianity's separateness and superiority to Judaism. Scratch the surface of much of the seemingly anti-Jewish works and one often finds some Christians attracted to Judaism, or people who want to maintain the heritage of Judaism and believe in Jesus (Ignatius *Phld., Magn., Barn.,* J. Chrysostom, Origen).

Probably the most striking conclusion I draw from the sources, however, is that Jews who did not share the belief in Jesus and Christians had very different ideas about when they became separate entities. I have attempted to schematize the materials on charts 1 and 2, below. Chart 1 indicates what I have interpreted to be the Jews' view of Christians as insiders or outsiders to the Jewish community, based on the incidents reported. Chart 2 shows how Christians seemed to see themselves relative to the Jewish community.

I am obviously reading between the lines, and in some cases, the material is simply unclear. Jews did not see Christians as clearly separate from their own community until at least the middle of the second century. By then, however, Justin's Trypho at least seems to know very little about Christians, though he had read the Gospels. *Diogn.,* from approximately the same period, says Jews thought of Christians as foreigners. *Mart. Pol.* certainly evinces no sympathy between Jews and Christians. Although all three are tendentious documents, they suggest that the Christian view of themselves as "other" than Jews was now shared by the Jews themselves.

Yet the vast majority of statements or actions attributed to Jews in our materials are or could be directed against fellow Jews, people who are still considered within the community of Israel.

Chart 1

Christians seen as:	**Insiders**	**Outsiders**	**Status Unclear**
Jews' View	1 Thess 2:14–16 (hinder Gentile mission)	Acts chart 4 (involve Romans)	Synoptics chart 4 (rumor of theft of Jesus' body)
	Paul's pursuit of the Way	John chart 1 (expulsion)	
	Persecution of Paul (39 stripes)	*Mart. Pol.*	John chart 1 (fear of Jews)
	Synoptics Chart 1 (Legal Observance)	*Diogn.* (foreigners)	
	Synoptics Chart 3 (floggings, sanhedrins)	Justin charts 1,2,4	John chart 3 (plot to kill Lazarus)
	Josephus, *Testimonium Flavianum*		Rev (slander)
	Josephus, *Ant.* 20.9.1 200–202.		*Gos. Pet.* (polemic)
	Acts Chart 1 (Conversions)		Justin chart 3 (verbal attacks)
	Acts Chart 1 (Neutral Curiosity)		Justin chart 5 (hatred)
	Acts Chart 2 (Tolerance)		
	Acts Chart 3 (Verbal Abuse)		
	Acts Chart 4 (warnings, beatings, imprisonment)		
	John Chart 4 (comforting of mourners)		
	Justin-Chart 6 (teachers discourage association with Christians; emissaries; Christianity as *hairesis*)		

Chart 2

Christians seen as:	Insiders	Outsiders	Status Unclear
Christians' View	Synoptics chart 3 (those who submit to floggings, sanhedrins)	1 Thess 2:14–16 Paul as persecutor, persecuted	Synoptics chart 1 (legal observance) Acts chart 2 (Curiosity)
	Acts 1 (Conversions)	Synoptics chart 2 (nonacceptance of the 12)	Acts chart 3 (Tolerance)
		Synoptics chart 3 (floggings, sanhedrins)	Rev
	inscriptions at Carthage		
	John chart 4 (comforting mourners)	Acts chart 3 (mob violence, verbal attack)	
		Acts chart 4 (warnings, beatings, detention)	
		John chart 1 (fear of Jews)	
		John chart 2 (expulsions)	
		John chart 3 (plots)	
		Mart. Pol.	
		Gos. Pet.	
		Justin	
		Diogn.	

Synagogue discipline and arguing over ritual practice, both early phenomena, are certainly only relevant to fellow Jews. The Sanhedrin's attempts to control Christians suggests they saw it as an internal matter. Slander and verbal abuse are often for one's closest associates. I do not know if disagreements about Jesus' status, especially the resurrection, led Jews to judge Christians heretics, or if they remained simply disagreements. The people who avenge James' death (*Ant.*) and the Pharisees who counsel tolerance of Christians (Acts) are clearly dealing with matters they see as internal.

The earliest example of Jews seeing Christians as outsiders occurs in Acts where Jews try to hand Christians over to Roman authorities. In the Fourth Gospel, written about the same time as Acts, Jews expel Christians from the synagogue and thereby withdraw whatever protection Rome afforded the Jews. Such actions represent an abandonment, a statement that these people are no longer part of us. Romans, of course, may continue to see Christians as part of Jewry, and part of the Jewish motive is to disabuse them of that idea. By 150–55, at least in the sources we have, the Jews see Christians as "other." They do not share the same assumptions about Scripture, they are foreigners, and they do not deserve protection from the Jewish community. Christians are still to be argued with and their claims about Scripture need to be countered, in part to ensure continued Jewish proselytism. When did Jews "read out" Christians from the people Israel? In John's community and some other places, they did as early as the end of the first century. In many places, the separation took place during the first half of the second century.[10]

While some Jewish actions against Christians before 150 are directed against fellow Jews, Christians do not interpret them that way. Almost from the outset Christians have a consciousness of themselves as distinct from other Jews. Paul's use of the term "persecution" for his punishment of the early church and his own subsequent suffering from synagogue discipline implies that he thought the punishment was unjustified. He held an identity different from the people administering it. Matthew feels no affinity with the people doing the same to fellow Christians in "their synagogues." He interprets his status to be an outsider.

The Acts material that reports mobs, beatings, and warnings

evinces a clear sense of "us" vs. "them" from the Christian point of view. The capstone of this attitude is the thrice-repeated judgment put in Paul's mouth, where he seems to "give up" on the Jews (13:46–47; 18:6; 28:25–28). John 9:22, as we have interpreted it, signals the author's self-separation from the synagogue that is not necessarily shared by all other Christians. The *Gospel of Peter* is propaganda, and evinces a total alienation from Judaism. Popular circles (if the legendary elements in the Matthean infancy and resurrection material and the *Gos. Pet.* are a guide) probably held stronger prejudices. The late sources, as I have shown, show that both sides viewed Jews and Christians as separate communities.

A large number of references are simply unclear and allow for several interpretations. Since I am using mainly Christian sources, we often cannot know what the Jews thought about their own actions and statements. Did Jews who argued against the resurrection, for example, think they were countering some worrisome trends among their own people, or did they consider the Christians a dangerous group to be ejected from the community at all costs? We do not know.

No doubt the social sciences can shed light on some of these processes—a larger parent group slow to let go of some eccentric, deviant members. As long as the parent group does not label the deviant member an outsider, there is hope of return. Theories of group behavior, conformity and deviance, labelling, and the effect of real or perceived persecution are all relevant. L. Festinger, for example, shows the larger group cannot exert influence on deviates if (1) the larger group loses its attractiveness and (2) the influence of some other group to which the deviate belongs is much stronger.[11] Both of these phenomena could help explain Christian secession from Judaism in our time period. The attitudes of the larger Jewish group might be illuminated by some of the work on new religious movements.[12] To avoid the dangers of reductionism and to give full weight to the vast literature on group behavior, however, this question deserves a full and separate treatment.

Individuals who are disaffected from a larger parent group often claim that they really represent the goals and values of the larger group and that the latter is misguided and corrupt. Most religious reformers from the Essenes to Luther do not see themselves as innovators,[13] but as returning the faith to its pristine state. In so doing they must deny the legitimacy of the larger group because both cannot be the true representation of the faith. Both cannot, for example, be the true Israel. Nor is pressure in the form of verbal assaults or physical actions calculated to make a deviant member feel warmly toward the parent group. Either the negative critique of the deviates by the parent group is accepted as legitimate, or the authority of the parent group must be rejected. Christians understandably chose the latter course. Jews, at least in some places, were slower to let go of members with ideas they found strange or dangerous and long-held hope of their return.

NOTES

INTRODUCTION

1. As, for example, D. Hare, *The Theme of Jewish Persecution of Christians in the Gospel of St. Matthew* (Cambridge: Cambridge University Press, 1967).
2. Two examples are W. Frend, *Martyrdom and Persecution in the Early Church* (Oxford: Blackwell, 1965) and J. Booth, *Jesus and the Laws of Purity* (Sheffield: JSOT, 1986).
3. This is not the place to review all New Testament scholarship and its evaluation of Judaism. Certain scholars, like W. D. Davies, E. P. Sanders, and K. Stendahl, however, are notable for their attempts to understand Judaism on its own terms, although their chief interest is explication of Christian texts.
4. See J. L. Martyn, *History and Theology in the Fourth Gospel* (2d ed.; Nashville: Abingdon, 1979); and W. D. Davies, *The Setting of the Sermon on the Mount* (Cambridge: Cambridge University Press, 1964) 270–76.
5. See E. M. Smallwood, *The Jews under Roman Rule* (2d ed.; Leiden: Brill, 1981); P. Schäfer, *Studien zur Geschichte und Theologie des rabbinische Judentums* (Leiden: Brill, 1978); S. Cohen, *From the Maccabees to the Mishnah* (Philadelphia: Westminster, 1987) 166–68; and B. Bokser, "Recent Developments in the Study of Judaism 70–200 C.E.," *SecCent* 3 (1983) 29–32. Two collections of articles in this vein are *Christianity, Judaism and other Greco-Roman Cults* (Festschrift M. Smith; ed. J. Neusner; Leiden: Brill, 1975); and *Jewish and Christian Self-Definition* (ed. E. P. Sanders et al.; 3 vols.; Philadelphia: Fortress, 1980-85).
6. M. Simon, *Verus Israel* (Oxford: Oxford University Press, 1986).
7. S. Riegel, "Jewish Christianity: Definitions and Terminology," *NTS* 24 (1978) 410–15; G. Buchanan, "Worship, Feasts and Ceremonies in the Early Jewish–Christian Church," *NTS* 26 (1980) 279–97; and B. Visotzky, "Prolegomenon to the Study of Jewish Christianities," *AJSRev* 14 (1989) 47–70.
8. The most influential of the modern works to delineate "the creation of an official attitude toward Judaism" by the church is James Parkes' *The Conflict of the Church and the Synagogue* (London: Soncino, 1934). More recent discussions include R. Ruether, *Faith and Fratricide* (New York: Seabury, 1974); J. Gager, *The Origins of Anti-Semitism* (New York: Oxford University Press, 1985); and H. Conzelmann, *Gentiles,*

Jews, Christians (Minneapolis: Augsburg Fortress, 1992). Collected articles on this topic appear in *Anti-Semitism and the Foundations of Christianity* (ed. A. Davies; New York: Paulist, 1979); *Kirche und Synagoge* (ed. K. Rengstorf and S. von Kortzfleisch; 2 vols.: Stuttgart: Klett, 1968-70); and *Anti-Judaism in Early Christianity* (2 vols.; ed. P. Richardson et al.; Waterloo: Wilfred Laurier University Press, 1986).

9. See J. Sevenster, *The Roots of Pagan Anti-Semitism in the Ancient World* (Leiden: Brill, 1975); L. Feldman, "Anti-Semitism in the Ancient World," and S. Cohen, "Anti-Semitism in Antiquity," in *History and Hate* (ed. D. Berger; Philadelphia: JPS, 1986) 15–42, 43–47 respectively. J. Gager stresses the ancients' positive evaluation of Judaism that accompanied the negative (*Origins,* 35–112) while J. Meagher argues that the hostile voice of the pagans was by far the stronger one ("As the Twig Is Bent: Anti-Semitism in Greco-Roman and Earliest Christian Times," *Foundations* 1–26). Evidence for proselytes and semi-proselytes to Judaism shows that it was not uniformly despised. See L. Feldman, *Jew and Gentile in the Ancient World* (Princeton: Princeton University Press, 1993).

10. L. Johnson has shown that, relative to other ancient examples of Jews' criticism of other Jewish groups, the Christian statements against the Jews are relatively tame, "The New Testament Anti-Jewish Slander and the Conventions of Ancient Polemic," *JBL* 108 (1989) 419–41.

11. One such attempt is the sympathetic assessment of pagan reactions to Christianity. See S. Benko, "Pagan Criticism of Christianity during the First Two Centuries A.D.," *ANRW* II/23.2, 1055–1118; R. Wilken, *The Christians as the Romans Saw Them* (New Haven: Yale University Press, 1984); and R. Lane Fox, *Pagans and Christians* (San Francisco: Harper and Row, 1986).

12. In the last few years, such mutual respect is in evidence in *Anti-Judaism* (ed. Richardson et al.); *Christians among Jews and Gentiles: Essays in Honor of Krister Stendahl on His Sixty-fifth Birthday* (ed. G. Nickelsburg and G. MacRae) *HTR* 79 (1986); and *To See Ourselves as Others See Us: Christians, Jews, "Others" in Late Antiquity* (ed. J. Neusner and E. Frerichs; Chico: Scholars Press, 1985). An individual work notable for this approach is A. Segal, *Rebecca's Children* (Cambridge: Harvard University Press, 1986).

13. H. Conzelmann's exhaustive treatment, *Gentiles, Jews, Christians,* surveys Greco-Roman literature about Jews and Judaism and Judaism's attitudes toward the Greco-Roman world, providing the backdrop for Jewish responses to Christians.

14. Extracting early traditions from rabbinic literature is particularly problematic. J. Neusner is pessimistic about the possibility of doing so ("The Use of Rabbinic Sources for the Study of Ancient Judaism," *Approaches to Ancient Judaism III,* ed. W. S. Green [Chico: Scholars Press, 1981] 1–17). Other scholars are more hopeful about delineating diverse source materials. See R. Kalmin, *Sages, Stories, Authors and Editors in Rabbinic Babylonia* (Providence: Brown University Press, forthcoming).

15. See M. Stern, *Greek and Latin Authors on Jews and Judaism* (2 vols.; Jerusalem: Israel Academy of Sciences and the Humanities, 1974–80).
16. See M. Whittaker, *Jews and Christians: Greco-Roman Views* (Cambridge: Cambridge University Press, 1984); S. Benko, "Pagan Criticism"; and R. Wilken, *The Christians as the Romans Saw Them.*
17. Scholars who disagree with my view include A. Momigliano, *Claudius* (Oxford: Clarendon, 1934) 32–35; E. M. Smallwood, *The Jews under Roman Rule* (2d ed.; Leiden: Brill, 1981) 211, n. 30; H. Leon, *The Jews of Ancient Rome* (Philadelphia: JPS, 1960) 25–27; and R. E. Brown, *Antioch and Rome* (New York: Paulist, 1982) 102.
18. Those who doubt that "Chrestus" should be understood as "Christus" include E. Koestermann ("Ein folgenschwerer Irrtum des Tacitus," *Historia* 16 [1967] 457–60); S. Benko ("The Edict of Claudius of A.D. 49 and the Instigator Chrestus," *ThZ* 25 [1969] 406–18); and D. Slingerland ("Chrestus-Christus?" *New Perspectives on Ancient Judaism* 4 [ed. A. Avery-Peck; Lanham: University Press of America, 1989] 133–44).
19. See an abstract of my paper, "Who were the Galileans in Bar Kochba's letter to Yeshua ben Galgula?" *SBL Abstracts* (Atlanta: Scholars Press, 1987) 258.

CHAPTER 1, THE PAULINE AND DEUTERO-PAULINE LETTERS

1. E. P. Sanders, *Paul, the Law, and the Jewish People* (Philadelphia: Fortress, 1983) 190–92. For a bibliographic summary of this view, see A. Hultgren, "Paul's Pre-Christian Persecutions of the Church: Their Purpose, Locale and Nature," *JBL* 95 (1976) 97–111, n. 1.
2. By the end of the first century, at least four different Christian attitudes toward Jewish Law are discernible. See R. E. Brown, "Not Jewish Christianity and Gentile Christianity, but Types of Jewish/Gentile Christianity," *CBQ* 45 (1983) 74–79.
3. Hultgren, "Persecutions," 99–102. See my article, "You Invent a Christ! Christological Claims as Points of Jewish-Christian Debate," *USQR* 44 (1991) 315–28.
4. I would resist the well-known model that draws a line of division between a party of Hellenists whose theology Stephen represents and a party of more conservative Hebrews. C. Hill has shown how tenuous are the connections necessary to build this model (*Hellenists and Hebrews* [Minneapolis: Fortress, 1992]). Yet Acts 8:1 suggests the apostles were distinguished in some way.
5. Segal, *Rebecca's Children*, 104–7.
6. R. Jewett argues that Zealots are pressuring the teachers in Galatia, who are forced to press their Gentile converts for circumcision. See "The Agitators and the Galatian Congregation," *NTS* 17 (1970–71) 198–212. Sanders simply says some non-Christian Jews are at work (*Paul, Law, People* 190–92).
7. e.g. *Ant.* 4.8.21 § 238; *m.Kil.* 8.3; *m.Ter.* 11.3; *m.Pesaḥ.* 7.11; *m.Mak.* 3.1–16.
8. Sanders, *Paul, Law, People,* 192.

9. Ibid., 190.

10. D. Georgi argues that these lists of self-authenticating achievements imitate the imperial *res gestae* (the *res gestae* of Augustus, *CIL* III.769–99), D. Georgi, *The Opponents of Paul in Second Corinthians* (Philadelphia: Fortress, 1986) 294, n. 122.

11. R. Hodgson demonstrates the frequency of the "tribulation list" throughout ancient Jewish and Greco-Roman literature, where the hero is legitimized by "labors" or tribulations. See Hodgson, "Paul the Apostle and First Century Tribulation Lists," *ZNW* 74 (1983) 59–80.

12. From the time of Julius Caesar, Jews had certain religious rights and protection, freedom of observance and worship, and exemption from emperor worship. A series of ad hoc enactments lent Judaism a semi-official status, but the term *religio licita* does not appear until Tertullian. Sources that show Judaism's special privileges appear in M. Whittaker, *Jews and Christians* (Cambridge: Cambridge University Press, 1984) 93–102.

13. The pastoral purpose of 1 Thessalonians is discussed by A. Malherbe, *Paul and the Thessalonians* (Philadelphia: Fortress, 1987).

14. G. Luedemann, drawing on J. Knox's reconstruction of the chronology of Paul's life, places the composition of 1 Thessalonians even earlier, at the beginning of the 40s (*Paul, Apostle to the Gentiles* [Philadelphia: Fortress, 1984] 3–4, 201).

15. B. Pearson, "I Thessalonians 2:13–16: A Deutero-Pauline Interpolation," *HTR* 64 (1971) 79–94.

16. K. Donfried, "Paul and Judaism: 1 Thess 2:13–16 as a Test Case," *Int* 38 (1984) 242–53; J. Orchard, "Thessalonians & the Synoptic Gospels," *Bib* 19 (1938) 19–42; and R. Schippers, "The Pre-Synoptic Tradition in 1 Thessalonians 2:13–16," *NovT* 8 (1966) 223–34.

17. P. Schubert, *Form and Function of the Pauline Thanksgivings* (Berlin: Töpelmann, 1939) 23.

18. J. Hurd, "Paul Ahead of His Time: 1 Thess 2:13–16," *Anti-Judaism in Early Christianity* (ed. P. Richardson et al.) 1.21–36 (Waterloo, Ont.: Wilfred Laurier University Press, 1986).

19. R. Jewett, *The Thessalonian Correspondence* (Philadelphia: Fortress, 1986) 74.

20. J. Coppens, "Miscellanées bibliques. LXXX. Une diatribe antijuive dans 1 Thess II, 13–16," *ETL* 51 (1975) 90–95; and R. Collins, "A Propos the Integrity of 1 Thess," *ETL* 55 (1979) 67–106.

21. The interpolation theory originated from R. Knopf's suggestion that v. 16 c is a marginal gloss, since *hē orgē* must mean the catastrophe of 70 C.E. (*Das nachapostolische Zeitalter: Geschichte der christlichen Gemeinden vom Beginn der Flavierdynastie bis zum Ende Hadrians* [Tübingen: Mohr, 1905] 139). F. C. Baur had earlier declared the whole letter inauthentic ("Die beiden Briefe an die Thessalonicher, ihre Unechtheit und Bedeutung für die Lehre der Parusie Christi," *Theologische Jahrbücher* 14 [1855] 141–68). For a summary of the issues of authenticity for both 1 & 2 Thess, see Jewett, *The Thessalonian Correspondence* (Philadelphia: Fortress, 1986) 3–18.

22. Coppens offers a number of other possible candidates for "the wrath"; Jewett ("Agitators," 205, n. 5) argues that it refers to the massacre of twenty to thirty thousand Jews following a disturbance in Jerusalem in 49 C.E. (*Ant.* 20.5.3 § 112; *J.W.* 2.12.1 §§ 224–27).

23. G. Fee argues that *arche* and *archon* always mean earthly agents in the New Testament (*The First Epistle to the Corinthians* [NICNT; Grand Rapids: Eerdmans, 1987] 103–4).

24. O. Cullman typifies the view that the "rulers" are both human and divine powers (*Christ and Time* [London: SCM, 1962] 191–95). W. Wink shows how either the political or the supernatural understanding of the term is possible (*Naming the Powers* [Philadelphia: Fortress, 1984] 40–45). Linguistically, however, Fee's case is stronger, since the term normally refers only to earthly powers.

25. Other examples of similar anti-Jewish canards. Josephus preserves a statement of Lysismachus: "Moses ... instructing them [the Israelites] to show goodwill to no man" (*Ag. Ap.* 1.34 § 309). Josephus claims Apion "would have it appear that we swear by the God who made heaven and earth and sea to show no goodwill to a single alien, above all to Greeks" (*Ag. Ap.* 2.10 § 121). Diodorus, probably citing Posidonius, states "They [the Jews] alone of all nations, refused to associate with any other people and considered them all as enemies" (*World Hist.* 34.1). Philostratus says, "For the Jews have long been in revolt not only against the Romans, but against all mankind too. Those who have devised an anti-social way of life...." (*Life of Apollonius of Tyana* 5:33). Celsus is quoted by Origen, "They [the Jews] pride themselves on the knowledge of some greater wisdom and shun the society of others as if they were not as pure as themselves" (*Contra Celsum* 5.41.4). For a discussion of pagan views of Jewish misanthropy, see Pearson, "1 Thess," 83, n. 25, and V. Tcherikover, *Hellenistic Civilization and the Jews* (New York: Atheneum, 1974) 367–69.

26. Recent summaries of the debate over authenticity appear in Jewett, *The Thessalonian Correspondence* (Philadelphia: Fortress, 1986) 36–46; R. Collins, "A Propos," 67–106; G. Okeke, "Fate," 127–32; and Hurd, "Paul Ahead of His Time," 23–27.

27. Tertullian, *Ag. Marcion* 15.

28. According to W. Horbury, the charge of "brigandage" in ancient usage was probably equivalent to sedition ("Christ as Brigand in Ancient Anti-Christian Polemic," *Jesus and the Politics of His Day* [ed. E. Bammel and C.F.D. Moule; Cambridge: Cambridge University Press, 1984]).

29. Some examples include *Barn.* 5.11–13; Justin, *1 Apol.* 35, 38, 40, 47, *Dial.* 108; Tertullian, *Ag. Jews* 13–14; *Apol.* 26; Origen, *Ag. Celsus* 1.47; 4.22; *Gos. Pet.* 1.1; 7.25.

30. O. Steck, *Israel und das gewaltsame Geschick der Propheten* (Neukirchen-Vluyn: Neukirchener Verlag, 1967) 276.

31. H.-J. Schoeps, "Die jüdischen Prophetenmorde," *Aus frühchristlicher Zeit* (Tübingen: Mohr, 1950) 126–43. See also B. H. Amaru, "The

Killing of the Prophets: Unraveling a Midrash," *HUCA* 54 (1983) 153–80.

CHAPTER 2, SYNOPTIC GOSPELS

1. Although W. Farmer and his adherents have questioned these hypotheses and revived the Griesbach hypothesis, most scholars remain unconvinced. See W. Farmer, *The Synoptic Problem* (New York: Macmillan, 1964) and "Modern Developments of Griesbach's Hypothesis," *NTS* 23 (1976–77) 275–95. R. Morgenthaler provides statistical support for the Two-Source hypothesis and the priority of Mark (*Statistische Synopse* [Zürich: Gotthelf, 1971]). F. Nierynck also shows that the technical relationship among the Synoptics supports these hypotheses (*The Minor Agreements of Matthew and Luke against Mark* [Leuven: Leuven University Press, 1974]).

2. The apocalyptic urgency and prophetic statements of the Temple's destruction (13:1–2, 7–8, 14) suggest a time of writing just before or just after 70. The lack of reflection on the destruction and expectation of imminent deliverance suggest little time could have elapsed since 70.

3. Mark's interest in Jerusalem and its fate and his use of traditions paralleled in Palestinian Jewish apocalyptic literature suggest a proximity to Palestine. But Mark's mistakes about Palestinian geography and his need to explain Aramaisms and Jewish customs (3:17, 5:41, 7:3–5, 11) preclude placing the Gospel's composition in Palestine itself. Syria, in the penumbra of Palestine, is an excellent candidate for Mark's provenance. For a discussion of issues of dating the Gospel, see J. Marcus, *The Mystery of the Kingdom of God: The Marcan Parable Chapter (Mark 4:1-34) and the Theology of the Gospel as a Whole* (Ph.D diss., Columbia University, 1985) 12–14; and H. C. Kee, *Community of the New Age: Studies in Mark's Gospel* (Philadelphia: Westminster, 1977) 100–101.

4. R. E. Brown and others evaluate positively a tradition of Papias (*Hist. eccl.*3.39.15) that Mark's Gospel was written at Rome (*Antioch and Rome* [New York: Paulist, 1985] 197). Marxsen has argued for Galilee as the place of origin because of its theological significance for Mark as the place of the imminent Parousia (*Mark the Evangelist* [Nashville: Abingdon, 1969] 92).

5. Though fewer clues help pinpoint the place of Matthew's composition, Antioch of Syria is an attractive candidate as a large Greek-speaking city with a considerable Jewish populace and an early Christian community (see J. Meier, *Antioch and Rome,* 15–27).

6. R. Bultmann, *History of the Synoptic Tradition* (3d ed.; New York: Harper and Row, 1963) 368–74.

7. C. Blomberg, *The Historical Reliability of the Gospels* (Leicester, UK: Inter-Varsity, 1987). The evangelical orientation of the author and the project does not preclude an attempt to evaluate other scholars on their own terms.

8. B. Mack, *A Myth of Innocence* (Philadelphia: Fortress, 1988).

9. Mack argues that Christians rationalized their loss of social status in

the Jewish community by imagining past conflicts where Jesus silences his Pharisaic opponents (*Myth*, 203–5).

10. We do not take such rigidly skeptical views of other ancient writers discussing events decades later, say, Josephus writing *Ant.* 20 years after the war against Rome, or Dio Cassius describing the three Jewish revolts at the end of the second century.

11. R. Bultmann, *History of the Synoptic Tradition*, 48.

12. Mark must explain Jewish customs to his readers (7:3–4, 11–13). He presupposes a woman's right to divorce her husband (10:11-12), which reflects Roman but not Jewish law. His emphasis on the gentile mission also hints at an audience that is predominantly Gentile, though there may be some Jewish Christians in it.

13. Lohmeyer, Wellhausen, Klostermann, Taylor, and Haenchen argue the original tradition included only the disciples of John. John the Baptist is associated with ascetic practices elsewhere in Mark (1:4–6; cf. Matt 3:4).

14. The Pharisees themselves left us no writings to inform us about their fasting practices. Josephus' brief descriptions of the *pharisaioi* do not mention fasting (*Ant.* 18.1.3 § 12; 13.5.9 § 171; *J.W.* 2.8.14 § 162-66; *Life* 2 § 12). Nor do any rabbinic sources associate the *perushim* with fasting, although one tradition says they abstained from meat and wine after the destruction of the Temple (*t.Soṭa* 15.11, 12). Christian sources report that the Pharisees fasted twice a week (*Did.* 8.1; Luke 18:12; also Matt 6:16) which conforms to later rabbinic custom. The Pharisees probably did fast, but perhaps not in a way that differed from many other Jews, and they do not seem to have been distinguished as Pharisees by this practice.

15. Most of the laws related to the observance of the Sabbath by rabbinic Jews have a limited Scriptural basis. They are characterized as "mountains hanging by a hair" (*m.Ḥag* 1.8) and reflect extra-scriptural developments. Josephus reports that the Pharisees observed traditions not written in the Law of Moses (*Ant.* 13.10.6 § 297).

16. Bultmann assigns vv. 1–8 to the level of the pre-Markan Palestinian church (*History of the Synoptic Tradition*, 18). Vv. 9–13 represent another unit, and vv. 15–23 seem to be Mark's interpretation of the tradition. These latter verses relate to Mark's stance toward tradition, however, and do not necessarily afford information about Jewish reactions to Christians.

17. A recent study suggests that the criticism which made an invidious distinction between the written law and the oral tradition, and downgraded oral tradition as mere human invention (Mark 7:8; Matt 15:6) was an anti-Pharisaic commonplace (A. Baumgarten, "The Pharisaic Paradosis," *HTR* 80 [1987] 63–77).

18. J. Booth, *Jesus and the Laws of Purity* (JSNT 13; Sheffield: JSOT, 1986) 63–65.

19. E. Haenchen, *Der Weg Jesu* (Berlin: de Gruyter, 1968) 263 n. 1; H. Anderson, *The Gospel of Mark* (London: Marshall, Morgan & Scott,

1976) 223; and D. Nineham, *Saint Mark* (Philadelphia: Westminster, 1963) 193.

20. The Tosefta reports that one of the four obligations required of the *ḥaver* was to eat ordinary food (*ḥullin*) in a state of ritual purity (*t.Dem.* 2.2, 10–14), so at least some people did not limit hand washing to priests in the Temple. The relationship between the *ḥaverim* and the Pharisees is a matter of dispute, and the *ḥaburah* may have been a subset within the Pharisees. A general summary of the issues appears in J. Neusner, "The Fellowship (Haburah) in the Second Jewish Commonwealth," *HTR* 53 (1960) 125–42.

21. In rabbinic literature, the *perushim* are pictured as being in conflict with the "People of the Land" (*Ammei ha-Aretz*), the former being more careful about ritual purity and/or more learned. See A. Oppenheimer, *The ʿAm Ha-Aretz* (Leiden: Brill, 1977).

22. Booth, *Purity,* 221–23.

23. See Mack, *Myth,* 179–92 for the results of an SBL 1981 group on the *chreia* and for a review of the arguments for the pronouncement stories as *chreia*. See also *Ancient Quotes and Anecdotes* (Sonoma, CA: Polebridge, 1989) and *Semeia* 20 (1981), which is devoted entirely to the study of pronouncement stories. Hultgren earlier maintained that the conflict stories are new in form and content and show no formal dependence on any other literary or popular forms of the period (*Adversaries,* 39). Given the work of Mack and others, this estimate needs revision.

24. Though some disagreement over terminology exists among Bultmann, Taylor, Dibelius, and Albertz, I take "conflict stories" or "controversy stories" (*Streitgespräche*) as a category within the larger category of "pronouncement stories."

25. B. Malina gives many examples of this kind of "deviant labelling" in the New Testament, and how the tradition neutralized these labels (*Calling Jesus Names* [Sonoma, CA: Polebridge, 1988] 3–5).

26. Scholars who place the situation after Jesus' time, in the period of the Gospel authors, include Haenchen (*Weg*); Lohmeyer (Markus, 272); Marxsen (*Mark* 158); and Nineham (*Mark* 348).

27. I assume the version in Matt 10:19 is closer to the original. It is easier to imagine that Luke might have added "synagogues" than that Matthew, who polemicizes against certain synagogues, might have removed it. J. Fitzmyer also judges "synagogues" a Lukan addition (*The Gospel According to Luke* (AB; Garden City: Doubleday, 1981–85] 963).

28. *Synedria* in Jewish sources is normally a body within Palestine, although one reference suggests they might have operated outside Palestine (*m.Mak.* 1:10). H. Mantel argues that this reference and *m.Sanh.* 5–6 show there were sanhedrins outside Palestine (*Studies in the History of the Sanhedrin* [Cambridge: Harvard University, 1965] 93). It is unclear to me whether these courts were set up outside Palestine or their jurisdiction merely extended beyond Palestine. Josephus uses the term both to signify the Great Sanhedrin, and in the nontechnical sense of

"council" (including a council of Romans assembled by the emperor). *Gerousia* is the more common term for local Jewish councils in the diaspora. We know little of the structure of these councils in the time of the Gospels, but later mishnaic materials describe local groups made up of three or twenty-three members who tried civil and capital cases (*m.Sanh.* 1.1–4).

29. The punishment of judicial flogging derives from Deut 25:2 and is attested by later mishnaic evidence (*m.Sanh.* 1.2; 3.6; 4.1; *m.Mak.* 3.4,7; *m.Ḥul.* 12.4). E. P. Sanders argues that such a discipline was meant to hold a member to the community, not to exclude him (*Paul, Law, People,* 192).

30. J. Gnilka, *Das Matthäusevangelium* (vol. 1; Freiburg: Herder, 1986) 376; G. Kilpatrick, *The Origins of the Gospel according to St. Matthew* (Oxford: Clarendon, 1946) 110; D. Hare, *The Theme of Jewish Persecution of Christians in the Gospel of St. Matthew,* 104–5; and J. Meier, *Law and History in Matthew's Gospel* (Rome: Biblical Institute, 1976) 13.

31. Some have postulated a more complicated redaction—namely that these sayings were derived from Matthew and Luke independently (Streeter, Manson, Haenchen, Beare). While possible, such a solution assumes a high degree of coincidence. Fitzmyer maintains they are both derived from Q (*Luke,* 943). Hare is probably correct that this was originally an anti-Pharisaic saying which Luke maintained and Matthew intensified by placing it in Jesus' mouth and adding explicit details of the persecution (*Theme,* 92).

32. O. Steck, *Israel und des gewaltsame Geschick der Propheten* (Neukirchen-Vluyn: Neukirchener Verlag, 1967). H.-J. Schoeps, "Die jüdischen Prophetenmorde," *Aus frühchristlichen Zeit* (Tübingen: Mohr[Siebeck], 1950) 126–43.

33. B. Garland, *The Intention of Matthew 23* (Leiden: Brill, 1979) 175–76.

34. H. Kosmala takes a minority view that this verse does not refer to the Jewish people as a whole but only to the crowd before Pilate, and it represents a legal formula by which they take responsibility for Jesus' execution ("His Blood on Us and Our Children," *ASTI* 7 [1968–69] 94–126).

35. Imprisonment is mentioned as punishment for two offenses in *t.Sanh.* 12.7-8. In CD 12.4, it is a substitute for the death penalty for transgressing a Sabbath law. Some of these references might also point to imprisonment by the Romans, with or without Jewish collusion.

36. In Matt 27:62–65, the Pharisees negotiate with Pilate on the Sabbath of Passover and worry about the third day specifically before the fact; in 28:11–15, the soldiers would circulate a tale of their own negligence. Perhaps Matthew's circumlocution of the word for Sabbath is meant to blur the unlikely fact of this event taking place on the Sabbath.

37. S. Krauss, *Das Leben Jesu nach jüdischen Quellen* (Berlin: Calvary, 1902) 170.

38. H. von Campenhausen, "The Events of Easter and the Empty Tomb," *Tradition and Life in the Church* (London: Collins, 1968) 66–68.
39. An interesting parallel occurs in *Mart. Pol.* 17.2 where the Jews are accused of persuading the authorities not to relinquish Polycarp's body to the Christians lest they begin to worship him instead of Jesus, perhaps by claiming his resurrection.
40. W. L. Craig takes the Matthean version of the guard at the tomb as more likely to be historical than the form in *Gos. Pet.* The Matthean version does not work very well as apologetic because it does not cover every possibility (e.g. it leaves a period of twelve hours from Friday evening until Saturday when the body might have been taken. *Gos. Pet.*, by contrast, is "failsafe apologetic" (W. L. Craig, "The Guard at the Tomb," *NTS* 30 [1984] 280). But the fact that Matt 28:11–15 is clumsy apologetic does not make it historical, nor should we expect too much logic and consistency from popular traditions.
41. The word *planaō* has a wide usage in later anti-Christian polemic, as well as within the New Testament (2 Cor 6:8; John 7:12, 47; 2 Tim 3:13). At Qumran, the equivalent word *mesi(y)t* is associated with error, seduction, and the devil. The tradition of the bribery of the guard at the tomb would have been an obvious Christian counter to the rumor of the theft of Jesus' body.
42. See my article, "You Invent a Christ!: Christological Claims as Points of Jewish-Christian Debate," *USQR* 44 (1991) 315–28.
43. Had these references been included, we would have seen more evidence that the claim of Jesus' messiahship was at issue (Mark 14:61; Matt 1:1–17; 22:42; 26:63; Luke 2:26; 3:23–38; 22:67). Similarly, his authority is a point of dispute (Mark 2:7; 11:28; Matt 9:2–3; 21:23; Luke 4:32; 20:2). Other themes reflected in disputes between Jesus and Jewish authorities include halakic observance (Mark 2:16; 3:2; 10:2; Matt 11:19; 12:10; 15:12; Luke 6:7; 11:38; 13:14), loyalty to the Temple (Mark 14:58; Matt. 26:61), the charge that Jesus has a demon (Mark 3:22; Matt 9:34; 12:24; Luke 11:15), and Jesus' pedigree (Matt 1:1–17; Luke 3:23-38).

CHAPTER 3, ACTS

1. H. Conzelmann, *Acts of the Apostles* (Hermeneia; Philadelphia: Fortress, 1987) xxxiii; J. Fitzmyer, *The Gospel According to Luke (I-IX)* (AB; Garden City: Doubleday, 1981) 53–57; E. Haenchen, *The Acts of the Apostles* (Philadelphia: Westminster, 1971) 3–49; M. Hengel, *Acts and the History of Earliest Christianity* (London: SCM, 1979) 66; P. Feine, J. Behm, W. Kümmel, *Introduction to the New Testament* (New York: Abingdon, 1966) 151; and G. Schneider, *Die Apostelgeschichte I* (Freiburg: Herder, 1980) 121.
2. Authors like J. Munck, F. F. Bruce, A. J. Mattill, and W. W. Gasque date Acts pre-70. They minimize the discrepancies between the Lukan Paul and the Paul of his letters and cite Luke's "failure" to explicitly mention the Neronian persecution, Paul's death, or the destruction of the Temple. Many of the arguments are from silence. Authors like J.

Knox and H. Koester who date Acts as late as 125–35 stress the discrepancies between the letters of Paul and the image of Paul in Acts,
attributing the discrepancies to a considerable distance in time.

3. Fitzmyer, *Gospel According to Luke,* 1:57.

4. Writing in the last decades of the century, Luke probably would not
have known directly of the inner workings of the Sanhedrin in the
30s (Acts 4:5–21; 5:27–40). Further, the dispute between the Hebrews
and Hellenists (6:1) jars the picture of unity that Acts promotes, so its
inclusion may point to a source. A. Harnack proposed the Antiochene
source and the Jerusalem source, recensions A and B (*The Acts of the
Apostles* (NTS 3; New York: Putnam's, 1909) 162–203. Others argue
that a travel journal, itinerary, or memoirs underlie the "we-passages."
E. Norden, *Agnostos Theos* (Leipzig: Teubner, 1913) 313–31; M.
Dibelius, *Aufsätze zur die Apostelgeschichte* (FRLANT 60; Göttingen:
Vandenhoeck & Ruprecht, 1951) 12–17; E. Trocmé, *Les Livre des Acts
et l'histoire* (Paris: Presses universitaires de France, 1957) 134–40; V.
Robbins argues that the author uses "we" in his narration of the sea
voyages because it is a convention of Hellenistic literature ("The We-
passages in Acts and Ancient Sea Voyages," *BR* 20 [1975] 5–18). For a
summary of the source question, see Dupont, *Livre et histoire;*
Schneider, *Apostelgeschichte* 89–95; or Haenchen, *Acts* 81–90. D.
Slingerland distinguishes between the first and second half of Acts and
attributes the more positive attitude toward Jews and Judaism in the
first half to the use of a Jewish-Christian source ("The Composition
of Acts: Some Redaction-Critical Observations," *JAAR* 56 [1988]
99–113).

5. Bruce, Dupont, Eltester, Hengel, Mattill, and Munck argue for Lukan
authorship. They explain the discordant details between the Paul of
Acts and the Paul of his own letters in various ways, such as a thirty-
year distance between the events and Luke's writing about them, a difference between Luke's view of Paul and Paul's own, Paul's "human-
ness" which left room for contradictions, Luke's failure to totally
understand Paul, and Luke's not possessing Paul's letters.

6. Skepticism about both the traditional identity of the author and the
overall reliability of Acts goes back to the Tübingen school of
Tendenzkritik. F. C. Baur and others say the Paul of Acts and the Paul
of the letters are totally incompatible, so the author could not have
been Paul's companion. Therefore Acts is written primarily to serve
Luke's theological agenda. This view is revived by Dibelius, and his
successors Conzelmann and Haenchen, who stress Luke as creative
author.

7. Note, for example, four recent studies on Acts, all of which focus on
some aspect of Luke's intention in composing Acts: R. Maddox, *The
Purpose of Luke-Acts* (Edinburgh: Clark, 1982); R. Brawley, *Luke-Acts
and the Jews* (SBL Monograph Series 33; Atlanta: Scholars Press, 1987);
Jack Sanders, *The Jews in Luke-Acts* (Philadelphia: Fortress, 1987); and
R. Pervo, *Profit with Delight* (Philadelphia: Fortress, 1987).

8. A notable exception is Hengel, who believes the author is Luke the

physician and Paul's companion, and that Acts is a relatively trustworthy "historical monograph." *Acts and the History of Earliest Christianity* (Philadelphia: Fortress, 1980).

9. Cadbury, *Making of Luke-Acts* 133; *Beginnings* vol. 2, 336.

10. The prologue form, too, is a Hellenistic convention and no guarantee of veracity. For parallel uses of individual words of Luke's prologue, see Cadbury, "Commentary on the Preface of Luke," *Beginnings*, vol. 2, 489–510.

11. Hengel, *Acts and Early Christianity*, 60.

12. Cadbury, *Making of Luke-Acts*, 133.

13. Bruce, *Acts Greek Text*, 15 and Gasque, *History of Criticism* 225–26, 247–258.

14. L. Donelson, "Cult Histories and the Sources of Acts," *Bib* 68 (1987) 1–21.

15. Pervo, *Profit with Delight*, 6.

16. An example is Diogenes Laertius' *Lives of Eminent Philosophers*. See C. Talbert, *Literary Patterns, Theological Themes and the Genre of Luke-Acts* (Missoula: Scholars Press, 1974).

17. J. Fitzmyer, *Gospel According to Luke* 16.

18. D.R.A. Hare, "The Rejection of the Jews in the Synoptic Gospels and Acts," *Anti-Semitism and the Foundations of Christianity* (ed. A. Davies; New York: Paulist, 1979) 27–47; P. Richardson, ed., *Anti-Judaism in Early Christianity* (Waterloo, Can.: Laurier, 1986); and R. Ruether, *Faith and Fratricide* (New York: Seabury, 1979) 64–95. Jack Sanders refers to "Luke's blanket hatred of the Jews as a group" (*The Jews in Luke-Acts* [Philadelphia: Fortress, 1987] 311. Compare Jervell, who maintains that the mission to the Jews is seen as successful in Acts ("The Divided People of God: The Restoration of Israel and Salvation for the Gentiles," *Luke and the People of God* [Minneapolis: Augsburg, 1972], 41–74); and R. Brawley, who argues that Luke has not "written off" the Jews (*Luke-Acts and the Jews*). Articles devoted to this question are gathered in *Luke-Acts and the Jewish People* (ed. J. Tyson; Minneapolis: Augsburg, 1988).

19. Pervo, *Profit with Delight*, 107–8.

20. The issue of the *sebomenoi*, or "God-fearers," has aroused considerable debate. A. T. Kraabel at one point argued no such group existed, but they were invented by Luke as a buffer group to help explain the transition of Christianity from a Jewish to a gentile religion ("The Disappearance of the God-fearers," *Numen* 28 [1981] 113–26). L. Feldman argues that a number of inscriptions support the existence of such a group ("Jewish 'Sympathizers' in Classical Literature and Inscriptions," *TAPA* 81 [1950] 200–8). The inscription at Aphrodisias suggests that, at least in that community, a group of Gentiles was in some way helpful to and enjoyed some status in the local Jewish community. See J. Reynolds and R. Tannenbaum, *Jews and God-fearers at Aphrodisias* (Cambridge: Cambridge Philological Society, 1987). The debate is summarized, with articles by the principal scholars, in *BAR* 12 (1986) 44–69. Josephus mentions the Jewish colony at Antioch,

which attracted and incorporated large numbers of Greeks (*J. W.* 7.3.3 § 45). See also S. Cohen, who concludes that "god-fearer" is not a technical term that always carries the same meaning ("Crossing the Boundary and Becoming a Jew," *HTR* 82 [1989] 13–33).

21. L. Levine, "The Second Temple Synagogue," *The Synagogue in Late Antiquity* (ed. L. Levine; Philadelphia: ASOR, 1987) 17.

22. J. Heinemann, "Preaching in the Talmudic Period," *EncJud* vol 13, cols. 994–98.

23. Aspects of the scene in 28:17–31 are historically improbable, including Paul's power to summon the community leaders twice and the Jewish leaders' polite but impartial interest. Paul's letter to the Romans shows there was a Christian group in the capital as early as the 50s. For a discussion of pre-Pauline Christianity in Rome, see W. Wiefel, "The Jewish Community in Ancient Rome and the Origins of Roman Christianity," *The Romans Debate* (ed. K. Donfried; Minneapolis: Augsburg, 1977) 100–19.

24. Brawley, *Luke-Acts and the Jews,* 156. See also Jervell, *Luke and the People of God,* 41–74.

25. Pervo, *Profit with Delight,* 34–37.

26. I assume Alexander is speaking in favor of the Christians because he is put forward to make a defense (*apologeisthai*) and shouted down by the pagan crowd. Were he merely joining in the anti-Christian fervor, Acts would not characterize his speech as a defense. He may, of course, simply be defending the Jewish community against attack because Paul and others are Jews.

27. Brawley, *Luke-Acts and the Jews,* 154.

28. Sanders, *Jews,* 242. See also J. Ziesler, "Luke and the Pharisees," *NTS* 25 (1979) 146–57; and R. Brawley, *The Pharisees in Luke-Acts* (Ph.D. thesis, Princeton Theological Seminary, 1978).

29. Scholars early on noted the combination of elements of lynch-justice and orderly court proceeding before the Sanhedrin in Stephen's trial. Many have attributed it to a conflation of conflicting sources. See Schneider, *Apostelgeschichte,* 431–40; 469–81. Since both mob violence and court action appear in the account, I classify Stephen's death in group c (spontaneous violence) and group d (legal measures).

30. Pervo, *Profit with Delight,* 32–33.

31. Ibid., 33–34.

32. Pervo cites Vergil and Apuleius, among others, *Profit with Delight,* 34–39.

33. R. Hodgson notes how common it was to boast of one's hardships. The trials of the ancient sage were recounted in "peristasis catalogues," where they legitimized the hero by showing his endurance and serenity in the face of suffering ("Paul the Apostle and First Century Tribulation Lists," *ZNW* 74 [1983] 59–80). See also J. T. Fitzgerald, *Cracks in Earthen Vessels* (SBLDS; Atlanta: Scholars Press, 1988).

34. The nature, competence, and constituency of the Sanhedrin is a mat-

ter of much debate. See Schürer-Vermes-Millar, *Jewish People,* v. 2, 199–226; and Cohen, *Maccabees to Mishnah,* 107–8.

35. Conzelmann, *Apostelgeschichte,* 51; Schneider, *Apostelgeschichte,* 1.433–34.

36. Smallwood, *Roman Rule,* 187–200. See *Ant.*18.6. §§ 144–47; §§ 155–60.

37. Sanders, *Jews,* 23; Haenchen, "The Book of Acts as Source Material," 278; and Conzelmann, *Apostelgeschichte,* 10.

38. He is called a "magus," the same term associated with Simon. "Magus" and "false prophet" are not identical terms, and the latter has a wider currency in the New Testament (Matt 7:15; 24:11,24; Mark 13:22; Luke 6:26; 2 Pet 2:1; 1 John 4:1; Rev 16:13). For the changing connotations of the word "magus," see A. Nock, "Paul and the Magus," *Beginnings* 5, 164–88.

39. An example is *Ag. Celsus* 1.28, which says Jesus learned magic in Egypt. See M. Smith, *Jesus the Magician* (New York: Harper & Row, 1978). For rabbinic and New Testament miracle stories, see P. Fiebig, *Jüdische Wundergeschichten des neutestament-lichen Zeitalters* (Tübingen: Mohr, 1911).

40. Ramsay, *Bearing,* 114–15.

41. Lucian (*Passing of Peregrinus,* 12–13) notes that the charlatan Peregrinus was part of a Christian group. A later rabbinic tradition shows that one of Jesus' followers was also accorded magical powers: Eliezer ben Dama is bitten by a snake and wants to be healed by someone using Jesus' name. Rabbi Ishmael prevents him to protect him from transgression, but does not suggest that the healer would be ineffective (*t.Ḥul.* 2.22).

42. Conzelmann, *Apostelgeschichte,* 111.

43. Compare Sanders, who implies that they stand for "evil Judaism" in Luke's portrayal (*Jews,* 281).

44. Josephus reports a Jew posing as a magician (*Ant.* 20.7.2 § 142). Lucian says "Fools fall for the spells of the Jews" (*Gout* 173). Apuleius ranks Moses as one of the "celebrated magicians" (*Apologia* 90).

45. Conzelmann, *Apostelgeschichte,* 111; Pervo, *Profit with Delight,* 63.

CHAPTER 4, JOHN

1. Scholars who date the Gospel 80–100 include C. K. Barrett, R. E. Brown, W. Kümmel, R. Kysar, N. Perrin, and D. Duling. Schnackenburg and others assume a connection to activities in the Yavnean period and increasingly hostile relations between "the Church and the Synagogue."

2. Brown identifies five stages of composition, *The Gospel according to John* (vol. 1; Garden City: Doubleday, 1966) xxxvi–xxxix. Schnackenburg also posits several stages when he considers the question of authorship (*The Gospel According to St. John* [New York: Herder & Herder, 1968] 91–102).

3. The term is proffered by D. M. Smith, *Johannine Christianity* (Columbia, S.C.; University of South Carolina Press, 1984) 184–85.

4. *History and Theology in the Fourth Gospel* (2d ed; Nashville: Abingdon, 1979). Although disagreement on particular points may exist, Martyn's basic conclusion is seconded by virtually every major Johannine scholar.

5. R. Scroggs, *Christology in Paul and John* (Philadelphia: Fortress, 1988) 79.

6. Ibid., 78. See also A. Segal, *Two Powers in Heaven* (Leiden: Brill, 1977).

7. J. Fitzmyer posits an Aramaic original behind this hymn, which would render *kyrios* as one of the names for God (*A Wandering Aramean* [Missoula: Scholars Press, 1979] 128). Even without the rendering into Aramaic, however, the hymn's implications of Jesus' divinity are unmistakable (cf. Phil 2:10–11; Isa 45:23).

8. Some examples include: C. K. Barrett, *The Gospel of John and Judaism* (London: SPCK, 1975); E. Grässer, "Die Antijüdische Polemik im Johannesevangelium," *NTS* 10 (1964–65) 74–90; R. Leistner, *Antijudaismus im Johannesevangelium?* (Bern: Lang, 1974); and S. Pancaro, *The Law in the Fourth Gospel* (NovTSup 42; Leiden: Brill, 1975). All the major commentaries contain some judgment on this issue.

9. R. Ruether, *Faith and Fratricide* (New York: Seabury, 1974) 111–16; J. Townsend, "The Gospel of John and the Jews," *Anti-Semitism and the Foundations of Christianity* (ed. A. Davies; New York: Paulist, 1979) 72–97; E. J. Epp, "Anti-Semitism and the Popularity of the Fourth Gospel in Christianity," *CCAR Jour* 22 (1975) 35–52; J. Leibig, "John and 'the Jews': Theological Anti-Semitism in the Fourth Gospel," *JES* 20 (1983) 211–34.

10. R. Bultmann, *The Gospel of John* (Philadelphia: Westminster, 1971) 86; R. Fuller, "'The Jews' in the Fourth Gospel," *Dialog* 16 (1977) 31–37; U. von Wahlde, "The Johannine 'Jews': A Critical Survey," *NTS* 28 (1982) 33–60; and R. A. Culpepper, "The Gospel of John and the Jews," *RevExp* 84 (1987) 273–88.

11. Several schools of thought exist on the identity of this group. One group of scholars maintains that the term "the Jews" designates the Jewish authorities opposed to Jesus while another group argues that the term stands for both the common people and the authorities. A third group sees "the Jews" as symbols of the world and its unbelief. They represent opposition to Jesus from any quarter—pagan or Jewish. John's purpose in leveling these distinct groups with a general term "the Jews" may be to link these enemies of Jesus to those Jews who trouble John's own people. Some suggest it is a geographic designation, "the Judeans." These positions are summarized by von Wahlde ("Johannine Jews," 34–41). As Culpepper and others note, the effect of using this general term to stand in for all the enemies of Jesus and his followers has been to project a certain anti-Judaism, regardless of which actual characters stand behind the term. See Culpepper, "Gospel and Jews," 275; and J. Ashton, "The Identity and Function of the *Ioudaioi* in the Fourth Gospel," *NovT* 27 (1985) 40–75.

12. Bultmann, Meeks, and others equate the term "the Jews" with the world (see Meeks, "The Man from Heaven in Johannine Sectarianism," *JBL* 91 [1972] 44–72). The terms are not wholly interchangeable. While "the Jews" may stand for "the world," I doubt that every reference to "the world" has the Jews in mind. Interestingly, in one case "the world" represents Jewish belief in Jesus (12:19).

13. Martyn, *History and Theology,* 38–62.

14. Scholars who link the use of *Birkat ha-Minim* to John's statements about expulsion of Christians from the synagogue include Barrett, Lindars, Schnackenburg, and Townsend. Others consider the curse to have been an anti-Christian measure, regardless of whether or not it is in the background of the Fourth Gospel (W. D. Davies, *The Setting of the Sermon on the Mount* [Cambridge: Cambridge University Press, 1966] 275–78). This argument appears as early as S. Krauss, "The Jews in the Works of the Church Fathers," *JQR* o.s. 5 (1892–93) 130–32.

15. The most comprehensive response to the theory that *Birkat ha-Minim* was broadly applied against Christians is R. Kimelman, "Birkat Ha-Minim and the Lack of Evidence for an Anti-Christian Jewish Prayer in Late Antiquity," *Jewish and Christian Self-Definition* (vol. 2; ed. E. P. Sanders et al.; Philadelphia: Fortress, 1981) 226–44. Others who doubt its widespread use as an anti-Christian prayer include Cohen (*Maccabees,* 227); P. Schäfer ("Die sogenannte Synode von Jabne," *Judaica* 31 [1975] 54–64, 116–24); and D. Hare (*Jewish Persecution* [Cambridge: Cambridge University Press, 1967] 54). For a summary of the debate, see R. Whitacre, *Johannine Polemic* (SBL Dissertation Series 67; Chico: Scholars Press, 1980) 7–10.

16. In the Cairo Geniza version, *noṣrim* and *minim* is in fact redundant if *minim* means only Christians. The term *noṣrim,* however, may not be original. Kimelman argues that had *noṣrim* been part of the original wording, rabbinic literature would have been more likely to refer to the blessing as *Birkat ha-Noṣrim* ("Birkat Ha Minim," 233).

17. See Townsend, "John and the Jews," 72–73 for a survey of John's use of typically Jewish symbols such as bread, light, water, life to apply to Jesus. Other religions also employ these symbols, of course, but in John's case, the most likely conduit for his use of them would be Judaism.

18. Martyn, *History and Theology,* 60.

19. S.J.D. Cohen, "The Significance of Yavneh: Pharisees, Rabbis and the End of Jewish Sectarianism," *HUCA* 55 (1984) 27–53.

20. J. Heinemann, *Prayer in the Talmud* (Berlin: de Gruyter, 1977) 225.

21. Some scholars propose an intermediate view of the relationship between the Blessing against the Heretics and the scenes of expulsion in the Fourth Gospel. R. Kysar suggests that the formulation of *Birkat ha-Minim* merely made official what had been happening informally for some time. It is this informal rejection of Christians that the Gospel reflects (*John* [Minneapolis: Augsburg, 1986] 14–15). R. E. Brown suggests that *Birkat ha-Minim* came at the end of a process that began

with hostility and expulsion (*Antioch and Rome*, 48, n. 111). W. Meeks suspects that the deterioration of relationships took place over time, perhaps culminating in the *Birkat ha-Minim*, but that John portrays this deterioration as a punctilear event ("Man from Heaven," 55, n. 40; cf. Martyn, *History and Theology*, 54–55, n. 69). J. A. Overman argues, as I do, that the benediction included Christians but was not aimed at them specifically. See his summary of scholarship on the issue in *Matthew's Gospel and Formative Judaism* (Minneapolis: Fortress, 1990) 48–62.

22. *Dial.* 38.1 says that the Jewish teachers ruled that Jews should not associate or converse with Christians. But this sounds like Jewish withdrawal from Christians, not active excommunication (though the outward effect would be similar). Justin, writing 155–60, describes a time when Judaism and Christianity are clearly separate entities.

23 An example in tannaitic literature equates killing the evildoer with service to God (*m.Sanh.* 10.6), though this is certainly hyperbole.

24. Brown, *Beloved Disciple*, 43.

CHAPTER 5, REVELATION

1. W. Kümmel, *Introduction*, 466–69; N. Perrin & D. Duling, *Introduction*, 113; E. Schüssler Fiorenza, *Invitation to the Book of Revelation* (Garden City: Doubleday, 1981) 62–63; and A. Yarbro Collins, "Dating the Apocalypse of John," *BR* 26 (1981) 33–45.

2. Many doubt that Domitian was responsible for a major persecution of Christians. The earliest explicit testimony is from Eusebius (*Hist. Eccl.* 3.17.1–3.20.7), who quotes the second-century Hegesippus. Pliny's letter to Trajan (*Letters* 10.96.2–5) lends indirect support because it alludes to a policy of testing and executing Christians which had been in place for some time, possibly from Domitian's reign. Pliny's statement in Bithynia in 112 that some people had given up their Christianity 20 years earlier (*Letters* 10.96.6) may mean they were pressured under Domitian's reign, but apostasy need not always signal outside persecution. See M. Charlesworth, "Some Observations on Ruler-Cult Especially in Rome," *HTR* 28 (1935) 32–34; and P. Keresztes, "The Jews, the Christians, and Emperor Domitian," *VC* 27 (1973) 22–23. The weakness of the evidence has led Yarbro Collins, J. Sweet, and others to doubt anything more than intermittent, local persecutions under Domitian. See A. Yarbro Collins, *Crisis and Catharsis* (Philadelphia: Westminster, 1984) 69–71; and J. Sweet, "Maintaining the Testimony of Jesus," *Suffering and Martyrdom in the New Testament* (ed. W. Horbury and B. McNeil; Cambridge: Cambridge University Press, 1981) 102. They suggest that the references to persecution are largely predictive and that Revelation warns its readers against accommodation to the Roman presence and seduction by its luxuries.

3. Domitian did not invent emperor worship, but Suetonius, Pliny, Dio Chrysostom, Tacitus, and Juvenal say that he promoted it far more than his predecessors, using the title *dominus et deus*, requiring magistrates to swear by the *divi* and the genius of the emperor, and encour-

aging offerings before his image. See Charlesworth, "Ruler-Cult," 32–35; Charlesworth, *CAH* 11.41–42; and K. Scott, *The Imperial Cult under the Flavians* (New York: Arno, 1975) 89–112. These Roman historians were partially motivated by a desire to flatter Trajan, Domitian's successor, however, and may have painted an unfairly negative picture. L. Thompson questions the picture of Domitian as a megalomaniacal tyrant, and cites a "provincial" tradition favorable to the emperor (Josephus, *Life* 76; *Sib. Or.* 12.125–32; "A Sociological Analysis of Tribulation in the Apocalypse of John," *Semeia* 36 [1986] 154–55, 162).

4. W. M. Ramsay, *The Letters to the Seven Churches of Asia* (New York: Hodder & Stoughton, 1914) 210–430.

5. No literal quotes appear in Revelation. However, the many examples and types of dependences are charted by R. H. Charles, *The Revelation of St. John* (2 vols.; ICC; New York: Scribner's, 1920) 1.lxv–lxxxvi.

6. Pergamum, referred to in 2:13 as a place of "Satan's throne," was a center of Roman administration and the imperial cult, and contained many monuments to the gods (Ramsay, *Seven Churches,* 283–90).

7. A few scholars, however, have understood this epithet to mean the opponents are Gentile Judaizers, Gentiles taking on some Jewish customs (J. Gager, *Origins,* 132; P. Prigent, *L'Apocalypse de Saint Jean* [CNT 14; Lausanne: Delachaux et Niestlé, 1981] 47–48). If their "slander" is denunciation of John's group before the Romans, however, they are probably not Judaizers. A Gentile adopting Jewish customs would be in an even more precarious position than a full-fledged Jew and would be better off to avoid the Roman authorities completely. During Domitian's reign, Rome was intolerant of Jewish conversion and proselytism even while it tolerated Judaism. Flavius Clemens and Flavia Domitilla—probably Jews or converts to Judaism—were accused of atheism, and, Dio tells us, "many others who were drifting into Jewish practices were condemned" (Dio Cassius, *Rom. Hist.* 57.14.1–2). Similarly, "impiety" (*asebeia*) and "adopting a Jewish life" both invoke the death penalty (Dio's *Rom. Hist.* 68.1.2).

8. Literally *thlipsis* means "pressure," but in the New Testament it is usually used in a figurative sense to mean "harassment" or "persecution."

9. In secular Greek literature, *blasphēmia* carries the sense of slander, calumny, or abusive speech, as well as speaking profanely of sacred things. In the New Testament, as in the LXX, it normally refers to a violation of God's majesty through an attack on his people (1 Cor 4:13; 1 Pet 4:4) or an attack on Jesus' messianic claims (Mark 15:29; Matt 27:39; Luke 22:64, 23:39). Elsewhere in Revelation, *blasphēmia* is used to refer to the activity of the beast (13:1, 5–6; 17:3), a symbol for Rome.

10. Minucius Felix, a third-century Christian writer, cites these charges against Christians in the name of a second-century pagan, Caecilius (*Octavius* 8.3–5; 9.1–6; 31.1–2). Typically pagans accused Christians of these vices, or Christians accused each other. In spite of various

complaints about Jewish rumors against Christians, these charges are
never attributed to Jews until Origen's time (*Contra Celsum* 6.27).
Justin identifies it as a pagan canard (*1 Apol.* 26.6). Trypho pointedly
says he does not believe these rumors (*Dial.* 10.2). See B. Visotzky,
"Overturning the Lamp," *JJS* 38 (1987) 72–80.

11. The charge of *maiestas,* or treason, had since Julius Caesar been a
fairly elastic term, including conspiracy, libel, or slander—anything
that detracts from the splendor of the people or her rulers. See *OCD*
640–41 and A. Jones, *The Criminal Courts of the Roman Republic and
Principate* (Totowa: Rowman and Littlefield, 1972) 106–7.

12. Smallwood, *The Jews Under Roman Rule,* 134–36. Jewish rights probably came from *ad hoc* confirmations of city laws which allowed Jews
to meet as *collegia* (S. Applebaum, "The Organization of the Jewish
Communities in the Diaspora," *The Jewish People in the First Century*
[ed. S. Safrai & M. Stern, in cooperation with D. Flusser & W. van
Unnik; Compendia Rerum Judaicarum ad Novum Testamentum;
Assen: van Gorcum, 1974] vol. 1, 460). Jews could not take these
rights for granted, since they were sometimes revoked, as under Gaius
(Philo, *Leg.* 44.353). No one calls Judaism a *religio licita* until
Tertullian.

13. *Fisci Judaici Calumnia Sublata;* H. Mattingly, *Coins of the Roman Empire
in the British Museum* (London: 1936) 3.15, 17, 19.

14. In both Smyrna and Philadelphia, the Christians are "have-nots," poor
or powerless, leading to speculation about the sociological factors at
work. Several scholars have examined Revelation as a whole using
theories of social deprivation, crisis, and forging of group identity. See
D. Aune, "The Social Matrix of the Apocalypse of John," *BR* 26
(1981) 16–31; L. Thompson, "Sociological Analysis," *Semeia* 36
(1986) 147–74; and A. Yarbro Collins, "Vilification," 308–20.

15. J. Sweet, "Maintaining the Testimony of Jesus: the Sufferings of
Christians in the Revelation of John," *Suffering and Martyrdom in the
New Testament* (ed. W. Horbury and B. McNeil; Cambridge:
Cambridge University Press, 1981) 102. One death is mentioned at
Pergamun, but it is not recent. Sweet doubts a major persecution of
Christians under Domitian.

16. Collins, *Crisis,* 86.

17. C. Cadoux, *Ancient Smyrna* (Oxford: Blackwell, 1938) 304–5. For
some later inscriptions, see L. Robert, *Hellenica* 11–12 (1960) 260–62;
CIJ 739; *CIJ* 742.

CHAPTER 6, JOSEPHUS

1. The above passages represent my translations of the Greek text in the
Loeb edition of Josephus. My reconstruction of a more original version of *TF* appears below.

2. The *Jewish Antiquities* is dated by Josephus himself to the thirteenth
year of Domitian, which corresponds to Sept. 93–Sept. 94. In spite of
certain problems, most scholars accept this date as reliable. The problems are outlined in E. Schürer, *The History of the Jewish People in the

Age of Jesus Christ (ed. G. Vermes and F. Millar; Edinburgh: Clark, 1973) 481–83, n. 47.

3. For the history of early skepticism about *TF*, see R. Eisler, *The Messiah Jesus and John the Baptist according to Flavius Josephus' Recently Rediscovered 'Capture of Jerusalem' and the other Jewish and Christian Sources* (London: Methuen, 1931), 40–49.

4. L. Feldman, "The *Testimonium Flavianum:* The State of the Question," *Christological Perspectives* (ed. R. Berkey and S. Edwards; New York: Pilgrim, 1982); "Flavius Josephus Revisited," *ANRW* II, 21.2, 821–62; "Christianity," *Josephus and Modern Scholarship (1937–1980)* (ed. L. Feldman; Berlin: de Gruyter, 1984) 673–707; P. Winter, "Excursus II—Josephus on Jesus and James," Schürer, *Jewish People,* 428–41; Z. Baras, "The *Testimonium Flavianum:* The State of Recent Scholarship," *Society and Religion in the Second Temple Period* (ed. M. Avi-Yonah and Z. Baras; World History of the Jewish People 8; Jerusalem : Massada, 1977) 303–13, 378–85; J. Meier, "Jesus in Josephus: A Modest Proposal," *CBQ* 52 (1990) 76–103.

5. Feldman, "State," 181; "Christianity," 690; Winter, "Josephus on Jesus," 432–33.

6. Eisler chronicles the history of Christian censorship of Jewish and other literature containing material considered unfavorable to Christianity (*Messiah Jesus,* 3–21, 63–72). Establishing the reality of such censorship of *TF* is central to Eisler's thesis of the greater reliability of Slavonic Josephus. Since Josephus is preserved only by the Church, some tampering would be likely.

7. Meier offers a similar reconstruction of *TF* in "Jesus in Josephus." A Modest Proposal," *CBQ* 52 (1990) 76–103.

8. Eisler suggests that something has been removed which read "*arche neon thorybon Iesous tis,* thus rendering the line "about this time arose an occasion for new disturbances, a certain Jesus. . . ." (*Messiah Jesus,* 50–51). Thackeray notes that *ginetai de* is normally used by Josephus to introduce a disaster of some kind (*Josephus: Man and Historian,* 142–43).

9. Agapius' version also has Jesus as "a wise man." Winter maintains that no Christian would have put this in, since it undermines Jesus' uniqueness, and that it is probably Josephan.

10. Heinichen's emendation, accepted by Eisler (*Messiah Jesus,* 53) and Thackeray (*Josephus: Man and Historian,* 145) changes "the true" ΤΑΛΗΘΗ to "the unusual," ΤΑΑΗΘΗ. I have adopted it here because it involves a minute change of one bar in magiscule writing, it fits better with the negative sensual connotations of *hēdonē,* and the mss. have elsewhere confused the two words in their adverbial form. A censor may have consciously changed what he found or a Christian scribe may have unconsciously read what he believed to be the case and substituted "the truth" for "the unusual."

11. *hēdonē* is a word with a long history and carries mostly negative overtones of sensual pleasure. *TDNT* compares it to the *yeṣer hara* in

Hebrew, but that comparison does not distinguish between the impulse to pleasure and pleasure itself.

12. Eisler and Bammel emend to *apēgageto*, "led astray," "seduced." This would certainly fit better with *hēdonē* and the emphasis on wonderworking. However the verb here, *epagō*, already has a slightly negative tinge, "to bring something on oneself." If it is the work of a Christian censor, one might expect a more positive term.

13. Note the absence of the line "He was the Messiah." Had Josephus believed this, we would expect some indication of it elsewhere. This seems to be the best argument against its inclusion, not "Could a loyal Pharisee(?) like Josephus have believed in Jesus?" "What about Akiba and Bar Kochba?" "Could the Roman lackey Josephus have included this?" and similar speculations. Eisler assumes something such as "he was believed to be the Messiah," as Jerome quotes it (*De Viris Illustribus* 13.14). The Arabic version uncovered by Pines has "he was perhaps the Messiah," a nonsensical statement from any point of view, probably reflecting an inadequate rendering from Syriac into Arabic (Pines, *Arabic TF,* 31).

14. Bammel's emendation to *apatēsantes*, "those who were misled, cheated" is unwarranted. He assumes a hostility in the original which may not have been there. In fact, J. Maier suggests the opposite tendency, that *TF* described one more in a series of obscure movements that suffered misfortune. The phrase cries out for some kind of closure, namely "did not cease to do what?" Some possibilities are "to rave," as Eisler submits, "to love him," as Thackeray has it, or simply "to exist," in keeping with the final sentence of *TF.*

15. Eisler (*Messiah Jesus* 62, n.1) says this may be an addition and that originally the line was more vague, leaving in doubt whether or not Jesus had died.

16. *phyle* is considered clearly disparaging by Eisler, Thackeray, and Bammel, but *BAG, TDNT,* and *LSJ* yield no negative associations with the word. It was most often used by Christians (and others) as a substitute for "nation" or to designate the twelve tribes of Israel.

17. There must have been some use of *Christos* in the original or this name would not make sense.

18. Eisler maintains that this statement "certainly does not imply a wish on the part of the author for their continued growth" (*Messiah Jesus,* 56), and Thackeray hears the word "unfortunately" barely held back by Josephus. Yet it may be a neutral statement, or Josephus may be expressing simple surprise that the ignominious death of their Messiah did not dampen the messianists' belief.

19. For a review of these sources, see M. Smith, *Jesus the Magician* (New York: Harper and Row, 1978) 45–67.

20. *Ant.*8.2.7 § 53; 10.11.2 § 237. See Rengstorf's concordance for a complete list of the uses of *sophos.*

21. A later Christian censor might have wanted to play down James' role. Some suggest political reasons, that James became an embarrassment because he had been a radical Zealot. Origen connects his death with

the fall of Jerusalem. Or a censor might have thought praise of James detracted too much from Jesus—something Origen complains about (*Comm. Matt.* 10.17). Or a later censor—as a member of a church no longer observant, or perhaps in conflict with Jewish Christians—might have wanted to mute the praise for the hero of the Jewish-Christian, law-observant Church. Lacking any evidence for Christian censorship, however, these speculations must remain speculations.

22. D. Rhoads discusses the delicate relation between the procurator and the high priest (*Israel in Revolution* [Philadelphia: Fortress, 1976] 89). Apparently the procurator was to be consulted whenever the Sanhedrin convened, and he alone was responsible for the death penalty. No doubt this was a sore point with the high priest and Sadducees. Perhaps Josephus is here merely taking a pro-Roman view and showing that no one agreed with Ananus' actions or conspired with him.

23. A. Baumgarten notes that Josephus regularly associates the Pharisees with *akribeia* ("The Name of the Pharisees," *JBL* 102 [1983] 413).

CHAPTER 7, THE MARTRYDOM OF POLYCARP

1. I have accepted B. Dehandschutter's reading of *asebeias* instead of *Asias, Martyrium Polycarpi* (Louvain: Louvain University, 1979). The charge of *asebeia* fits perfectly with the charges in the rest of the sentence of disloyalty to the gods and discouraging sacrifice and worship of the gods and the emperor, charges brought against Christians in Trajan's (and possibly Domitian's) time. *Asebeias* can also claim to be the more difficult reading (and therefore more likely to be original). A Christian scribe might change it to *Asias*, but the reverse seems unlikely. Dehandschutter dissents from the standard view that MS. M is the most reliable and prefers a group of MSS., B C H P V.

2. The spectrum of opinion on *Mart. Pol.*'s date ranges from 155 to 177. The earlier date is attested to by inferior evidence but fits better with the correspondence between Polycarp and Ignatius of Antioch and with Irenaeus' statement that Polycarp knew John at Ephesus, as Chadwick notes (*The Early Church* [Penguin: Harmondsworth, 1967] 30). For a brief discussion of dating, see Musurillo, *Christian Martyrs,* xiii, or Dehandschutter, *Polycarpi,* 280–81.

3. H. von Campenhausen posits five stages of reworkings ("Bearbeitungen und Interpolationen des Polykarpmartyriums," *Sitzungberichte der Heidelberger Akademie der Wissenschaften* 3 [1957] 5–48). With the exception of 17.2, his work does not affect the passages cited.

4. H. Delehaye, *Les Passions des Martyrs et les Genres littéraires* (Brussels: Bureaux de la Société des Bollandistes, 1921) 19.

5. The earliest inscription (ca. 123–24 C.E.) cites "the former Judeans" as contributing money to embellish and extend public buildings in Smyrna (*CII* 742; *IGR* iv.1431). Two other inscriptions from second- and third-century Smyrna show people purchasing tombs with the expectation that the local government would guarantee their ownership

(*IGR* iv.1387; *CII* 741; *IGR* iv.1452). The fine on trespassers was to be divided between the royal treasury and the Jewish community. Further, L. Robert reports an inscription that shows the secretary (*grammateus*) of the Smyrnean Jewish community to have been a Roman citizen, who freely used public archives and facilities ("Inscriptions D'Asie Mineure a Leyde," *Hellenica* 11–12 [1960] 260–62).

6. J. Parkes, *Conflict*, 136; W. Schoedel, *Apostolic Fathers*, 67.

7. Parkes, *Conflict*, 137; I. Abrahams, *Studies in Pharisaism and the Gospels*, 2.67. Neither would I suggest the opposite extreme, like C. Cadoux, who says the Jews were more available to join in the persecution since it was their Sabbath and they were free from work (*Ancient Smyrna* [Oxford: Blackwell, 1938] 361).

8. Parkes, *Conflict*, 137.

9. See H. Fischel, "Martyr and Prophet," *JQR* 37 (1946/7) 265–80, 363–86. Fischel shows the extent to which the roles of the prophet and the martyr are combined, including the granting of prophetic visions to the martyr.

10. Fischel, "Martyr and Prophet," 376–84.

11. An exception is Pseudo-Pionius, a spurious work set in Smyrna a century after Polycarp's death. Even in that work, however, the Jews offer Christians the shelter of the synagogue.

12. Parkes, *Conflict*, 145. For the legends of Agricola and Vital, see Ambrose, *Exhort. Virg.* 1.1.6–8, *PL* 16, col. 353 and Paulinus of Milan, *Vita Ambrosii* 29, *PL* 14, col. 39. For the legends of Hermes, Aggaeus and Caius, Vincent and Orantius see *Acta Sanctorum* Jan 4 and Jan 22. The bodies of Hermes, Aggaeus, and Caius are said to have been thrown unwittingly into a Jewish sepulchre. Agricola and Vital, however, are buried with the permission of the Jews. In the case of Vincent and Orantius, a space in the crypt is purchased from the Jews. These acts are placed in the late third–early fourth century. I do not argue the historicity of the burial accounts, but only wish to show portrayals of Jews in certain martyr-acts. Christian graves in Jewish cemeteries in North Africa are reported by A. Delattre, but not all scholars agree on their Christian character (*Gamart ou la nécropole juive de Carthage* [Lyons: Mougin-Rusand, 1895]).

13. J. Lightfoot argues that the artificiality of other parallels suggests their conformity to reality, e.g. a police captain named Herod, or a slave who divulges information under torture as a "stand-in" for Judas. A fabricator would have been less obvious (*The Apostolic Fathers* Part 2, vol. 1 [London: Macmillan, 1885] 597). This reasoning attributes much skill to the fabricator, however. Surely some authors were clumsier than others. In the case of the references to Jews, however, the parallels are not so much clumsy as remote.

14. H. von Campenhausen, *Bearbeitungen und Interpolationen des Polykarpmartyriums* (Heidelberg: Universitätsverlag, 1957) 24–26. He argues that the material from *Ioudaion* to *lambanein* is interpolated, and the original read "these things were at the provocation and urging of the ignorant ones."

15. von Campenhausen, *Bearbeitungen,* 30–31.
16. Simon, *Verus Israel,* 151.

CHAPTER 8, THE GOSPEL OF PETER

1. Scholars who argued this view include J. A. Robinson, H. Swete, T. Zahn, L. Vaganay, and K. Beyschlag. A summary of opinions on this issue appears in J. D. Crossan, *The Cross that Spoke* (San Francisco: Harper and Row, 1988) 13–15.
2. A. von Harnack, *Bruchstücke des Evangeliums und der Apokalypse des Petrus* (Leipzig: Hinrichs, 1893) 32–47; P. Gardner-Smith, "The Gospel of Peter," *JTS* 27 (1926) 255–71.
3. R. Cameron, *The Other Gospels* (Philadelphia: Westminster, 1982) 77–78; J. D. Crossan, *Four Other Gospels* (Minneapolis: Winston, 1985) 132–81; J. Denker, *Die Theologiegeschichtliche Stellung des Petrusevangelium* (Frankfurt: Lang, 1975) 31–57; and H. Koester, "Apocryphal and Canonical Gospels," *HTR* 73 (1980) 105–30.
4. *Gos. Pet.* depicts certain events also found in the Synoptic Gospels; the scene of the mockery (Mark 14:65; 15:16–20; Matt 27:29–30; *Gos. Pet.* 3.6–9), the superscription on the cross (Mark 15:26; Matt 27:37; Luke 23:38; *Gos. Pet.* 4.11), the division of Jesus' garments (Mark 15:24; Matt 27:35; Luke 23:34; *Gos. Pet.* 4.12), the drink given to Jesus (Mark 15:23, 36; Matt 27:34; *Gos. Pet.* 5.16), the empty tomb (Mark 16:5; Matt 28:2; Luke 24:2–4; *Gos. Pet.* 13.55–56). The Gospel of Matthew and *Gos. Pet.* share the elements of Pilate's hand washing, the earthquake, and setting a guard at the tomb to prevent theft, and attempting to suppress reports of the resurrection by influencing Pilate and the Roman soldiers (Matt 27:24, 50, 64; 28:13–15; *Gos. Pet.* 1.1, 6.21, 8.30–31, 11.47–49). The Gospel of Luke and *Gos. Pet.* both record the mention of Herod's participation (Luke 23:6–12; *Gos. Pet.* 1.1–2), the repentance of one of those crucified with Jesus (Luke 23:39–43; *Gos. Pet.* 4.13), and the remorse of the spectators (Luke 23:48; *Gos. Pet.* 8.28). With the Gospel of John, *Gos. Pet.* shares the naming of Mary Magdalene alone (John 20:1; *Gos. Pet.* 12.50), people motivated by "fear of the Jews" (John 9:22; 20:19; *Gos. Pet.* 12.48, 50, 52), and Jesus' burial in a garden (John 9:41; *Gos. Pet.* 6.24).
5. Brown offers the analogy of a modern-day Christian congregant asked to tell the story of the Passion from memory. The basic outline of the story and certain key phrases would be there, but elements from several Gospels would probably be combined ("The Gospel of Peter," 335–36).
6. The only firm termini are the destruction of the Jerusalem Temple (70 C.E.) and Serapion's testimony around 190–200 that the Gospel had already acquired some status in certain circles in nearby Rhossus.
7. Vaganay rehearses the reasons he judges the Gospel unhistorical (*Évangile de Pierre,* 141–47). See also Mara, *Évangile de Pierre,* 29–33. Crossan, however, judges the substance of it to be the oldest preserved Christian account of the Passion.
8. Typical elements identified by H. Delehaye are expanded by H.

Musurillo in *The Acts of the Christian Martyrs* (Oxford: Clarendon, 1972) lii–liii.

9. Also a punishment on its own (Suetonius, *Aug.* 67; *Tib.* 44), breaking the legs of a crucified criminal would hasten death by asphyxiation. See H. Hutzig, "Crux" in Pauly-Wissowa, v. 8, cols. 1728–31. In the second-century *Acts of Andrew* (Narr. 22, *Mart.* II.1, Hennecke-Schneemelcher vol. 1, 417) the proconsul orders his soldiers to crucify Andrew and not to break his legs, "intending in that way to make the punishment more severe." The only archaeological remains of a crucified victim show his legs were broken, but a further evaluation of V. Tzaferis' initial report ("Jewish Tombs at and Near Giv'at ha-Mivtar, Jerusalem," *IEJ* 20 [1970] 18–32) by J. Zias and E. Sekeles concludes that his legs were broken after death and not as part of his execution ("The Crucified Man from Giv'at ha-Mivtar: A Reappraisal," *IEJ* 35 [1985] 22–27). So we are still in doubt as to whether the *crurifragium* was normally performed.

10. See W. L. Craig, who compares *Gos. Pet*'s version with the Matthean version, noting that the former is airtight, leaving no possibility that the body could have been stolen and making clear that the Jews witnessed Jesus' resurrection ("The Guard at the Tomb," *NTS* 30 [1984] 273–81).

11. Swete, *Euangelion,* 13; and Vaganay, *Évangile,* 272.

CHAPTER 9, THE CHRISTIAN APOLOGISTS

1. H. Marrou produces a table of scholarly proposals for the date of *Diogn.,* ranging from pre-70 to the sixteenth century, although the vast majority fall in the second century (*A Diognète* [SC 33; Paris: Cerf, 1951] 242–43). See also P. Andriessen, "L'apologie de Quadratus conservée sous le titre d'Epitre à Diognète," *Recherches de théologie ancienne et médiévale* 13 (1946) 5–39, 125–49, 237–60; 14 (1947) 121–56; L. Barnard, "The Epistle ad Diognetum: Two Units from One Author?" *ZNW* 56 (1965) 130–37; and H. Meecham, *The Epistle to Diognetus* (Manchester: Manchester University Press, 1949) 16–19.

2. Frend, *Martyrdom and Persecution,* 258–59.

3. The word *hos* does not here seem to mean "as if" (Smyth, *Greek Grammar,* 670–71). The author does not imply elsewhere that Christians really are not outsiders to Judaism and the Jews are mistaken in treating them so. He draws very clear distinctions between Christians and Jews.

4. Dating of both works relies on the ascription of *1 Apol.* to Antonius Pius (ruled 137–62) and Justin's mention of the *1 Apol.* in *Dial.* A virtual consensus on dating exists among scholars, including J. Juster, L. Barnard, N. Hyldahl, and E. Osborn.

5. Virtually no modern writer thinks that Trypho can be identified as the rabbi Tarphon of rabbinic literature because Tarphon is too early, too learned, and too anti-Christian (Osborn, *Justin* 12–13).

6. A. Hulen claims Trypho is merely a tool for Justin to lay out his own

arguments ("The 'Dialogues with the Jews' as Sources for the Early Jewish Argument against Christianity," *JBL* 51 [1932] 63).

7. Several scholars believe that some sort of debate actually took place. A. Harnack does not venture to date the encounter (*Judentum und Judenchristentum in Justins Dialog mit Trypho* [TU d.r. 39; Leipzig: Hinrichs, 1913] 53). L. Barnard places it 30 years before the writing of *Dial.* (*Justin Martyr* [Cambridge: Cambridge University Press, 1967] 19).

8. Wilde suggests that Justin only knew about Jews and Judaism from the LXX (*Treatment,* 104). Sigal ("Inquiry," 75) and Barnard ("The Old Testament and Judaism in the Writings of Justin Martyr," *VT* 14 [1964] 406) maintain that Justin represents mid–second-century Judaism fairly accurately. A judgment on this issue depends on how much we hold Justin's mistakes about Judaism against him (e.g. the Pharisees are a heretical sect of the Jews). G. Stanton maintains that Justin at least transmits some genuine Jewish allegations against Christians ("Aspects of Early Christian-Jewish Polemic and Apologetic," *NTS* 31 [1985] 377–92). See also Hulen, "Dialogues," 58–70.

9. See B. Visotzky, "Overturning the Lamp," *JJS* 38 (1987) 72–80. Visotzky argues that these charges are formulaic in Christian, pagan, and rabbinic literature.

10. My thanks to K. Katz for this information and for allowing me to read his unpublished paper, "Form and Convention in *Dialogue with Trypho*" (delivered at the Jewish Theological Seminary, February 1987). See also G. Bowersock, *Greek Sophists of the Roman Empire* (Oxford: Clarendon, 1969); and *Approaches to the Second Sophistic* (University Park: American Philological Association, 1974).

11. See M. Hoffman, *Der Dialog bei den christlichen Schriftstellern der ersten vier Jahrhunderts* (Berlin: Akademie, 1966); and B. Voss, *Der Dialog in der frühchristlichen Literatur* (Munich: Fink, 1979).

12. Stanton, "Aspects," 379.

13. O. Skarsaune argues that Justin's use of proof-texts shows at least two layers of tradition. The earliest stratum is a group of texts which Jewish Christians used to address fellow Jews. These texts prove Jesus from Scripture and use intra-Israel critiques like the killing of the prophets and suffering as God's punishment. The second layer of tradition shows these texts used and supplemented by gentile Christians to illustrate Israel's unworthiness and justify the triumph of gentile Christianity (*The Proof from Prophecy: A Study in Justin Martyr's Proof-Text Tradition* [Leiden: Brill, 1987] 326–28). This is an attractive thesis, since it solves the paradox of Justin's sharp polemic against Judaism and appropriation of her status and her Scripture. Whatever the original milieu of Justin's sources, however, he appropriates their verses and uses them as ammunition against Judaism. I do not think he is battling Jewish Christians because he professes to know about and tolerate their law-observance.

14. See my article, "'You Invent a Christ!': Christological Claims as Points of Jewish-Christian Dispute," *USQR* 44 (1991) 315–28.

15. Stanton, "Aspects," 379.
16. S. Katz, "Issues," 46–47.
17. R. Kimelman points out that in Palestinian texts a *min* means a deviant Jew, and is a general term that may include someone who professes Jesus ("Birkat Ha-Minim," 228–32). Kimelman also notes that no reference in Justin includes both the term "curse" and a description of it happening within Jewish prayer, 235–36.
18. Scholars who, along with Kimelman, minimize the significance and specificity of *Birkat ha-Minim* as an anti-Christian prayer include E. Schürer (*History* 2.462–63); A. Marmorstein ("The Attitude of the Jews towards Early Christianity," *The Expositor* 49 [1923] and "The Amidah of the Public Fast Days," *JQR* n.s. 15 [1925] 409–18); S. Katz, ("Issues," 63–76); and P. Schäfer ("Die sogenannte Synode von Jabne," *Judaica* 31 [1975]).
19. Scholars who take this view include S. Krauss ("The Jews in the Works of the Church Fathers," *JQR* 5 [1893] 122–57; M. Simon (*Verus*, 234–36); W. D. Davies (*The Setting of the Sermon on the Mount* [Cambridge: Cambridge University Press, 1964] 275–79); Frend (*Martyrdom*, 179); and J. L. Martyn (*History and Theology in the Fourth Gospel* [Nashville: Abingdon, 1968] 50–62).
20. Baumgarten, "The Pharisaic *Paradosis*," *HTR* 80 (1987) 63–77.
21. Nilson, "Dialogue," 539.

CHAPTER 10, JEWISH AND CHRISTIAN WRITERS AFTER 150 c.e.

1. H. Chadwick, *Origen Contra Celsum* (Cambridge: Cambridge University Press, 1953) xxiv.
2. See Chadwick, *Contra Celsum* 31, n.3; and J. Maier, *Jesus von Nazareth in der talmüdischen Uberlieferung* (Darmstadt: Wissenschaftliche Buchgesellschaft, 1978). Maier maintains that the Pantera stories in Jewish sources were originally about some anonymous second-century figure and tradition attached them to Jesus only much later.
3. Apparently this image derives from a proverb and means "to fight over nothing." See Plato, *Phaedrus* 260c. Possibly Celsus is employing a double entendre because pagans associated Jews with worship of an ass (*Ag. Ap.* 2.7.79–81) and later, Christians as well (Tertullian, *Ad Nationes* 1.14; the well-known graffito of Jesus as a crucified donkey from the Roman Palatine hill).
4. For a survey of the attitudes toward Jews and Judaism in the Church Fathers, see S. Krauss, "The Jews in the Works of the Church Fathers," *JQR* o.s. 5 (1893) 122–57; 6 (1894) 82–99, 225–61; J. Parkes, *Conflict* 125–95; R. Ruether, *Faith and Fratricide*, 117–82; D. Efroymson, "The Patristic Connection," *Foundations*, ed. A. Davies, 98–117; and A. L. Williams, *Adversus Judaeos*, 3–90.
5. N. de Lange, *Origen and the Jews* (Cambridge: Cambridge University Press, 1976) 85.
6. Matthew 1:18–19 may reflect the charge of illegitimacy. In general the infancy narratives implicitly refute attacks on Jesus' legitimacy and pedigree. See R. E. Brown, *Birth* 143, 534–42.

7. A review of early Jewish sources does not yield any example of the charge of cannibalism or blood-libel against Christians. See B. Visotzky, "Overturning the Lamp," *JJS* 38 (1989) 75–77.

8. W. Frend, "A Note on Terullian and the Jews," *Studia Patristica* 10 (1970) 291–96.

9. Frend, *Martyrdom and Persecution,* 374.

10. See the discussion of the ossuaries at Gamart in North Africa in A.-L. Delattre, *Gamart ou la nécropole juive de Carthage* (Lyons: Mougin-Rusand, 1895); and Y. Le Bohec, "Inscriptions juives et judaisantes de l'Afrique romaines," *Antiquités Africaines* 17 (1981) 183–86, inscriptions 34 and 46.

11. Various surveys of rabbinic references to Christianity with varying conclusions include R. T. Herford, *Christianity in Talmud and Midrash* (London: Williams and Norgate, 1903); H. Strack, *Jesus die Häretiker und die Christen* (Leipzig: Hinrichs, 1910); J. Maier, *Jesus von Nazareth in der talmüdischen Überlieferung* (Darmstadt: Wissenschaftliche Buchgesellschaft, 1978); and L. Schiffman, "At the Crossroads: Tannaitic Perspectives on the Jewish-Christian Schism," *Jewish and Christian Self-Definition* 2 (ed. E. P. Sanders et al.; Philadelphia: Fortress, 1981) 115–56.

12. J. Lightstone, "Christian Anti-Judaism in Its Judaic Mirror," *Anti-Judaism in Early Christianity* (vol. 2; ed. S. Wilson; Waterloo: Wilfred Laurier, 1986) 103–32.

13. Nicodemus is identified as ruler (*archōn*) in John 3:1 and a teacher (*didaskalos*) in 3:10. In 1:38 John translates the term "rabbi" as "teacher." The titles are also equated in Matt 23:8, where a certain antipathy is implied. R. E. Brown (*John,* 74–75) cites epigraphical evidence that *didaskalos* was used as a title in the first century. If it stands for the term "rabbi," then the New Testament usage may have been typical. Nicodemus is never called "rabbi," however. It is possible that rabbis were called teachers, but not all teachers were rabbis. Further, many epigraphical rabbis are not identifiable as ones from the later talmudic materials. They possess neither the same names, nor the same ideas about pagan art. See S. Cohen, "Epigraphical Rabbis," *JQR* 72 (1981–82) 1–17.

14. See A. Segal, *Two Powers in Heaven* (SJLA 25; Leiden: Brill, 1977).

15. See B. Visotzky ("Prolegomenon," *AJSRev* 14 [1989] 47–70) who argues the "Ten Tribes" are Jewish Christians.

16. In Christian literature, this term often means an ascetic, a "monk" or "nun." See "A philosopher-nun" in *New Documents Illustrating Early Christianity,* v. 4 (ed. G. Horsley; N.S.W., Australia: Macquarie University Press, 1987) 257–59.

17. In fact this verse does not appear in our text of the Gospels.

18. For a discussion of the passage and its parody of Matt 5:14–17, see Visotzky, "Lamp," 78–79.

19. See R. Beckwith, "The Date of the Closing of the Canon," *Mikra* (ed. M. J. Mulder; Philadelphia: Fortress, 1988) 58–61.

20. It would surely make a difference if the Christians referred to were

Jewish or Gentile. The Christian healers and interpreters in rabbinic literature are obviously Christian Jews. The women whom Eusebius says are scourged in the synagogue are Christian Jews. The arguments over Jesus' pedigree are probably between Jews and other Jews who believe in Jesus. In many cases, however, we do not know if the Christians are of Jewish or Gentile origin, e.g. the *philosoph* who judges Imma Shalom's case, those whom Tertullian says suffer persecution, or those who are accused of misusing Scripture in Eusebius. Even the Jewish puzzlement over law-observance could be directed at gentile Christians, wondering how they can claim some aspects of Hebrew Scripture but not others. Origen himself is a Gentile; both the incidents he reports may have been between Jews and Christian Jews.

CHAPTER 11, MAJOR TRENDS DETECTED

1. See n. 10 in the previous chapter. Some literary evidence, though of a hagiographic character, supports the idea of Christian martyrs buried in Jewish cemeteries. See the legends of Agricola and Vital in Ambrose, *Exhort. Virg.* 1.1.6-8 (*PL* 16, col. 353) and Paulinus of Milan, *Life of St. Ambrose* 29 (*PL* 14, col. 39) and the legends of Hermes, Aggaeus, Caius, Vincent of Saragossa, and Orantius in *Acta Sanctorum,* Jan. 4, Jan. 22.
2. Haenchen, *Acts,* 272–74.
3. It is not clear if Christians could avoid punishment by declaring themselves outside the Jewish community. They could hardly appeal to the Romans for protection, since they would have had to argue on the basis of their separation from Judaism and give up the protection afforded to the Jews.
4. Christological issues, particularly the resurrection, probably played a role from the very start. The resurrection narratives contain certain apologetic touches that underscore the physical reality of Jesus' resurrection, such as Jesus eating a broiled fish (Luke 24:42–43) or Thomas touching Jesus' side and hands (John 20:27–28). It is hard to know, however, whether or not these touches are responding directly to Jewish objections. See D. Juel (*Messianic Exegesis* [Philadelphia: Fortress, 1988]), who argues that Scriptural reflection on Jesus as the crucified and risen Messiah was the focus of earliest Christian reflection. The tension between this image and the more traditional Jewish eschatological figure produced the distinctive Christian kerygma and earliest attempts at self-definition.
5. R. E. Brown, *The Birth of the Messiah* (Garden City: Doubleday, 1977) 143–53, 517–33.
6. Philo speaks of the planting of virtues by God in the human soul by using as analogies the conception of the patriarchs without human intervention, but the material is highly allegorical (*Cherubim* 12–15). See P. Grelot, "La naissance d'Isaac et celle de Jésus," *NRT* 94 (1972) 462–87, 561–85. Other questionable parallels are discussed by Brown (*Birth* 524–25, n. 21).

7. See R. Scroggs, *Christology in Paul and John* (Philadelphia: Fortress, 1988) 78–84.

8. The notion of testimony books employed by Christians in their debates with Jews, first proposed by J. Rendel Harris, is now largely discarded (*Testimonies* [Cambridge: Cambridge University Press, 1919]). Yet the recurrence of certain verses suggests that certain texts were regularly used in polemics with Jews. See B. Lindars, *New Testament Apologetic* (London: SCM, 1961) 13–31; and C. H. Dodd, *According to the Scriptures* (London: Nisbet, 1952).

9. For other examples of ancient references to Jewish missionary work, see L. Feldman, "Anti-Semitism in the Ancient World," *History and Hate* (ed. D. Berger; Philadelphia: Jewish Publication Society, 1986) 34–36. For an alternate view, see S. McKnight, *Light Among the Gentiles* (Minneapolis: Fortress Press, 1991).

10. If Justin's use of *hairesis* reflects Jewish views of Christians, then Christians may still have been seen as something of a Jewish group, although an illegitimate one (depending on whether *hairesis* means "sect" or "heresy" and whether all heresies rendered people apostates). Further, if Jews needed to be warned about Christians, as Justin also asserts, then there is still significant contact. In other words, the withdrawal of Jews from Christians may still have been in process in Justin's time.

11. L. Festinger, S. Schachter and K. Bach, *Social Pressures in Informal Groups* (Stanford: Stanford University Press, 1950) 103–4.

12. Much of the work on new religious movements has been on such matters as how to keep people out of them or get them back. The underlying assumption seems to be that these movements are by definition illegitimate. See T. Robbins, *Cults, Converts and Charisma* (London: International Sociological Association, 1988).

13. Christians evince a strong claim to be "new" in some non-polemical situations. Paul speaks of the "new creation" in 2 Cor 5:17. For Hebrews, the "new covenant" is central. In polemical situations, however, Christians claimed the antiquity of biblical Israel.

BIBLIOGRAPHY

GENERAL

Bammel, E. "Christian Origins in Jewish Tradition." *NTS* 13 (1967) 317-35.

Baum, G. *The Jews and the Gospel: A Re-examination of the New Testament.* London: Bloomsbury, 1961.

————. *Is the New Testament Anti-Semitic?* Glen Rock: Paulist, 1965.

Benko, S. "The Edict of Claudius of A.D. 49 and the Instigator Chrestus." *ThZ* 25 (1969) 406-18.

————. "Pagan Criticism of Christianity during the First Two Centuries A.D." *ANRW* II/23.2, 1055-1118.

————. *Pagan Rome and the Early Christians.* London: Batsford, 1984.

Bloch, M. *The Historian's Craft.* Manchester: Manchester University Press, 1954.

Bokser, B. "Recent Developments in the Study of Judaism 70-200 C.E." *Second Cent* 3 (1983) 1-68.

Booth, J. *Jesus and the Laws of Purity.* Sheffield: JSOT, 1986.

Brown, R. E. *The Birth of the Messiah.* Garden City: Doubleday, 1977.

Brown, R. E., and J. P. Meier. *Antioch and Rome.* New York: Paulist, 1983.

Callan, T. *Forgetting the Root.* New York: Paulist, 1986.

Carr, E. H. *What Is History?* London: Macmillan, 1961.

Cohen, S. *From the Maccabees to the Mishnah.* Philadelphia: Westminster, 1987.

————. "Anti-Semitism in Antiquity." In *History and Hate.* Ed. D. Berger, 43-47. Philadelphia: Jewish Publication Society, 1986.

Conzelmann, H. *Gentiles, Jews, Christians.* Minneapolis: Augsburg Fortress, 1992.

Davies, A., ed. *Anti-Semitism and the Foundations of Christianity.* New York: Paulist, 1979.

Davies, W. D. *The Setting of the Sermon on the Mount.* Cambridge: Cambridge University Press, 1964.

de Vogué, M. "Sur les nécropole juive de Carthage." *RArch* 13 (1889) 163-86.

Delattre, A.-L. *Gamart ou la nécropole juive de Carthage.* Lyons: Mougin-Rusand, 1895.

Dunn, J. *The Partings of the Ways.* London: SCM, 1991.

Evans, C., and D. Hagner. *Anti-Semitism and Early Christianity.* Minneapolis: Fortress, 1993.

Feldman, L. "Anti-Semitism in the Ancient World." In *History and Hate.* Ed. D. Berger, 15–42. Philadelphia: Jewish Publication Society, 1986.

Festinger, L., S. Schachter, and K. Bach. *Social Pressures in Informal Groups.* Stanford: Stanford University Press, 1950.

Fisher, D. H. *Historian's Fallacies.* London: Routledge and Kegan Paul, 1971.

Fox, R. *Pagans and Christians.* San Francisco: Harper and Row, 1986.

Frend, W. *Martyrdom and Persecution in the Early Church.* Oxford: Blackwell, 1965.

Gadamer, H.-G. *Truth and Method.* New York: Seabury, 1975.

Gager, J. *The Origins of Anti-Semitism.* New York: Oxford University Press, 1983.

Goldstein, M. *Jesus in Jewish Tradition.* New York: Macmillan, 1950.

Gooch, G. P. *History and Historians in the Nineteenth Century.* 2d. ed. London: Longmans, Green, 1952.

Goodman, M. "Jewish Proselytizing in the First Century." In *The Jews among Pagans and Christians.* Ed. J. Lieu, J. North, and T. Rajak. London: Routledge, 1992.

Goppelt, L. *Christentum und Judentum in ersten und zweiten Jahrhundert.* Gütersloh: Bertelsman, 1955.

Grant, R. "The Social Setting of Second Century Christianity." In *Jewish and Christian Self-Definition.* Vol. 1. Ed. E. P. Sanders, A. Baumgarten, and A. Mendelson. Philadelphia: Fortress, 1980.

Guterman, S. *Religious Toleration and Persecution in Ancient Rome.* London: Aiglon, 1951.

Hare, D. *The Theme of Jewish Persecution of Christians in the Gospel of St. Matthew.* Cambridge: Cambridge University Press, 1967.

Harnack, A. *The Mission and Expansion of Christianity.* London: Williams & Norgate, 1904.

Herford, R. T. *Christianity in Talmud and Midrash.* London: Williams & Norgate, 1903.

Horbury, W. "The Benediction of the Minim and early Jewish-Christian Controversy." *JTS* 33 (1982) 19–61.

––––––. "A Critical Examination of the Toledoth Jeshu." Ph.D. diss., Cambridge University, 1970.

Janne, H. "Impulsore Chresto." *Annuaire de l'Institut de Philologie et d'Histoire Orientales* 2 (1934) 531–53.

Johnson, L. "The New Testament Anti-Jewish Slander and the Conventions of Ancient Polemic." *JBL* 108 (1989) 419–41.

Juel, D. *Messianic Exegesis.* Philadelphia: Fortress, 1988.

Juster, J. *Les Juifs dans l'empire Romain.* 2 vols. Paris: Guethner, 1914.

Katz, S. "Issues in the Separation of Judaism and Christianity after 70 C.E.: A Reconsideration." *JBL* 103 (1984) 43–76.

Klassen, W. "Anti-Judaism in Early Christianity: The State of the Question." In *Anti-Judaism in Early Christianity.* 2 vols. Ed. P. Richardson, D. Granskou, and Stephen Wilson, 1.1-19. Waterloo, Laurier, 1986.

Krauss, S. "The Jews in the Works of the Church Fathers." *JQR* 5 (1893) 122–57.

————. *Das Leben Jesu nach jüdischen Quellen*. Berlin: Calvary, 1902.

Le Bohec, Y. "Inscriptions juives et judaisantes de l'Afrique romaines." *Antiquités Africaine* 17 (1981) 165–207.

Le Clerq, H. *Afrique Chrétienne*. Paris: Lecoffre, 1904.

Leon, H. *The Jews of Ancient Rome*. Philadelphia: Jewish Publication Society, 1960.

Lieu, J., J. North, and T. Rajak. *The Jews among Pagans and Christians in the Roman Empire*. London: Routledge, 1992.

Lindars, B. *New Testament Apologetic*. London: SCM, 1961.

McKnight, S. *A Light among the Gentiles*. Minneapolis: Fortress, 1991.

Maclennan, R. *Early Christian Texts on Jews and Judaism*. Brown Judaic Series 194. Atlanta: Scholars Press, 1990.

Maier, J. *Jesus von Nazareth in der talmüdischen Uberlieferung*. Darmstadt: Wissenschaftliche Buchgesellschaft, 1978.

————. *Jüdische Auseinandersetzung mit dem Christentum in der Antike*. Darmstadt: Wissenschaftliche Buchgesellschaft, 1982.

Mason, S. "Pharisaic Dominance before 70." *HTR* 83 (1990) 363–81.

Meagher, J. "As the Twig Is Bent: Anti-Semitism in Greco-Roman and Earliest Christian Times." In *Anti-Semitism and the Foundations of Christianity*. Ed. A. Davies, 1-26. New York: Paulist, 1979.

Meeks, W., and R. Wilken. *Jews and Christians in Antioch in the First Four Centuries of the Common Era*. SBLSBS 13. Missoula: Scholars Press, 1978.

Momigliano, A. *Claudius*. Oxford: Clarendon, 1934.

Monceaux, P. *Histoire littéraire de l'Afrique Chrétienne*. Paris: Ministre de l'Institution Publique et des Beaux-Arts, 1901.

Neusner, J., ed. *Christianity, Judaism and other Greco-Roman Cults*. Festschrift M. Smith. Leiden: Brill, 1975.

Neusner, J., and E. Frerichs, eds. *"To See Ourselves as Others See Us": Christians, Jews and 'Others' in Late Antiquity*. Chico: Scholars Press, 1985.

Nickelsburg, G., and G. MacRae, eds. *Christians among Jews and Gentiles: Essays in Honor of Krister Stendahl on His Sixty-fifth Birthday*. HTR 79 (1986).

Parkes, J. *The Conflict of the Church and the Synagogue*. London: Soncino, 1934.

Rengstorf, K., and S. von Kortzfleisch. *Kirche und Synagoge*. 2 vols. Stuttgart: Klett, 1970.

Riegel, S. "Jewish Christianity: Definitions and Terminology." *NTS* 24 (1978) 410–15.

Robbins, T. *Cults, Converts and Charisma*. London: International Sociological Association, 1988.

Rokeah, D. "Anti-Judaism in Early Christianity." *Immanuel* 16 (1983) 50–64.

————. *Jews, Pagans and Christians in Conflict*. Jerusalem: Magnes, 1982.

Ruether, R. *Faith and Fratricide*. New York: Seabury, 1974.

Sanders, E. P., A. Baumgarten, A. Mendelson, and B. Meyer, eds. *Jewish and Christian Self-Definition*. 3 vols. Philadelphia: Fortress, 1980–85.

Schäfer, P. *Studien zur Geschichte und Theologie des rabbinischen Judentums*. Leiden: Brill, 1978.

Schiffman, L. *Who Was a Jew? Rabbinic and Halakhic Perspectives on the Jewish-Christian Schism*. Hoboken: Ktav, 1985.

Schlatter, A. *Synagoge und Kirche bis zum Bar Kochba-Aufstand*. Stuttgart: 1966.

Segal, A. *Rebecca's Children*. Cambridge: Harvard University Press, 1986.

———. "Studying Judaism with Christian Sources." *USQR* 44 (1991) 267–86.

Setzer, C. "You Invent a Christ!: Christological Claims as Points of Jewish-Christian Dispute." *USQR* 44 (1991) 315–28.

Sevenster, J. *The Roots of Anti-Semitism in the Ancient World*. Leiden: Brill, 1975.

Siker, J. *Disinheriting the Jews*. Louisville: Westminster/John Knox, 1991.

Simon, M. *Verus Israel*. ET. Oxford: Oxford University Press, 1986.

Slingerland, D. "Chrestus-Christus?" In *New Perspectives on Ancient Judaism 4*. Ed. A. Avery-Peck, 133-44. Lanham: University Press of America, 1989.

Smallwood, E. M. *The Jews under Roman Rule*. 2d. ed. Leiden: Brill, 1981.

Snyder, G. *Ante Pacem*. Macon: Mercer, 1985.

Stanton, G. "Aspects of Early Christian-Jewish Polemic and Apologetic." *NTS* 31 (1985) 377–92.

Stern, M. *Greek and Latin Authors on Jews and Judaism*. 2 vols. Jerusalem, Israel Academy of Sciences and Humanities, 1974, 1980.

Visotzky, B. "Prolegomenon to the Study of Jewish Christianities." *AJS Rev* 14 (1989) 47–70.

Whittaker, M. *Jews and Christians: Greco-Roman Views*. Cambridge: Cambridge University Press, 1984.

Wiefel, W. "The Jewish Community in Ancient Rome and the Origins of Roman Christianity." In *The Romans Debate*. Ed. K. Donfried, 100-19. Minneapolis: Augsburg, 1977.

Wild, R. "The Encounter between Pharisaic and Christian Judaism: Some Early Gospel Evidence." *Nov Test* 27 (1985) 105–24.

Wilde, R. *The Treatment of the Jews in the Greek Christian Writers*. Washington: Catholic University Press, 1949.

Wilken, R. "The Christians as the Romans (and Greeks) Saw Them." *Jewish and Christian Self-Definition*, vol. 1. Ed. E.P. Sanders, 100-25. Philadelphia: Fortress, 1980.

———. *The Christians as the Romans Saw Them*. New Haven: Yale University Press, 1984.

Williams, A. L. *Adversus Judaeos*. Cambridge: Cambridge University Press, 1935.

Wilson, S. *Jewish-Christian Relations 70–170 C.E.* Minneapolis: Fortress, forthcoming.

CHAPTER 1, PAULINE AND DEUTERO-PAULINE LETTERS

Amaru, B. "The Killing of the Prophets: Unraveling a Midrash." *HUCA* 54 (1983) 153–80.

Barth, M. *Ephesians*. Garden City: Doubleday, 1974.

Bassler, J., ed. *Pauline Theology*. Minneapolis: Fortress, 1991.

Baur, F. C. "Die beiden Briefe an die Thessalonicher, ihre Unechtheit und Bedeutung für die Parusie Christis." *Theologische Jahrbücher* 14 (1855) 141–68.

———. *Paul, the Apostle of Jesus Christ*. 2d. ed.. London: Williams & Norgate, 1875–76.

Boers, H. "The Form Critical Study of Paul's Letters: 1 Thessalonians as a Case Study." *NTS* 22 (1975–76) 140–58.

Bornkamm, G. "The Letter to the Romans as Paul's Last Will and Testament." In *The Romans Debate*. Ed. K. Donfried, 17-31. Minneapolis: Augsburg, 1977.

———. "The Heresy of Colossians." In *Conflict at Colossae*. Ed. F. Francis and W. Meeks. Missoula: Society of Biblical Literature, 1973.

———. *Paul*. New York: Harper & Row, 1971.

Bruce, F. F. *The Epistles to the Colossians, to Philemon and to the Ephesians*. Grand Rapids: Eerdmans, 1984.

Bultmann, R. *Der Stil der paulinischen Predigt und die kynische-stoische Diatribe*. FRLANT. Göttingen: Vandenhoeck & Ruprecht, 1910.

Collins, R. "A Propos the Integrity of 1 Thessalonians." *ETL* 55 (1979) 67–106.

Coppens, J. "Miscellanées bibliques. LXXX. Une diatribe antijuive dans 1 Thess II, 13-16." *ETL* 51 (1975) 90–95.

Cullmann, O. *Christ and Time*. London: SCM, 1962.

Davies, W. D. *Jewish and Pauline Studies*. Philadelphia: Fortress, 1984.

Dibelius, M., and H. Greeven. *An die Kolosser, Epheser und Philemon*. HZNT. Ed. H. Leitzmann and G. Bornkamm. Tübingen: Mohr (Siebeck), 1953.

Donfried, K. "Paul and Judaism: 1 Thessalonians 2:13-16 as a Test Case." *Interpretation* 38 (1984) 242–53.

———. "False Presuppositions in the Study of Romans." In *The Romans Debate*. Ed. K. Donfried. Minneapolis: Augsburg, 1977.

———. *The Romans Debate*. Minneapolis: Augsburg, 1977.

Eckart, K.-G. "Der zweite echte Brief des Apostels Paulus an die Thessalonicher." *ZTK* 58 (1961) 30–44.

Fee, G. *The First Epistle to the Corinthians*. NICNT. Grand Rapids: Eerdmans, 1987.

Fitzgerald, J. T. *Cracks in Earthen Vessels: An Examination of Hardships in the Corinthian Correspondence*. SBLDS. Atlanta: Scholars Press, 1988.

Fraikin, D. "The Rhetorical Function of the Jews in Romans." In *Anti-Judaism in Early Christianity*. Ed. P. Richardson, 91-105. Waterloo: Wilfred Laurier, 1986.

Francis, F., and W. Meeks. *Conflict at Colossae*. Missoula: Society of Biblical Literature, 1973.

Funk, R. "The Apostolic Parousia: Form and Significance." In *Christian History and Interpretation*. Festschrift J. Knox. Ed. W. Farmer et al., 249-68. Cambridge: Cambridge University Press, 1967.

Gager, J. *The Origins of Anti-Semitism*. Oxford: Oxford University Press, 1985.

Gaston, L. "Paul and the Torah." In *Anti-Semitism and the Foundations of Christianity*. Ed. A. Davies, 48-71. New York: Paulist, 1979.

Haacker, K. "Paulus und das Judentum." *Judaica* 33 (1977-79) 161-77.

Hare, D.R.A. *The Theme of Jewish Persecution of Christians in the Gospel according to St. Matthew*. Cambridge: Cambridge University Press, 1967.

Hodgson, R. "Paul the Apostle and First Century Tribulation Lists." *ZNW* 74 (1983) 59-80.

Hooker, M. "Were there False Teachers in Colossae?" In *Christ and Spirit in the New Testament*. Ed. B. Lindars and S. Smalley, 315-31. Cambridge: Cambridge University Press, 1973.

Horbury, W. "Christ as Brigand in Ancient Anti-Christian Polemic." In *Jesus and the Politics of His Day*. Ed. E. Bammel and C.F.D. Moule. Cambridge; Cambridge University Press, 1984.

Hultgren, A. "Paul's Pre-Christian Persecutions of the Church: Their Purpose, Locale and Nature." *JBL* 95 (1976) 97-111.

Hurd, J. "Paul Ahead of his Time: 1 Thess 2:13-16." In *Anti-Judaism in Early Christianity*. Vol. 1. Ed. P. Richardson et al., 21-36. Waterloo, Can.: Wilfred Laurier, 1986.

Jewett, R. *The Thessalonian Correspondence*. Philadelphia: Fortress, 1986.

Käsemann, E. *Commentary on Romans*. Grand Rapids: Eerdmans, 1980.

_____ . "Ephesians and Acts." In *Studies in Luke-Acts*. Festschrift P. Schubert. Ed. L. Keck and J. L. Martyn, 288-297. Nashville: Abingdon, 1966.

Knopf, R. *Das nachapostolische Zeitalter: Geschichte der christlichen Gemeinden vom Beginn der Flavierdynastie bis zum Ende Hadrians*. Tübingen: Mohr, 1905.

Koester, H. "1 Thessalonians-Experiment in Christian Writing." In *Continuity and Discontinuity in Church History*. Festschrift D. Williams. Ed. F. Church and T. George, 33-44. Leiden: Brill, 1979.

_____ . "Apostel und Gemeinde in den Briefen an die Thessalonicher." In *Kirche*. Festschrift G. Bornkamm. Ed. D. Lührmann and G. Strecker, 287-98. Tübingen: Mohr (Siebeck), 1980.

_____ . *Introduction to the New Testament*. Vol. 2. Philadelphia: Fortress, 1982.

Lightfoot, J. "The Colossian Heresy." In *Conflict at Colossae*. Ed. F. Francis and W. Meeks, 13-57. Missoula: Society of Biblical Literature, 1973.

Lohse, E. *Colossians and Philemon*. Philadelphia: Fortress, 1971.

Luz, U. *Das Geschichtsverständnis des Paulus*. Kaiser: München, 1968.

Lyonnet, S. "Paul's Adversaries in Colossae." In *Conflict at Colossae*. Ed. F. Francis and W. Meeks, 147-61. Missoula: Society of Biblical Literature, 1973.

Manson, T. W. "St. Paul's Letter to the Romans- and Others." *BJRL* 31(1948) 224-40. Reprinted in K. Donfried, *The Romans Debate* 1-16.

Moule, C.F.D. *The Epistles of Paul the Apostle to the Colossians and to Philemon*. Cambridge: Cambridge University Press, 1957.

Munck, J. *Christ and Israel: An Interpretation of Romans 9-11*. Philadelphia: Fortress, 1967.

_____ . *Paul and the Salvation of Mankind*. London: SCM, 1959.

Mussner, F. *Der Brief an die Kolosser.* Düsseldorf: Patmos, 1965.

Okeke, G. "1 Thess 2:13-16: The Fate of the Unbelieving Jews." *NTS* 27 (1980) 127-36.

Orchard, J. "Thessalonians and the Synoptic Gospels." *Biblica* 19 (1938) 19-42.

Pearson, B. "I Thessalonians 2:13-16: A Deutero-Pauline Interpolation." *HTR* 64 (1971) 79-94.

Percy, E. *Die Probleme der Kolosser-und-Epheserbriefe.* Lund: Gleerup, 1946.

Pobee, J. *Persecution and Martyrdom in the Theology of Paul.* JSNT 6. Sheffield: JSOT, 1985.

Richardson, P. *Israel in the Apostolic Church.* Cambridge: Cambridge University Press, 1969.

Richardson, P., ed. *Anti-Judaism in Early Christianity.* 2 vols. Waterloo, Can: Wilfred Laurier, 1986.

Rigaux, B. *Les Epitres aux Thessaloniciens.* Paris: Gabalda, 1956.

Roetzel, C. *The Letters of Paul: Conversations in Context.* 2d. ed. Atlanta: John Knox, 1982.

Sanders, E. P. *Paul, the Law, and the Jewish People.* Philadelphia: Fortress, 1983.

Schippers, R. "The Pre-Synoptic Tradition in 1 Thessalonians 2:13-16." *NovT* 8 (1966) 223-34.

Schlier, H. *Christus und die Kirche im Epheserbriefe.* Tübingen: Mohr, 1930.

———. *Der Brief an die Epheser.* 2d. ed. Düsseldorf: Patmos, 1958.

———. *Principalities and Powers in the New Testament.* New York: Herder, 1961.

Schoeps, H.-J. "Die jüdischen Prophetenmorde." In *Aus frühchristlicher Zeit,* 126-43. Tübingen: Mohr (Siebeck), 1950.

Schmithals, W. "The Historical Situation of the Thessalonian Epistles." In *Paul and the Gnostics,* 128-318. Nashville: Abingdon, 1972.

———. *Der Römerbrief als historisches Problem.* Gütersloh: Mohn, 1975.

Schubert, P. *Form and Function of the Pauline Thanksgivings.* Berlin: Töpelmann, 1939.

Schweizer, E. *The Letter to the Colossians.* Minneapolis: Augsburg, 1976.

Scroggs, R. "The Political Dimensions of Anti-Judaism in the New Testament." Unpublished paper.

Steck, O. *Israel und das gewaltsame Geschick der Propheten.* Neukirchen-Vluyn: Neukirchener, 1967.

Stendahl, K. "Paul and the Introspective Conscience of the West," In *Paul among Jews and Gentiles.* 78-96. Philadelphia: Fortress, 1976.

Stuhlmacher, P. "Der Abfassungszweck des Römerbrief." *ZNW* 77 (1986) 180-93.

Tcherikover, V. *Hellenistic Civilization and the Jews.* New York: Atheneum, 1974.

Weatherly, J. "The Authenticity of 1 Thessalonians 2.13-16: Additional Evidence." *JSNT* 42 (1991) 79-98.

Whittaker, M. *Jews and Christians: Graeco-Roman Views.* Cambridge: Cambridge University Press, 1984.

Wiefel, W. "The Jewish Community in Ancient Rome and the Origins of

Roman Christianity." *The Romans Debate.* Ed. K. Donfried. Minneapolis: Augsburg, 1977.

Wilckens, U. "Über Abfassungszweck und Aufbau des Römerbriefs." In *Rechtfertigung als Freiheit,* 110-70. Neukirchen-Vluyn: Neukirchener, 1974.

Yates, R. "Colossians and Gnosis." *JSNT* 27 (1986) 49–68.

Zeller, D. *Juden und Heiden in der Mission des Paulus.* Stuttgart: Katholisches Bibelwerk, 1973.

CHAPTER 2, THE SYNOPTIC GOSPELS

Aichinger, H. "Quellenkritische Untersuchung der Perikope vom Ahrenraufen am Sabbat. Mark 2:23-28 par Matt 12:1-8 par Luk 6:1-5." In *Jesus in der Verkündigung der Kirche.* Ed. A. Fuchs, 110-53. Freistadt: Plochl, 1976.

Anderson, H. *The Gospel of Mark.* London: Marshall, Morgan and Scott, 1976.

Baumgarten, A. "The Pharisaic Paradosis." *HTR* 80 (1987) 63–77.

———. "*Korban* and the Pharisaic Paradosis." *JANES* 16–17 (1984–85) 5–17.

Beare, F. *The Gospel according to Matthew.* Oxford: Blackwell, 1981.

Blomberg, C. *The Historical Reliability of the Gospels.* Downers Grove, Ill: Inter-Varsity, 1987.

Booth, J. *Jesus and the Laws of Purity.* JSNT 13. Sheffield: JSOT, 1986.

Bowker, J. *Jesus and the Pharisees.* Cambridge: Cambridge University Press, 1973.

Bultmann, R. *The History of the Synoptic Tradition.* 3d ed. New York: Harper and Row, 1963.

Craig, W. "The Guard at the Tomb." *NTS* 30 (1984) 273–81.

Ebeling, H. "Die Fastenfrage (Mark 2:18-22)." *TSK* 108 (1937–38) 387–96.

Fitzmyer, J. *The Gospel according to Luke.* 2 vols. Garden City: Doubleday, 1981–85.

Garland, D. *The Intention of Matthew 23.* Leiden: Brill, 1979.

Gnilka, J. *Das Matthäusevangelium.* Freiburg: Herder, 1986.

———. *Das Evangelium nach Markus,* vol. 2. Zürich: Benziger, 1979.

Haenchen, E. *Der Weg Jesu.* Berlin: de Gruyter, 1968.

———. "Matthaus 23." *ZTK* 48 (1951) 38–63.

Hare, D. *The Theme of Jewish Persecution of Christians in the Gospel according to St. Matthew.* Cambridge: Cambridge University Press, 1967.

Hartmann, L. *Prophecy Interpreted: The Formation of Some Jewish Apocalyptic Texts and the Eschatological Discourse of Mark 13.* Coniectanea Biblica, New Testament Series 1. Lund: Gleerup, 1966.

Hengel, M. "Mark 7:3 *pygmē:* die Geschichte einer exegetischen Aporie und der Versuch ihrer Lösung." *ZNW* 9 (1969) 182–98.

Hultgren, A. *Jesus and his Adversaries.* Minneapolis: Augsburg, 1979.

Kee, A. "The Question about Fasting." *NT* 11 (1969) 161–73.

Kee, H. C. *Community of the New Age: Studies in Mark's Gospel.* Philadelphia: Westminster, 1977.

———. "Mark's Gospel in Recent Research." *Int* 32 (1978) 353–68.

Kilpatrick, G. *The Origins of the Gospel according to St. Matthew.* Oxford: Clarendon, 1946.

Kosmala, H. "His Blood on Us and Our Children." *ASTI* 7 (1968–69) 94–126.

Krauss, S. *Das Leben Jesu nach jüdischen Quellen.* Berlin: Calvary, 1902.

Kümmel, W. *Introduction to the New Testament.* Nashville: Abingdon, 1975.

Lamprecht, J. *Die Redaktion der Markus-Apokalypse.* Analecta Biblica 28. Rome: Pontifical Biblical Institute, 1967.

Levine, A. J. *The Social and Ethnic Dimensions of Matthean Salvation History.* New York: Mellen, 1988.

Lohmeyer, E. *Das Evangelium des Markus.* Göttingen: Vandenhoeck & Ruprecht, 1954.

———. *Das Evangelium des Matthäus.* Göttingen: Vandenhoeck & Ruprecht, 1956.

Lührmann, D. "Die Pharisäer und die Schriftgelehrten im Markusevangelium." *ZNW* 78 (1987) 169–85.

Mack, B. *A Myth of Innocence.* Philadelphia: Fortress, 1988.

Malina, B. *Calling Jesus Names.* Sonoma, CA: Polebridge, 1988.

Marcus, J. *The Mystery of the Kingdom of God. The Marcan Parable Chapter (Mark 4:1-34) and the Theology of the Gospel as a Whole.* Ph.D. thesis, Columbia University, 1985.

Marxsen, W. *Mark the Evangelist.* Nashville: Abingdon, 1969.

Meier, J. *Law and History in Matthew's Gospel.* Rome: Biblical Institute, 1976.

———. *Matthew.* Wilmington, DE: Glazier, 1980.

Montefiore, C. *The Synoptic Gospels.* London: Macmillan, 1909.

Morgenthaler, R. *Statistische Synopse.* Zürich: Gotthelf, 1971.

Muddiman, J. "Jesus and Fasting." *Jésus aux origines de la Christologie.* Ed. J. Dupont, 271-81. Leuven: Leuven University Press, 1975.

Neusner, J. *The Pharisees: Rabbinic Perspectives.* Leiden: Brill, 1973.

———. "The Fellowship (Haburah) in the Second Jewish Commonwealth." *HTR* 53 (1960) 125-42.

Nierynck, F. *The Minor Agreements of Matthew and Luke Against Mark.* Leuven: Leuven University Press, 1974.

Nineham, D. *Saint Mark.* Philadelphia: Westminster, 1963.

Oppenheimer, A. *The 'Am Ha-Aretz.* Leiden: Brill, 1977.

Perrin, N., and D. Duling. *The New Testament: An Introduction.* New York: Harcourt, Brace, Jovanovich, 1982.

Rivkin, E. "Defining the Pharisees: The Tannaitic Sources." *HUCA* 40 (1969) 205-49.

Robbins, V. "The Chreia," *Greco-Roman Literature and the New Testament.* SBLSBS 21. Atlanta: Scholars Press, 1988.

———. "Pronouncement Stories from a Rhetorical Perspective." *Forum* 4 (1988) 3-32.

Sanders, E. *The Tendencies of the Synoptic Tradition.* Cambridge: Cambridge University Press, 1969.

———. *Paul, the Law, and the Jewish People.* Philadelphia: Fortress, 1983.

Sanders, Jack. *The Jews in Luke-Acts.* Philadelphia: Fortress, 1987.

Schweizer, E. *The Good News according to Mark.* Atlanta: John Knox, 1970.

Tannehill, R. "Introduction: The Pronouncement Story and its Types." *Semeia* 20 (1981) 1–14.

———. "Varieties of Synoptic Pronouncement Stories." *Semeia* 20 (1981) 101–19.

Trocmé, E. *The Formation of the Gospel according to Mark.* Philadelphia: Westminster, 1975.

von Campenhausen, H. "The Events of Easter and the Empty Tomb." In *Tradition and Life in the Church,* 42-89. London: Collins, 1968.

CHAPTER 3, THE BOOK OF ACTS

Anderson, G. *Ancient Fiction: The Novel in the Greco-Roman World.* Totowa, NJ: Barnes and Noble, 1984.

Brawley, R. *The Pharisees in Luke-Acts.* Ph.D. thesis, Princeton Theological Seminary, 1978.

———. *Luke-Acts and the Jews.* SBL Monograph Series 33. Atlanta: Scholars Press, 1987.

Bruce, F. F. "Chronological Questions in the Acts of the Apostles." *BJRL* 68 (1986) 273–95.

———. *The Acts of the Apostles: The Greek Text with Introduction and Commentary.* London: Tyndale, 1951.

Cadbury, H. J. *The Book of Acts in History.* New York: Harper & Brothers, 1955.

———. *The Making of Luke-Acts.* New York: Macmillan, 1927.

———. *The Style and Literary Method of Luke.* HTS 6. Cambridge: Harvard University Press, 1920.

———, and K. Lake. *The Beginnings of Christianity,* vols. 4–5. Ed. F. Foakes Jackson and K. Lake. London: Macmillan, 1933.

Conzelmann, H. *Die Apostelgeschichte.* HZNT 7. Tübingen: Mohr (Siebeck), 1963.

———. *Heiden-Juden-Christen. Auseinandersetzung in der Literatur der hellenistisch-römischen Zeit.* Tübingen: Mohr (Siebeck), 1981.

Dibelius, M. *Aufsätze zur die Apostelgeschichte.* FRLANT 60. Göttingen: Vandenhoeck & Ruprecht, 1951.

Donelson, L. "Cult Histories and the Sources of Acts." *Biblica* 68 (1987) 1–21.

Dunn, J. *Unity and Diversity in the New Testament.* London: SCM, 1977.

Dupont, J. *Les Sources du Livre des Actes. état de la question.* London: Darton, Longman & Todd, 1964.

Feldman, L. "Jewish 'Sympathizers' in Classical Literature and Inscriptions." *TAPA* 81 (1950) 200–208.

Fitzmyer, J. *The Gospel according to Luke (I-IX).* Garden City: Doubleday, 1981.

———. "Paul." *NJBC* 1329-37.

Gasque, W. *A History of the Criticism of the Acts of the Apostles.* Tübingen: Mohr (Siebeck), 1975.

George, A. "Israel dans l'oeuvre de Luc." *RB* 75 (1968) 481–525.

Guterman, L. *Religious Toleration and Persecution in Ancient Rome.* London: Aiglon, 1951.

Harnack, A. *The Acts of the Apostles.* New Testament Studies 3. New York: Putnam's, 1909.

Haenchen, E. *The Acts of the Apostles.* Philadelphia: Westminster, 1971.

————. "The Book of Acts as Source Material for the History of Early Christianity." *Studies in Luke-Acts.* Ed. L. Keck, and J. L. Martyn, 258-78. Philadelphia: Fortress, 1966.

Hengel, M. *Acts and the History of Earliest Christianity.* Philadelphia: Fortress, 1979.

————. *Die Zeloten.* Leiden: Brill, 1961.

Hill, C. *Hellenists and Hebrews.* Minneapolis: Fortress, 1993.

Jackson, F. Foakes, and K. Lake. *The Beginnings of Christianity,* 5 vols. London: Macmillan, 1922-33.

Jervell, J. "The Problem of Traditions in Acts." In *Luke and the People of God,* 19-39. Minneapolis: Augsburg, 1972.

————. "The Divided People of God." In *Luke and the People of God,* 41-74. Minneapolis: Augsburg, 1972.

Judge, E. "The Decrees of Caesar at Thessalonica." *Ref Theol Rev* 30 (1971) 1-7.

Katz, S. "Issues in the Separation of Judaism and Christianity after 70 C.E.: A Reconsideration." *JBL* 103 (1984) 43-76.

Keck, L., and J. L. Martyn. *Studies in Luke-Acts.* festschrift P. Schubert. Nashville: Abingdon, 1966.

Knox, J. *Chapters in a Life of Paul.* New York: Abingdon, 1950.

————. "Acts and the Pauline Letter Corpus." In *Studies in Luke-Acts.* Ed. L. Keck and J. L. Martyn 279-87. Philadelphia: Fortress, 1966.

Koester, H. *Introduction to the New Testament,* vol. 2. Philadelphia: Fortress, 1982.

Kraabel, A. T. "The Disappearance of the God-fearers." *Numen* 28 (1981) 113-26.

Lake, K., and H. J. Cadbury. *The Beginnings of Christianity,* vols. 4-5. Ed. F. Foakes Jackson and K. Lake. London: Macmillan, 1933.

Leon, H. *The Jews of Ancient Rome.* Philadelphia: JPS, 1960.

Levine, L. *The Synagogue in Late Antiquity.* Philadelphia: ASOR, 1987.

Loisy, A. *Les Actes des Apôtres.* Paris: Nourry, 1920.

Lüdemann, G. *Paul, Apostle to the Gentiles: Studies in Chronology.* Philadelphia: Fortress, 1984.

Maddox, R. *The Purpose of Luke-Acts.* Edinburgh: Clark, 1982.

Mattill, A. "The Date and Purpose of Luke-Acts: Rackham Reconsidered." *CBQ* 40 (1978) 335-50.

————. *A Classified Bibliography of Literature on the Acts of the Apostles.* Leiden: Brill, 1966.

————. "Luke as a Historian in Criticism since 1840." Ph.D diss., Vanderbilt University, 1959.

Munck, J. *The Acts of the Apostles.* Garden City: Doubleday, 1967.

Nock, A. "Paul and the Magus." In *The Beginnings of Christianity,* 5:164-88. London: Macmillan, 1933.

Norden, E. *Agnostos Theos*. Leipzig: Teubner, 1913.

Pervo, R. *Profit with Delight*. Philadelphia: Fortress, 1987.

Ramsay, W. *St. Paul the Traveler and Roman Citizen*. New York: Putnam's, 1896.

———. *The Bearing of Recent Discovery on the Trustworthiness of the New Testament*. Grand Rapids: Baker, 1953.

Reardon, B. "The Second Sophistic and the Novel." *Approaches to the Second Sophistic*. Ed. G. Bowersock, 23-29. University Park: Pennsylvania State University, 1974.

Reynolds, J., and R. Tannenbaum. *Jews and God-fearers at Aphrodisias*. Cambridge, Eng.: Cambridge Philological Society, 1987.

Robbins, V. "The We-passages in Acts and Ancient Sea Voyages." *BR* 20 (1975) 5–18.

Sanders, Jack T. *The Jews in Luke-Acts*. Philadelphia: Fortress, 1987.

———. "Who Is a Jew and Who Is a Gentile in Acts." *NTS* 37 (1991) 434–55.

Schneider, G. *Die Apostelgeschichte* 2 vols.. Freiburg: Herder, 1980-82.

Schwartz, J. "Ben Stada and Peter in Lydda." *JSJ* 21 (1990) 1-18.

Sherwin-White, A. *Roman Society and Roman Law in the New Testament*. Oxford: Clarendon, 1963.

Slingerland, D. "Chrestus: Christus?" *New Perspectives on Ancient Judaism*. Ed. A. Avery-Peck, 133-44. Lanham: University Press of America, 1989.

———. "The Composition of Acts: Some Redaction-Critical Observations." *JAAR* 56 (1988) 99–113.

Smith, M. *Jesus the Magician*. New York: Harper and Row, 1978.

Tiede, D. *Prophecy and History in Luke-Acts*. Philadelphia: Fortress, 1980.

Trocmé, E. *Les livres des Acts et l'histoire*. Paris: Presses universitaires de France, 1957.

Tyson, J. "The Jewish Public in Luke-Acts." *NTS* 30 (1984) 574–83.

———. ed. *Luke-Acts and the Jewish People*. Minneapolis: Augsburg, 1988.

Vielhauer, P. "On the Paulinism of Acts." *Studies in Luke-Acts*. Ed. L. Keck and J. L. Martyn, 33-50. Philadelphia: Fortress, 1966.

Wiefel, W. "The Jewish Community in Ancient Rome and the Origins of Roman Christianity." *The Romans Debate*. Ed. K. Donfried, 100-19. Minneapolis: Augsburg, 1977.

Ziesler, J. "Luke and the Pharisees." *NTS* 25 (1978–79) 146–57.

CHAPTER 4, THE GOSPEL OF JOHN

Ashton, J. "The Identity and Function of the *Ioudaioi* in the Fourth Gospel." *NovT* 27 (1985) 40–75.

Barrett, C. K. *The Gospel of John and Judaism*. London: SPCK, 1975.

———. *The Gospel according to St. John*, 2d. ed. Philadelphia: Westminster, 1978.

Bassler, J. "The Galileans: A Neglected Factor in Johannine Community Research." *CBQ* 43 (1981) 243–57.

Brown, R. E. *The Gospel according to John (I-XXI)*, 2 vols. AB. Garden City: Doubleday, 1966-70.

_____ . *The Community of the Beloved Disciple.* New York: Paulist, 1979.

_____ . "The Problem of Historicity in John." *CBQ* 24 (1962) 1–14.

Cohen, S.J.D. "The Significance of Yavneh: Pharisees, Rabbis and the End of Jewish Sectarianism." *HUCA* 55 (1984) 27–53.

Culpepper, R. A. "The Gospel of John and the Jews." *RevExp* 84 (1987) 273–88.

Davies, W. D. *The Setting of the Sermon on the Mount.* Cambridge: Cambridge University Press, 1964.

Fortna, R. *The Gospel of Signs.* Cambridge: Cambridge University Press, 1970.

Fuller, R. "'The Jews' in the Fourth Gospel." *Dialog* 16 (1977) 31–37.

Grässer, E. "Die antijüdische Polemik im Johannesevangelium." *NTS* 11 (1964–65) 74–90.

Haenchen, E. "Aus der Literatur zum Johannesevangelium 1929-1956." *TRev* N.F. 23 (1955) 295–335.

Hare, D.R.A. *The Theme of Jewish Persecution of Christians in the Gospel according to St. Matthew.* Cambridge: Cambridge University Press, 1967.

Heinemann, J. *Prayer in the Talmud.* Berlin: de Gruyter, 1977.

Horbury, W. "The Benediction of the *Minim* and early Jewish-Christian Controversy." *JTS* 33 (1982) 19–61.

Kimelman, R. "*Birkat Ha-Minim* and the Lack of Evidence for an Anti-Christian Jewish Prayer in Late Antiquity." *Jewish and Christian Self-Definition,* vol. 2. Ed. E. P. Sanders, A. Baumgarten, and A. Mendelson, 226–44. Philadelphia: Fortress, 1981.

Kysar, R. *The Fourth Evangelist and His Gospel: An Examination of Contemporary Scholarship.* Minneapolis: Augsburg, 1975.

_____ . "The Gospel of John in Current Research." *RelSRev* 9 (1983) 314–23.

_____ . *John.* Minneapolis: Augsburg, 1986.

Leistner, R. *Antijudaismus im Johannesevangelium?.* Bern: Lang, 1974.

Lindars, B. *The Gospel of John.* NCBC. Grand Rapids: Eerdmans, 1972.

_____ . "The Persecution of Christians in John 15:18—16:4a." In *Suffering and Martyrdom in the New Testament.* Ed. W. Horbury and B. McNeil, 48-69. Cambridge: Cambridge University Press, 1981.

Malatesta, E. *St. John's Gospel 1920-1965.* Analecta Biblica 32. Rome: Pontifical Biblical Institute, 1967.

Martyn, J. L. *History and Theology in the Fourth Gospel,* 2d. ed. Nashville: Abingdon, 1979.

_____ . "Glimpses into the History of the Johannine Community." In *L'Evangile de Jean.* Ed. M. de Jonge, 149-75. Gembloux: Duculot, 1977.

Meeks, W. "Am I a Jew?-Johannine Christianity and Judaism." In *Christianity, Judaism and Other Greco-Roman Cults: Studies for Morton Smith at Sixty,* pt. 1. Ed. J. Neusner 163-86. Leiden: Brill, 1975.

_____ . "The Man from Heaven in Johannine Sectarianism." *JBL* 91 (1972) 44–72.

Moda, A. "Quarto Vangelo 1966-72. Una selezione bibliografica." *RevistB* 22 (1974) 53–86.

Overman, J. A. *Matthew's Gospel and Formative Judaism.* Minneapolis: Fortress, 1990.

Painter, J. "John 9 and the Interpretation of the Fourth Gospel." *JSNT* 28 (1986) 31–61.

———. "The Farewell Discourses and the History of Johannine Christianity." *NTS* 27 (1980–81) 525–43.

Pancaro, S. *The Law in the Fourth Gospel.* Supp. to *NovT*Sup 42. Leiden: Brill, 1975.

Schäfer, P. "Die sogenannte Synode von Jabne." *Judaica* 31 (1975) 54–64, 116–24.

Schnackenburg, R. *The Gospel according to St. John.* New York: Herder and Herder, 1968.

Scroggs, R. *Christology in Paul and John.* Philadelphia: Fortress, 1988.

Smith, D. M. *Johannine Christianity.* Columbia, SC: University of South Carolina, 1984.

———. "The Life Setting of the Gospel of John." *RevExp* 85 (1988) 433–44.

Stemberger, G. "Die sogenannte Synode von Jabne." *Kairos* 19 (1977) 14–21.

Thyen, H. "Aus der Literatur zum Johannesevangelium." *TRev* 39 (1974) 1–69, 222–52, 289–330; 42 (1977) 211–70.

Townsend, J. "The Gospel of John and the Jews: The Story of a Religious Divorce." In *Anti-Semitism and the Foundations of Christianity.* Ed. A. Davies, 72-97. New York: Paulist, 1979.

von Wahlde U. "The Johannine 'Jews': A Critical Survey." *NTS* 28 (1982) 33–60.

Wengst, K. *Bedrängte Gemeinde und verherrlichter Christus.* Biblische Theologische Studien 5. Neukirchen-Vluyn, 1981.

Whitacre, R. *Johannine Polemic.* SBL Dissertation Series 67. Chico: Scholars Press, 1982.

CHAPTER 5, REVELATION

Applebaum, S. "The Organization of the Jewish Communities in the Diaspora." In *The Jewish People in the First Century.* Ed. S. Safrai & M. Stern, in cooperation with D. Flusser & W. van Unnik. Compendia Rerum Judaicarum ad Novum Testamentum. Assen: van Gorcum, 1974.

Aune, D. "The Social Matrix of the Apocalypse of John." *BR* 26 (1981) 16–32.

Cadoux, C. *Ancient Smyrna.* Oxford: Blackwell, 1938.

Charles, R. H. *The Revelation of St. John.* ICC. New York: Scribner's, 1920.

Charlesworth, M. P. "Some Observations on Ruler-Cult Especially in Rome." *HTR* 28 (1935) 26–42.

D' Aragon, J. L. "The Apocalypse." *JBC* 64 467–93.

Jones, A.H.M. *The Criminal Courts of the Roman Republic and Principate.* Totowa: Rowman and Littlefield, 1972.

Karrer, M. *Die Johannesoffenbarung als Brief.* Göttingen: Vandenhoeck & Ruprecht, 1986.

Keresztes, P. "The Jews, the Christians, and Emperor Domitian." *VC* 27 (1973) 1–28.

Lohmeyer, E. *Die Offenbarung des Johannes.* Tübingen: Mohr (Siebeck), 1953.

Mattingly, H. *Coins of the Roman Empire in the British Museum.* London: Printed by order of the Trustees, 1936.

Ramsay, W. M. *The Letters to the Seven Churches of Asia.* New York: Hodder & Stoughton, 1914.

Schüssler-Fiorenza, E. *Invitation to the Book of Revelation.* Garden City: Doubleday, 1981.

Sherwin-White, A. *The Letters of Pliny: A Historical and Social Commentary.* Oxford: Blackwell, 1966.

Scott, K. *The Imperial Cult under the Flavians.* New York: Arno, 1975.

Smallwood, E. M. *The Jews under Roman Rule,* 2d. ed. Leiden: Brill, 1981.

————. "Domitian's Attitude Towards Jews and Judaism." *Classical Philology* 51 (1956) 1–13.

Stern, M. *Greek and Latin Authors on Jews and Judaism,* 3 vols. Jerusalem: Israel Academy of Sciences and Humanities, 1974–84.

Sweet, J.P.M. "Maintaining the Testimony of Jesus: the Suffering of Christians in the Revelation of John." In *Suffering and Martyrdom in the New Testament.* Ed. W. Horbury and B. McNeil, 101–17. Cambridge: Cambridge University Press, 1981.

Thompson, L. "A Sociological Analysis of Tribulation in the Apocalypse of John." *Semeia* 36 (1986) 147–74.

Visotzky, B. "Overturning the Lamp." *JJS* 38 (1987) 72–80.

Wardman, A. *Religion and Statecraft Among the Romans.* Baltimore: Johns Hopkins University Press, 1982.

Wilken, R. *The Christians as the Romans Saw Them.* New Haven: Yale University Press, 1984.

Yarbro Collins, A. *The Apocalypse.* NT Message 22. Wilmington, DE: Glazier, 1979.

————. "The Political Perspective of the Revelation to John." *JBL* 96 (1977) 241–56.

————. "Dating the Apocalypse of John." *BR* 26 (1981) 33–45.

————. *Crisis and Catharsis.* Philadelphia: Westminster, 1984.

————. "Insiders and Outsiders in the Book of Revelation and Its Social Context." In *To See Ourselves As Others See Us.* Ed. J. Neusner & E. Frerichs, 187–218. Chico, CA: Scholars Press, 1985.

————. "Vilification and Self-Definition in the Book of Revelation." *HTR* 79 (1986) 308–20.

CHAPTER 6, JOSEPHUS

Attridge, H. *The Interpretation of Biblical History in the Antiquitates Judaicae of Flavius Josephus.* Missoula: Scholars Press, 1976.

Bammel, E. "Zum Testimonium Flavianum." In *Josephus-Studien.* Ed. O. Betz et al. Göttingen: Vandenhoeck & Ruprecht, 1974.

Baras, Z. "The Testimonium Flavianum and the Martyrdom of James." In *Josephus, Judaism and Christianity.* Ed. L. Feldman and G. Hata. Detroit: Wayne State University Press, 1987.

———. "The *Testimonium Flavianum.* The State of Recent Scholarship." In *Society and Religion in the Second Temple Period,* 378-85. World History of the Jewish People 8. Jerusalem: Massada, 1977.

Barish, D. "The *Autobiography* of Josephus and the Hypothesis of a Second Edition of his *Antiquities.*" HTR 7 (1978) 61-75.

Baumgarten, A. "The Name of the Pharisees." *JBL* 102 (1983) 411-28.

Bell, A. "Josephus the Satirist? A Clue to the Original Form of the Testimonium Flavianum." *JQR* 67 (1976) 16-22.

Birdsall, J. N. "The Continuing Enigma of Josephus' Testimony about Jesus." *BJRL* 67 (1985) 609-22.

Brandon, S. *The Fall of Jerusalem and the Christian Church.* London: SPCK, 1957.

———. "The Death of James the Just: A New Interpretation." In *Studies in Mysticism and Religion.* Festschrift G. Scholem. Ed. E. Urbach et al. Jerusalem: Magnes, 1967.

Broshi, M. "The Credibility of Josephus." *JJS* 33 (1982) 379-84.

Cohen, S. *Josephus in Galilee and Rome: His Vita and Development as a Historian.* Leiden: Brill, 1979.

Cornfeld, G., B. Mazar, and P. Maier. *The Jewish War.* Grand Rapids: Zondervan, 1982. Contains appendix on *TF.*

Drexler, H. "Untersuchungen zur Josephus und zur Geschichte des judische Aufstandes 66-70." *Klio* 19 (1925) 277-312.

Dubarle, A.-M. "Le témoignage de Josephe sur Jesus d'apres la tradition indirecte." *RB* 80 (1973) 481-513.

Eisler, R. *The Messiah Jesus and John the Baptist according to Flavius Josephus' Recently Rediscovered 'Capture of Jerusalem'.* London: Methuen, 1931; German original 1929.

———. "Flavius Josephus on Jesus called the Christ." *JQR* 21 (1930-31) 1-60.

Feldman, L. *Josephus and Modern Scholarship(1937-1980).* Berlin; New York: de Gruyter, 1984.

———. "Scholarship on Josephus." *ANRW* II 21.2 (1984) 763-862.

———. "The *Testimonium Flavianum*: The State of the Question." In *Christological Perspectives.* Ed. R. Berkey and S. Edwards. New York: Pilgrim, 1982.

———, and G. Hata, eds., *Josephus, Judaism and Christianity.* Detroit: Wayne State University Press, 1987.

Heinemann, I. "Josephus' Method in the Presentation of *Jewish Antiquities* Zion 5 (1940) 180-203 (Heb.).

Hoffman, R. *Jesus Outside the Gospels.* Buffalo: Prometheus, 1984.

Laqueur, R. *Der jüdische Historiker Flavius Josephus.* Giessen: 1920; repr. Darmstadt: Wissenschaftliche Buchgesellschaft, 1970.

Lieberman, S. *Greek in Jewish Palestine.* New York: Jewish Theological Seminary, 1965.

――――. *Hellenism in Jewish Palestine.* New York: Jewish Theological Seminary, 1962.

Maier, J. *Jesus von Nazareth in der talmüdischen Ueberlieferung.* Darmstadt: Wissenschaftliche Buchgesellschaft, 1978.

Meier, J. "Jesus in Josephus: A Modest Proposal." *CBQ* 52 (1990) 76–103.

Neusner, J. *Rabbinic Traditions about the Pharisees before 70,* 3 vols. Leiden: Brill, 1971.

Nodet, E. "Jesus et Jean-Baptiste selon Josephe." *RB* (July, Oct 1985) 321–48, 497–524.

Pines, S. *An Arabic Version of the Testimonium Flavianum.* Jerusalem: Israel Academy of Sciences and Humanities, 1971.

Rajak, T. *Josephus: The Historian and His Society.* London: Duckworth, 1982.

Rengstorf, K. *A Complete Concordance to Flavius Josephus,* 2 vols. and suppl. Leiden: Brill, 1973f.

Rhoads, D. *Israel in Revolution.* Philadelphia: Fortress, 1976.

Schalit, A. *Namenwörterbuch zu Flavius Josephus.* Leiden: Brill, 1968.

――――. *Zur Josephus-Forschung.* Darmstadt: Wissenschaftliche Buchgesellschaft, 1973.

Schreckenberg, H. *Bibliographie zu Flavius Josephus.* Leiden: Brill, 1968; suppl. 1979.

――――. *Die Flavius-Josephus-Tradition in Antike und Mittelalter.* Leiden: Brill, 1972.

――――. *Rezeptionsgeschichtliche und textkritische Untersuchungen zu Flavius Josephus.* Leiden: Brill, 1977.

Schürer, E. *The History of the Jewish People in the Age of Jesus Christ.* Trans. and ed. G. Vermes and F. Millar. Edinburgh: Clark, 1973.

Shutt, R. *Studies in Josephus.* London: SPCK, 1961.

Smith, M. *Jesus the Magician.* San Francisco: Harper and Row, 1978.

Thackeray, H. *Josephus: The Man and the Historian.* New York: 1929; repr. New York: Ktav, 1967.

Vermes, G. "The Jesus Notice of Josephus Re-examined." *JJS* 38 (1987) 1–10.

Winter, P. "Josephus on Jesus." *Jour. Hist. Studies* 1 (1968) 289–302; revised and repr. as "Excursus 2-Josephus on Jesus and James." In E. Schürer. *The History of the Jewish People in the Age of Jesus Christ.* Trans. and ed. G. Vermes and F. Millar; Edinburgh: 1973.

Zeitlin, S. "The Christ Passage in Josephus." *JQR* 18 (1928) 231–51.

――――. "The Hoax of the Slavonic Josephus." *JQR* 39 (1948-9) 171–80.

CHAPTER 7, THE MARTYRDOM OF POLYCARP

Altaner, B. *Patrology.* Freiburg: Herder, 1960.

Barnard, L. *Studies in the Apostolic Fathers and their Background.* Oxford: Blackwell, 1966.

――――. "In Defense of Pseudo-Pionius' Account of St. Polycarp's Martyrdom." In *Kyriakon: festschrift J. Quasten.* Ed. P. Granfield and J.-A. Jungmann, 192-204. Münster: Aschendorff, 1970.

Barnes, T. "A Note on Polycarp." *JTS* 18 (1967) 433–37.

————. "Pre-Decian Acta Martyrium." *JTS* 19 (1968) 509–31.

Bauer, W. *Orthodoxy and Heresy in Earliest Christianity.* Philadelphia: Fortress, 1971.

Bihlmeyer, K. *Die Apostolischen Väter,* 2d. ed. With W. Schneemelcher. Tübingen: Mohr(Siebeck), 1956.

Cadoux, C. *Ancient Smyrna: A History of the City from the Earliest Times to 324 A.D.* Oxford: Blackwell, 1948.

Campenhausen, H. von. *Bearbeitungen und Interpolationen des Polykarpmartyriums.* Sitzungsberichte der Heidelberger Akademie 3. Heidelberg: Universitätsverlag, 1957.

————. *Die Idee des Martyriums in der alten Kirche.* Göttingen: Vandenhoeck and Ruprecht, 1936.

Chadwick, H. *The Early Church.* Penguin: Harmondsworth, 1967.

Delehaye, H. *Les passions des martyrs et le genres litteraires.* Brussels: Société des Bollandistes, 1921.

————. *Sanctus: Essai sur le culte des saints dans l'antiquité.* Subsidia Hagiographica 17. Brussels: Société des Bollandistes, 1927.

————. *Les origines de culte des martyrs.* Subsidia Hagiographica 20. Brussels: Société des Bollandistes, 1933.

Fischel, H. "Martyr and Prophet." *JQR* 37 (1946/47) 265–80, 363–86.

Frend, W. L. *Martyrdom and Persecution in the Early Church.* Oxford: Blackwell, 1965.

Goodspeed, E. *A History of Early Church Literature.* Rev. and enl. R. Grant. Chicago: University of Chicago Press, 1942.

Grant, R. *The Apostolic Fathers.* New York: Nelson, 1964.

Grégoire, H., and P. Ongels. "La véritable date du martyre de S. Polycarpe." *Analecta Bollandiana* 69 (1951) 1–38.

————. et al. *Les persecutions dans l'empire Romain.* Academie royale de Belgique: Classe des lettres et des sciences morales et politiques: mémoires, 1st ed. vol 46/1; 2nd ed. rev. vol. 56/5; Brussels: Palais des Académies, 1951, 1964.

Gustafsson, B. "Eusebius' Principles in Handling His Sources as Found in His Church History, Books I-VII." Studia Patristica IV. *Texte und Untersuchungen* 79 (1961) 429–41.

Halton, T., and R. Sider. "A Decade of Patristic Scholarship 1970-1979." *Classical World* 76 (1982) 65–127; (1983) 313–83.

Harnack, A. *The Mission and Expansion of Christianity in the First Three Centuries.* (Trans. and ed. J. Moffatt. London, 1904; New York: Torchbook, 1961.

Knopf, R. *Ausgewählte Märtyrakten,* 3d. ed. rev. G. Krueger. Tübingen, 1929.

————. *Die Lehre der zwölf Apostel. Die zwei Clemensbriefe: Apostolische Väter* I. *HNT.* Tübingen, 1920.

Koester, H. *Synoptische Überlieferung bei den Apostolischen Vätern.* TU 65. Berlin, 1957.

Lightfoot, J. *The Apostolic Fathers I. S. Clement of Rome.* 2 vols. New York: Olms, Hildesheim, 1890.

———. *The Apostolic Fathers II. S. Ignatius, S. Polycarp* 2d. rev. ed. London: 1889.

Manns, F. *Essais sur le Judéo-Christianisme.* Jerusalem: Franciscan Printing Press, 1977.

Marrou, H. "La date du martyre de S. Polycarpe." *An Boll* 71 (1953) 5–20.

Musurillo, H. *The Acts of the Christian Martyrs.* Oxford: Clarendon, 1972.

Perler, O. "Das vierte Makkabäerbuch, Ignatius von Antiochien und die ältesten Martyrerberichte." *Rivista di archeologia cristiana* 29 (1949) 47–72.

Quasten, J. *Patrology* 3 vols. Utrecht: Spectrum 1950–60.

Schoedel, W. *The Apostolic Fathers: vol. 5, Polycarp, Martyrdom of Polycarp, Fragments of Papias.* Camden: Nelson, 1967.

Telfer, W. "The date of martyrdom of Polycarp." *JTS* n.s. 3 (1952) 79–83.

Zahn, T. *Ignatii et polycarpi: Epistolae Martyria fragmenta (Patrum Apostolicorum Opera 2.* Ed. O. de Gebhardt, A. Harnack, and T. Zahn. Leipzig: Hinrichs, 1876.

CHAPTER 8, THE GOSPEL OF PETER

Bauckham, R. "The Two Fig Tree Parables in the Apocalypse of Peter." *JBL* 104 (1985) 269–87.

———. "The Martyrdom of Enoch and Elijah: Jewish or Christian?" *JBL* 95 (1976) 454–55.

———. "The Apocalypse of Peter: An Account of Research." *ANRW* 25.6. Berlin: de Gruyter, 1988. 4712–50.

Beyschlag, K. *Die verborgene Uberlieferung von Christus.* Siebenstern Taschenbuchs 132. Munich: Siebenstern, 1969.

Bowersock, G. "A Roman Perspective on the Bar Kochba War." In *Approaches to Ancient Judaism.* Ed. W. S. Green, 131–41. Chico: Scholars Press, 1980.

Brown, R. E. "*The Gospel of Peter* and Canonical Gospel Priority." *NTS* 33 (1987) 321–43.

Cameron, R. *The Other Gospels: Non-Canonical Gospel Texts.* Philadelphia: Westminster, 1982.

Crossan, J. D. *Four Other Gospels.* Minneapolis: Winston, 1985.

———. *The Cross that Spoke.* San Francisco: Harper & Row, 1988.

Delehaye, H. *Les Passions des Martyrs et les Genres littéraire.* Brussels: Bureaux de la Société des Bollandistes, 1921.

Denker, J. *Die theologiegeschichtliche Stellung des Petrusevangelium.* Frankfurt: Lang, 1975.

Fischel, H. "Martyr and Prophet." *JQR* 37 (1946–47) 265–80, 363–86.

Gardner-Smith, P. "The Gospel of Peter." *JTS* 27 (1926) 255–71.

———. "The Date of the Gospel of Peter." *JTS* 27 (1926) 401–407.

Hennecke, E. *New Testament Apocrypha,* 2 vols. Ed. W. Schneemelcher. Philadelphia: Westminster, 1959-64.

Koester, H. "Apocryphal and Canonical Gospels." *HTR* 73 (1980) 105–30.

Lowe, M. "IOVDAIOI of the Apocrypha." *NovT* 23 (1981) 56–90.

Mara, M. *Evangile de Pierre.* SC 201. Paris: Cerf, 1973.

McCant, J. "The Gospel of Peter: Docetism Reconsidered." *NTS* 30 (1984) 258–73.

Massaux, E. *Influence de l'Evangile de saint Matthieu sur la littérature chrétienne avant saint Irénée.* Gembloux: Duculot, 1950.

Musurillo, H. *The Acts of the Christian Martyrs.* Oxford: Clarendon, 1972.

Robinson, J. A., and M. R. James. *The Gospel according to Peter and the Revelation of Peter.* London: Clay, 1892.

Schäfer, P. "Rabbi Aqiva and Bar Kokhba." In *Approaches to Ancient Judaism.* Ed. W. S. Green, 113–30. Chico: Scholars Press, 1980.

_____. *Der Bar-Kochba Aufstand.* Tübingen: Mohr (Siebeck) 1981.

Schaeffer, S. "An Annotated Bibliography on the Gospel of Peter." Unpublished manuscript, May 1987.

Schmidt, D. "The Peter Writings: Their Redactors and Their Relationships." Ph.D diss., Northwestern University, 1972.

Schmidt, K. *Kanonische und Apokryphe Evangelion und Apostelgeschichten.* Basel: Majer, 1944.

Sekeles, E., and J. Zias. "The Crucified Man from Giv'at ha-Mivtar: A Reappraisal." *IEJ* 35 (1985) 22–27.

Spitta, F. "Die Petrus-Apokalypse und der zweite Petrusbrief." *ZNW* 12 (1911) 237–42.

Tzaferis, V. "Jewish Tombs at and near Giv at ha-Mivtar, Jerusalem." *IEJ* 20 (1970) 18–32.

_____. "Crucifixion-The Archaeological Evidence." *BAR* 11 (1985) 44–53.

Vaganay, L. *Evangile de Pierre.* EB. 2d. ed. Paris: Gabalda, 1930.

Vielhauer, P. "Die Petrus-Apokalypse." In *Geschichte der urchristlichen Literatur* 507–13. Berlin: de Gruyter, 1975.

Wienel, H. "Offenbarung des Petrus." In *Neutestamentliche Apokryphen* 2d. ed. Ed. E. Hennecke; Tübingen: Mohr (Siebeck), 1924.

Yarbro Collins, A. "The Early Christian Apocalypses." *Semeia* 14 (1979) 61–121.

Zias, J., and E. Sekeles. "The Crucified Man from Giv'at ha-Mivtar: A Reappraisal." *IEJ* 35 (1985) 22–27.

CHAPTER 9, THE CHRISTIAN APOLOGISTS

Andriessen, P. "L'apologie de Quadratus conservée sous le titre d'Epitre à Diognète." *Recherches de théologie ancienne et médiévale* 13 (1946) 5–39, 125–49, 237–60; 14 (1947) 121–56.

Barnard, L. "The Old Testament and Judaism in the Writings of Justin Martyr." *VT* 14 (1964) 375–406.

_____. "The Epistle ad Diognetum: Two Units from One Author?" *ZNW* 56 (1965) 130–37.

_____. *Justin Martyr.* Cambridge: Cambridge University Press, 1967.

Bokser, B. Z. "Justin Martyr and the Jews." *JQR* 64 (1973) 96–122, 204–11.

Bowersock, G. *Greek Sophists of the Roman Empire.* Oxford: Clarendon, 1969.

———, ed. *Approaches to the Second Sophistic*. University Park: American Philological Association, 1974.

Brandle, R. *Die Ethik der 'Schrift an Diognet'*. Zürich: Theologischer Verlag, 1975.

Chadwick, H. *Early Christian Thought and the Classical Tradition*. Oxford: Clarendon, 1966.

———. "Justin Martyr's Defence of Christianity." *BJRL* 47 (1965) 275-97.

Goodenough, E. *The Theology of Justin Martyr*. Jena: Frommann, 1923; reprinted Amsterdam: Philo, 1968.

Goodspeed, E. *Die ältesten Apologeten*. Göttingen: Vandenhoeck & Ruprecht, 1914.

Grant, R. *Greek Apologists of the Second Century*. Philadelphia: Westminster, 1988.

Greer, R., and J. Kugel. *Early Biblical Interpretation*. Philadelphia: Westminster, 1986.

Harnack, A. *von Judentum und Judenchristentum in Justin's Dialog mit Trypho 47-92*. *TU* 39. Leipzig: Hinrichs, 1913.

Hoffman, M. *Der Dialog bei den christlichen Schriftstellern der ersten vier Jahrhunderts*. Berlin: Akademie, 1966.

Horbury, W. "The Benediction of the *Minim* and Early Jewish-Christian Controversy." *JTS* n.s. 33 (1982) 19-61.

Hulen, A. "The 'Dialogues with the Jews' as Sources for the Early Jewish Argument against Christianity." *JBL* 51 (1932) 58-70.

Hyldahl, N. *Philosophie und Christentum*. Copenhagen: Munksgaard, 1966.

Juster, J. *Les Juifs dans l'empire Romain*. Paris: Guethner, 1914.

Katz, K. "Form and Convention in *Dialogue with Trypho*." Paper delivered at the Jewish Theological Seminary, February 1987.

Katz, S. "Issues in the Separation of Judaism and Christianity after 70 C.E.: A Reconsideration." *JBL* 103 (1984) 43-76.

Kimelman, R. "*Birkat Ha-Minim* and the Lack of Evidence for an Anti-Christian Jewish Prayer in Late Antiquity." In *Jewish and Christian Self-Definition*. Ed. E. P. Sanders et al., 226-44. Philadelphia: Fortress, 1981.

Krauss, S. "The Jews in the Works of the Church Fathers." *JQR* 5 (1893) 122-57; 6 (1893) 82-99, 225-61.

Marmorstein, A. "The Attitudes of the Jews towards Early Christianity." *The Expositor* 49 (1923) 383-89.

———. "The Amidah of the Public Fast Days." *JQR* n.s. 15 (1925) 409-18.

———. "Jews and Judaism in the Earliest Christian Apologies." *The Expositor* 8th series 17 (1919) 73-80, 100-116.

Marrou, H. *A Diognète*. *SC* 33. Paris: Cerf, 1951.

Meecham, H. *The Epistle to Diognetus*. Manchester: Manchester University Press, 1949.

Nilson, J. "To Whom Is Justin's Dialogue with Trypho Addressed?" *TS* 38 (1977) 538-46.

Osborn, E. *Justin Martyr*. Tübingen: Mohr (Siebeck) 1973.

Sigal, P. "An Inquiry into Aspects of Judaism in Justin's Dialogue with Trypho." *Abr Nahrain* 18 (1978–79) 74–100.

Schwartz, J. "L'Epitre a Diognète." *RHPhR* 48 (1968) 46–53.

Skarsaune, O. *The Proof from Prophecy: A Study in Justin Martyr's Proof-Text Tradition.* Leiden: Brill, 1987.

Stanton, G. "Aspects of Early Christian-Jewish Polemic and Apologetic." *NTS* 31 (1985) 377–92.

Stylianopoulos, T. *Justin Martyr and the Mosaic Law.* Missoula, MT: Scholars Press, 1975.

Thierry, J. *The Epistle to Diognetus.* Leiden: Brill, 1964.

Trakatellis, D. "Justin Martyr's Trypho." *HTR* 79 (1986) 289–97.

van Winden, J. *An Early Christian Philosopher.* Leiden: Brill, 1971.

Visotzky, B. "Overturning the Lamp." *JJS* 38 (1987) 72–80.

Voss, B. *Der Dialog in der frühchristlichen Literatur.* Munich: Fink, 1979.

Wilson, S. "Justin's Trypho." Paper delivered at the Society for Biblical Literature Annual Meeting, San Francisco, November 22, 1992.

CHAPTER 10, JEWISH AND CHRISTIAN WRITERS AFTER 150 C.E.

Andresen, C. *Logos und Nomos: Die Polemik des Kelsos wider das Christentum.* Arbeiten zur Kirchengeschichte 30. Berlin: de Gruyter, 1955.

Aziza, C. *Tertullien et le Judaisme.* Nice: Faculté des lettres et des Sciences Humaines, 1977.

Baer, Y. "Israel, the Christian Church and the Roman Empire from the Time of Septimus Severus to the Edict of Toleration of 313." *Scripta Hierosolymitana* 7 (1961) 79–149.

Bardy, G. "Les traditions juives dans l'oeuvre d'Origène." *RB* 34 (1925) 217–52.

Baskin, J. "Rabbinic-Patristic Exegetical Contacts in Antiquity." In *Approaches to Ancient Judaism V.* Ed. W. S. Green, 53-80. Atlanta: Scholars Press, 1985.

Beckwith, R. "The Date of the Closing of the Canon." *Mikra.* Ed. M. Mulder, 58-61. Philadelphia: Fortress, 1988.

Bietenhard, H. *Caesarea, Origenes und die Juden.* Stuttgart: Kohlhammer, 1974.

Benko, S. "Pagan Criticism of Christianity during the First Two Centuries A.D." *ANRW* II23.2, 1055–1118.

―――. "The Edict of Claudius of A.D. 49 and the Instigator Chrestus." *ThZ* 25 (1969) 406–18.

―――. *Pagan Rome and the Early Christians.* London: Batsford, 1984.

Bickerman, E. "The Name of Christians." *HTR* 42 (1949) 109–24.

Chadwick, H. *Early Christian Thought and the Classical Tradition.* Oxford: Clarendon, 1966.

―――. *Origen: Contra Celsum.* Cambridge: Cambridge University Press, 1953.

Cohen, S.J.D. "Epigraphical Rabbis." *JQR* 72 (1981–82) 1–17.

de Lange, N. *Origen and the Jews.* Cambridge: Cambridge University Press, 1966.

Efroymsen, D. *Tertullian's Anti-Judaism and Its Role in His Theology.* Ph.D. diss., Temple University, 1976.

———. "The Patristic Connection." In *Anti-Judaism and the Foundations of Christianity.* Ed. A. Davies, 98-117. New York: Paulist, 1979.

———. "A Note on Tertullian and the Jews." *Studia Patristica* 10 (1970) 291-96.

Herford, R. T. *Christianity in Talmud and Midrash.* London: Williams and Norgate, 1903.

Hoffmann, R. *Celsus: On the True Doctrine.* New York: Oxford University Press, 1987.

Kalmin, R. *Sages, Stories, Authors and Editors in Rabbinic Babylonia.* Providence: Brown University Press, forthcoming.

Klijn, A.F.J., and G. Reinink. *Patristic Evidence for Jewish-Christian Sects.* Leiden: Brill, 1973.

Koetschau, P. *Contra Celsum. Die griechischen christlichen Schriftsteller der ersten drei Jahrhunderte* Bde II-III. Leipzig: Hinrichs, 1889.

La Piana, G. "Foreign Groups in Rome during the First Centuries of the Empire." *HTR* 20 (1927) 183-403.

Lifshitz, B. "L'Origine du Nom des Chretiens." *VC* 16 (1962) 65-70.

Lightstone, J. "Christian Anti-Judaism in Its Judaic Mirror: The Judaic Context of Early Christianity Revised." In *Anti-Judaism in Early Christianity,* vol. 2. Ed. S. Wilson, 103-32. Waterloo: Wilfred Laurier, 1986.

Maier, J. *Jesus von Nazareth in der talmüdischen Überlieferung.* Darmstadt: Wissenschaftliche Buchgesellschaft, 1978.

———. *Jüdische Auseinandersetzung mit dem Christentum in der Antike.* Darmstadt: Wissenschaftliche Buchgesellschaft, 1982.

Markus, R. *Christianity in the Roman World.* London: Thames and Hudson, 1974.

Mattingly, H. "The Origin of the Name *Christiani.*" *JTS* 9 (1958) 26-37.

Neusner, J. "The Use of Rabbinic Sources for the Study of Ancient Judaism." In *Approaches to Ancient Judaism III.* Ed. W. S. Green, 1-17. Chico: Scholars Press, 1981.

Schiffman, L. "At the Crossroads: Tannaitic Perspectives on the Jewish-Christian Schism." In *Jewish and Christian Self-Definition,* vol. 2. Ed. E. P. Sanders et al. 115-56. Philadelphia: Fortress, 1981.

Schwartz, J. "Ben Stada and Peter in Lydda." *JSJ* 21 (1990) 1-18.

Scramuzza, V. *The Emperor Claudius.* Cambridge: Harvard University Press, 1940.

Segal, A. F. *Two Powers in Heaven.* SJLA 25. Leiden: Brill, 1977.

Sevenster, J. *The Roots of Pagan Anti-Semitism in the Ancient World.* Leiden: Brill, 1975.

Strack, H. *Jesus, die Häretiker und die Christen.* Leipzig: Hinrichs, 1910.

INDEXES

APOCRYPHA

JEWISH WRITERS

Philo

Josephus

MODERN AUTHORS